THE BLUE CLIFF RECORD

VOLUME ONE

The Blue Cliff Record

Translated from the Chinese *Pi Yen Lu* by
Thomas and J. C. Cleary

Foreword by Taizan Maezumi Roshi

SHAMBHALA
Boulder & London
1977

SHAMBHALA PUBLICATIONS INC.
1123 Spruce Street
Boulder, Colorado 80302

© 1977 by Thomas & J. C. Cleary
Foreword © 1977 Shambhala Publications Inc.
Designed by Hal Hershey
ISBN 0-87773-094-6
LCC 78-146511

Distributed in the United States by Random House
and in Canada by Random House of Canada Ltd.

Distributed in the Commonwealth by Routledge &
Kegan Paul Ltd., London and Henley-on-Thames

Printed in the United States of America

Contents

Biographical Supplement

Foreword

Boundless wind and moon—the eye within eyes,
Inexhaustible heaven and earth—the light beyond light,
The willow dark, the flower bright—ten thousand
  houses;
Knock at any door—there's one who will respond.

This verse is known as the Preface to *The Blue Cliff Record*. Although the name of the book is taken from the place where it was written, all heaven and earth is nothing but the mass of this Blue Cliff. The hundred cases selected by Hsueh Tou for *The Blue Cliff Record* are as ten thousand and eighty-four thousand, which are the numbers of dharmas expounded by Shakyamuni Buddha. The innumerable dharmas revealed by him are to be found in each case of *The Blue Cliff Record*.

There are numerous ways to read a book: skimming, memorizing, careful study, quiet reading, reading aloud, reading with the body, reading with the mind, and reality-reading. It is this last kind of reading which *The Blue Cliff Record* requires. In this mode, you yourself become the case, and in so doing, the Blue Cliff of ancient China stands revealed as your very life, right here in this time and place.

Since the translators have already ably discussed the form and compilation of the book in their introduction, it is unnecessary for me to cover the same ground. But I should like to mention one thing: that the first person to introduce this text to Japan was Kigen Dōgen Zenji, founder of the Soto School of Japanese Zen. In 1227, at age 26, Dōgen Zenji had completed five years of study in China and was preparing for his return to Japan. But shortly before leaving, he discovered a copy of *The Blue Cliff Record,* and was so impressed that he spent his entire last night in China sitting up and hand-copying it. The hand-copied manuscript, known as the *Ichiya Hekigan* or *"One-Night Blue Cliff Record,"* is now treasured and housed at Daijoji Monastery in Japan.

As mentioned in the Introduction, around 1140 Ta Hui

burned the original, published by his teacher Yuan Wu in 1128. The familiar version of the present day is the edition of 1300, based upon remaining handwritten copies and two previously published versions. The manuscript Dōgen Zenji brought back to Japan some seventy years earlier was probably based on one of the two previous versions, or on a handwritten copy of the day.

The Blue Cliff Record has become almost uniquely revered among Zen Buddhists as a model koan text, especially noted for its subtlety and profundity in both form and content. Interestingly enough, another koan collection, the Book of Equanimity (J.: Shōyō Roku) parallels it in form and level of sophistication. Unlike The Blue Cliff Record, which was compiled and refined by masters of the Rinzai and Ummon Schools, the Book of Equanimity is a product of the Soto lineage, and is primarily associated with that school. Nonetheless, The Blue Cliff Record appears to have been widely appreciated by Soto masters, although the Book of Equanimity failed to gain much prominence among teachers of the Rinzai School.

It is noteworthy that Dōgen Zenji selected twenty-four cases from The Blue Cliff Record, nearly a fourth of the total number of cases, for inclusion in his own three-hundred-case collection of koans entitled the Shinji Shōbōgenzō ("The Shōbōgenzō in Chinese"). This is not to be confused with the Kaji Shōbōgenzō ("The Shōbōgenzō in Japanese"), which most modern readers think of when they mention the Shōbōgenzō. This latter work is heavily based upon koan interpretations and commentaries by Dōgen Zenji.

We mention this because of an unfortunately widespread impression nowadays that Dōgen Zenji and the Soto School represent a non-koan or even anti-koan orientation within Zen. In fact, nothing could be further from the truth. Like Ta Hui of the Lin Chi School, Dōgen Zenji was critical of the abuses of koan study common in his day. These abuses, which essentially involved a stereotyped and overly intellectual use of koans, led Dōgen Zenji to express his concern lest the clarity and vigor of Zen students fall into deeper decline. Similarly, Ta Hui's burning of The Blue Cliff Record was an expression of his concern over the misuse of koans, rather than any fundamental objection to the use of koans, verses, or commentaries as such.

Avoiding sectarian prejudice, misunderstanding, or biased views of koans, I sincerely wish that *The Blue Cliff Record*, one of the most wonderful dharma-treasures of the world's Eastern heritage, will at last be fully appreciated by, and benefit, its Western readers.

This tremendous work of translating *The Blue Cliff Record* has not previously been done by American scholars and is to be highly appreciated and praised. Western Zen Buddhists have waited a long time for a competent translation of this major text; they need wait no longer.

Moreover, I appreciate the extra effort expended to translate Master Tung Shan's *Five Ranks* and Master Fen Yang's *Eighteen Categories of Questions*. While it is true that Hsueh Tou was the first to append appreciatory verses to *The Blue Cliff Record*, nonetheless it was Fen Yang who first began the practice of composing such verses for koans in general. So readers may find these appended works of some special interest.

Regarding actual practice, I firmly believe that this translation is a milestone and will immensely benefit those who are sincerely engaged in the practice and enlightenment of the Buddha-way. Since Zen students must deal with these cases meticulously and in great detail, it can be seen how indispensable is a translation such as this. These cases are, after all, more than mere anecdotes of historical or philosophical interest. They are the living record of generations of enlightened practice. It is my sincere hope that, in appreciating these cases along with the verses, commentaries, and capping-phrases, the reader will be enriched in his understanding of the practice and accomplishment of *Anuttara Samyak Sambodhi*, the Supreme and Unexcelled Enlightenment.

A famous expression comes to mind:

"Before attaining enlightenment,
*   mountains are mountains, rivers are rivers.*

At the moment of enlightenment,
*   mountains are no longer mountains, nor are rivers rivers.*

But after accomplishing enlightenment,
*   mountains are mountains, rivers are rivers."*

This expression deals with three stages of practice. It is vital that the reader understand that the "mountains are mountains, rivers are rivers" experience *after* enlightenment is not at all the same as *before* such a realization. We cannot dispense with the "mountains are no longer mountains, nor are rivers rivers" aspect, which requires that the individual clearly realize his own true nature.

Although we know that all animate and inanimate beings are intrinsically buddhas, mere knowing is not enough. Dōgen Zenji says, "This dharma, (enlightened life) is abundantly inherent in each individual; nevertheless, without practice it will not be revealed, and without enlightenment it will not be realized."

The Blue Cliff Record reveals to us what enlightenment is, what the enlightened life is, how the patriarchs and masters of old struggled with it, attained it, actualized it, and accomplished it.

Penetrating the Blue Cliff, you will open ". . . the eye within eyes," and realizing life through the Blue Cliff, you yourself will become a torch, ". . . the light beyond light."

Being so, you will find no door at which to knock, nor any door to be opened.

Taizan Maezumi Roshi
Zen Center of Los Angeles
September, 1976

Preface

The introductory essay in this volume is intended to introduce some aspects of the tradition behind the classic Ch'an Buddhist *kung an* collection *Pi Yen Lu* which is presented here in English translation as *The Blue Cliff Record*, in the first of three parts.

The Chinese and Japanese pronunciations Ch'an and Zen are used in this volume because they are most familiar to Westerners, and it has been the Chinese and Japanese traditions of Ch'an which have thus far indirectly and directly most affected the early growth of Zen in the West. Ch'an also existed and exists in Korea and Vietnam, and contacts between these traditions and Western students have begun; for all of these, however, Chinese Ch'an is the ancestral tradition, and this will be our focus in the introduction to this volume.

Our primary aim is not historical record or doctrine as they are conventionally understood. Some books have touched on the subject, but there is as yet hardly any information in Western languages about Ch'an Buddhist teaching and history, and there are not enough authentic Ch'an texts translated to make a modern historiography practical or clearly show what Ch'an may mean in the present day.

When Buddhism crossed civilization boundaries in the past, translation, study, and practice were carried on for centuries before native schools of Buddhism emerged to present the teachings in new, currently useful forms. Western civilization has pretensions to objective scholarship and knowledge, with advanced techniques of information retrieval, but with all this has been slow to find out anything much about the Buddhist teachings, a part of the human heritage which cannot be claimed or relegated to any particular culture or time. An old description of five kinds of ch'an, or meditation, depicts the lowest as that of those seeking heavenly states; the next is that of the ordinary person who sees cause and effect and practices for the betterment of mental and physical health. Without going on to speak of the rest, it is obvious that these first two are with us now, and we can no longer be content with crude generalities, sectarian claims, or impressionistic accounts of the nature of Ch'an Buddhism. The aim of this volume is to present an authentic Ch'an text unencumbered by attempted explanations based on preconceptions regarding the text itself or the mental state of the reader.

Though we have sketched an outline of early to medieval Chinese Ch'an, since Ch'an is not a doctrinal school, generalizations about its historical forms are of limited usefulness; in an attempt to amend the shortcomings of a general approach, therefore, this volume includes excerpts from the lives and sayings of the Ch'an masters appearing in the main cases of volume one, based on materials from several collections of sayings, biographies, and "transmission of the lamp" records. Though the introduction is in the beginning, the reader may find it as interesting or useful to begin anywhere in the book.

Ch'an expression is usually very concentrated, and most recorded sayings of Ch'an masters come from people in special communities where the level of effort would be more intense than that of much of ordinary life in society. The reader must see through whatever cultural peculiarities are inevitable in an eight hundred and fifty year old book from another civilization; in doing so the reader must also see through present cultural peculiarities of thought and action, an effort which is itself a task of meditation. This book is not presented as a fossil embedded in the dust of a distant past, for the essence of Ch'an, the essence of mind, is timeless and placeless.

Introduction

The Blue Cliff Record is a translation of the Chinese Ch'an Buddhist classic *Pi Yen Lu*,[1] a collection of one hundred anecdotes of sayings and doings mainly from traditional accounts of Ch'an teachers and disciples, illustrated in verse and prose by outstanding Ch'an masters of later times. This set of one hundred *kung an*, "public cases"[2] of ancient events, was compiled by the eminent Sung dynasty Ch'an master Hsueh Tou Ch'ung Hsien (980–1052); Hsueh Tou pointed out the import of each story with verses and additional remarks of his own, as aid and guidance for observation and contemplation. About sixty years after Hsueh Tou's death, another excellent Ch'an teacher, Yuan Wu K'e Ch'in (1063–1135), gave a series of talks elucidating the original anecdotes and the verses of Hsueh Tou's collection. The anecdotes, Hsueh Tou's verses, and Yuan Wu's introductions, remarks, and commentaries all together form *The Blue Cliff Record*, named after the abode on Mt. Chia in Hunan where Yuan Wu once delivered his talks. This book has long been considered as one of the finest works of Ch'an literature, and defies adequate description short of its own presentation.

The Buddha Gautama, Shakyamuni, whom all Buddhists regard as their ancestor, invented and adapted various teachings and techniques to liberate people; he was likened to a skilled physician giving specific medicines to cure certain diseases. It is said, therefore, that there is no fixed teaching. Yet in spite of outward differences resulting from necessary adaptation to different situations, capacities of understanding and personality configurations, the real Buddha Dharma, the teaching of the enlightened ones, is of one uniform flavor, the flavor of liberation. Just as many streams lead to the ocean, where they merge into the uniform flavor of salt, goes the ancient metaphor, so do the teachings of enlightenment lead to the ocean of enlightenment and merge into the uniform flavor of liberation. When this essence is lost, and people enshrine relics of past method for a sense of personal satisfaction, righteousness, or comfort, then it is said that the medicine has become a disease. It is the practice of Ch'an and all real Buddhism to cut through all ploys of egoism in all its guises, "holy" or "profane," to break up stultifying material and intellectual idolatry.

A Ch'an master once wrote that the wise enshrine the miraculous bones of the ancients within themselves; that is, they do not regard teachings of ways to enlightenment as an external body of knowledge or information to be possessed as an acquisition or believed or revered as inflexible dogma, but rather apply it as far as possible to themselves and their situations, vivifying the way of enlightenment with their own bodies and lives, not just in their thoughts. It is therefore a matter of course that new Buddhist literature has been produced; for the Buddhist canon is not closed, as long as people continue the search for enlightenment. This is where a consideration of Buddhist history has some meaning: to help us see what ages and what is ageless.

As many Buddhist texts and practitioners entered Chinese civilization during the first millennium A.D., overtly representing different trends of thought and action, Chinese Buddhists developed, through study and practical application and experimentation, systems of organization, analysis, interpretation, meditation, and ritual. Several Buddhist schools arose in China between the fifth and seventh centuries, including the four major schools known as T'ien T'ai, Hua Yen, Pure Land (Ching T'u), and Ch'an. The schools based on specific scriptures and treatises and commentaries by Indian and Chinese masters were referred to in Ch'an jargon as "doctrinal schools" or "teaching schools."

The principal scriptures of the T'ien T'ai school are the *Saddharmapundarika* ("Lotus of Truth") and *Mahaparinirvana* ("Great Decease"); of the Hua Yen, the *Avatamsaka* ("Garland"); of the Pure Land, the *Sukhavativyuha* ("Lay of the Land of Bliss"). Ch'an students generally read these scriptures, as well as others such as the *Vajracchedika* ("Diamond Cutter"), *Surangama* ("Heroic Going"), *Vimalakirtinirdesa* ("Teaching of Vimalakirti"), and *Lankavatara* ("Descent into Sri Lanka"); thus, the study of classical Buddhist scriptures and treatises and the practice of various meditation methods were in the background of Ch'an studies, directly or indirectly, whether or not living masters of the other schools were in existence. Later followers of the teaching schools often concentrated on the works of the Chinese founders, who analyzed, synthesized, and organized the numerous and extensive Buddhist teachings, presenting them in a crystallized form for current use. Ch'an students did likewise, concentrating on the great Ch'an masters, but kept contact with other forms of Buddhist teaching, ancient and contemporary.

Ch'an was referred to by its followers as the "school of the patriarchs" because it was transmitted by a living succession of human exemplars; not a school of doctrine, or philosophical or scholastic interpretation, it was not based on any particular scripture, but on the direct experience of the enlightened mind, by whatever means currently necessary. There were many professional lecturing monks who specialized in certain texts or groups of texts, but Ch'an teachers originally did not make systematic explanations of Buddhist texts or traditional teachings; many students learned about Buddhism in the lecturing halls before coming to Ch'an study. Ch'an teachers drew freely on the ancient "Teachings," using quintessential passages from the scriptures to illustrate points in the course of their talks to students, much in the same way as they came to use sayings and anecdotes of earlier Ch'an masters. One of the attachments that Ch'an teachers had to deal with when doctrinal Buddhism became too institutionalized and formally traditionalized was the attachment of externalists and intellectuals to names and forms which had come to be hallowed.

During the fifth and sixth centuries meditation studies developed considerably in China, especially in the northern kingdoms. Early meditation adepts were generally ascetics and strict disciplinarians, often living in secluded mountain areas or in monasteries surrounding distinguished teachers or practicing alone. Recitation of scriptures, spells, and devotional formulas was carried to great lengths by some early meditators, and has been used to a greater or lesser extent throughout Ch'an history.

Ch'an tradition recognizes Bodhidharma (4–6 c. A.D.) as its first patriarch in China. He came to China in the late fifth or early sixth century[3] and traveled around for over fifty years, teaching when the occasion arose. Bodhidharma is said to have used the *Lankavatara* scripture in his teaching; this scripture represents teachings of the Yogacara, or "yoga practice" school, which says that reality as we conceive it is only mental, and uses meditational techniques of yoga to break mental attachments to mental processes which cause our discomfort and confusion. Shakyamuni Buddha used ancient techniques of yoga, but only to break concrete and abstract attachments and realize *moksha*, freedom, not to attain supposedly higher states. We have several documents purported to record teachings of Bodhidharma; the standard slogan of later times was that he pointed directly to the human mind, and undoubtedly used various methods to accomplish this. Bodhidharma is said to have had four adept disciples in China, and by the seventh century was recognized as one of the few meditation teachers of early times who inspired a continuing living succession.

Bodhidharma's principal heir Hui K'e (486–593), the second patriarch, and his successor Seng Ts'an (d. 606), the third patriarch, still living in a time of disunity and strife in what had been the Chinese empire, seem to have wandered around, engaging in local activity but never establishing any fixed abode as teaching centers. Hui K'e spent many years in Yeh, a metropolis in the northeast quarter of China, and is said to have met ten enlightened students over the years. After large numbers of monks and nuns were made to return to lay life, and monastic properties were taken by the governments in northern China around 577, Hui K'e spent the last sixteen years of his life dressed as a layman, even though the bans were later lifted, and the Buddhist communities resumed their growth and prosperity. He was opposed by an established Buddhist teacher, as Bodhidharma had been opposed by both Indian and Chinese lecturers, for unorthodox teachings and methods, and eventually killed. Seng Ts'an, of whom almost nothing is known, was also a layman when he met Hui K'e, who was his teacher for ten years in the mountains of Anwei, evidently near the close of the sixth century. He is said to have written the long poem *Hsin Hsin Ming*[4] which has always been popular and is considered the first classic of Chinese Ch'an.

The fourth patriarch of Ch'an, Tao Hsin (580–651), settled down on a mountain in central China for over thirty years, and a community of five hundred people eventually gathered around him. This community maintained its own livelihood, and Tao Hsin ignored the invitations of the T'ang imperial court, which usually richly patronized Buddhists. Tao Hsin is said to have spent two years on a journey to south China in later life. He wrote a book about standards of conduct for bodhisattvas, those following the path of knowledge of reality; he also wrote a book on meditation, outlining various methods and their effects, referring to various scriptural sources.[5] Ch'an had not been widespread during the times of the earlier patriarchs, but with Tao Hsin it came to be known all over China.

Tao Hsin was a strict teacher and only approved of one successor out of his many disciples; this was Hung Jen (602-675), the fifth patriarch. Hung Jen was with Tao Hsin from the age of seven until his late thirties, working by day and meditating by night. Among Hung Jen's eleven enlightened successors were Shen Hsiu (602–706) and Hui Neng (638–713): Shen Hsiu, a learned monk as well as a meditation master, was considered the sixth patriarch in the tradition of the so-called northern school of Ch'an; Hui Neng, an illiterate wood-cutter, was considered the sixth patriarch in the tradition of the so-called southern school. Teachers of the northern school worked mostly in or near urban areas of north China, especially the western capital of T'ang, Ch'ang An. These lineages died out by the end of the T'ang dynasty. There is a saying in Ch'an that each generation must go beyond its predecessors for the transmission to continue.

Some documents of the northern school were brought to Japan by the pilgrim Saicho in the early ninth century; Saicho had actually met Ch'an people of the so-called ox head (Niu T'ou) and northern schools, and included several texts documenting the inclusion of Ch'an as the Bodhidharma Sect in the four transmissions or heritages claimed by Tendai Buddhism in Japan, along with the philosophy and cessation of thought and observation of reality practices of T'ien T'ai, esoteric ritual, art, spells, and scriptures of tantric Buddhism, and precepts for bodhisattvas. The Bodhidharma Sect was brought to life for a time by Dainichi Nonin and some dedicated students and successors. Nonin was a Tendai student who specialized in Ch'an meditation and had such profound realization that he began to teach with effect. Many of the students of his successors and their successors eventually joined the Zen master Dogen (1200–1253), who returned from China in 1227 and gradually began to write and teach. Criticized for not having a teacher's bequest, Nonin sent two disciples to China with a statement of his realization, and was acknowledged by a Lin Chi master, of the southern school; so the reality behind Ch'an is not sectarian.

Hui Neng had become enlightened in his mid-twenties while a poor woodcutter in the frontier lands of south China. He later traveled north to see Hung Jen, and became a workman in Hung Jen's community at Huang Mei. Hung Jen recognized Hui Neng's enlightenment and after a short time passed on to him the robe and bowl of Bodhidharma as symbols of the patriarchate; he did this in secret, it is said, and sent Hui Neng away, fearing the jealous wrath of the monks because Hui Neng was a peasant from the uncivilized far south with no formal training in Buddhism. After fifteen years of wandering, Hui Neng reappeared in south China, became ordained as a Buddhist monk, and began to teach at Pao Lin monastery near the source of Ts'ao Ch'i, the Ts'ao Valley River. He awakened many people, and most of the teachers who appear in *The Blue Cliff Record* were descended from Hui Neng.

Little is known of most of Hui Neng's immediate disciples, but in the succeeding generation there appeared two great masters, Shih T'ou Hsi Ch'ien (700–790) and Ma Tsu Tao Yi (709–788), under whom Ch'an began to flourish in China as never before. From these two masters were descended the so-called "Five Houses and Seven Sects" of Ch'an which arose from the ninth to eleventh centuries. Descended from Ma Tsu were the Kuei-Yang and Lin Chi houses, named after *Kuei* Shan Ling Yu (771–854), *Yang* Shan Hui Chi (813–890), and *Lin Chi* Yi Hsuan (d. 867); during the eleventh century two great masters of Ch'an in the Lin Chi house, Huang Lung Hui Nan (1002–1069) and Yang Ch'i Fang Hui (d. 1049), were so influential and produced so many enlightened successors that their lineages became known as the Huang Lung and Yang Ch'i sects, or streams. From Shih T'ou were descended the Ts'ao-Tung, Yun Men, and Fa Yen houses, named after *Tung* Shan Liang Chieh (807–869), *Ts'ao*-Shan Pen Chi (840–901), *Yun Men* Wen Yen (d. 949), and *Fa Yen* Wen Yi (885–958). Referred to as schools, sects, houses, or clans of Ch'an, they were not sects in the sense of membership, but were terms of respect given later to successions of living masters, called after the reference names of their distinguished ancestors.

The five houses era was the most original and creative period of Ch'an teaching, source of much illustrative material and symbolic method used in later times. A considerable body of sayings and writings of the patriarchs and eminent heirs of the five houses and seven sects has been preserved. The living succession of the Kuei-Yang, the earliest house, died out in the tenth century, after five generations; Kuei Shan's *Admonitions*, a short treatise for Ch'an students, was used in Ch'an communities for over a thousand years. Te Kuang, a Lin Chi master in the second generation after Yuan Wu, sent this book over to Dainichi Nonin in Japan, and it was the first Ch'an book to be printed in that country.

The Fa Yen house also lasted about a century, while the Yun Men house, extremely effective for several generations after Hsueh Tou, lasted for some three hundred years and preserved and transmitted a great deal of Ch'an literature. The Lin Chi house, especially the Yang Ch'i branch, eventually became the most powerful and long lived Ch'an succession in China, while the Ts'ao Tung, not as prominent, nevertheless continued to exist and play a part in the Ch'an work for many centuries.

The Kuei-Yang and Lin Chi houses were both descended from Ma Tsu's great heir Pai Chang Huai Hai (720–814), who wrote the "Pure Rules for Ch'an Gardens" and uttered the famous dictum "One day without working is a day without eating." Pai Chang is known for having formally established a unique Ch'an monastic system. By the time of Kuei Shan, the monasteries were so wealthy and populous and so many monks were lazy and decadent that Kuei Shan wrote his little book warning about the deception of abundant offerings and supplies, criticizing the "rice bags" and "clothes hangers" who joined monastic life for food, clothing, and shelter without seriously trying to awaken to reality.

The Yun Men and Fa Yen houses were descended from the powerful master Te Shan Hsuan Chien (d. 867) and his successor Hsueh Feng Yi Ts'un, a great teacher of over sixty enlightened disciples. Te Shan was famous for his use of the staff to strike students; Hsueh Feng once had a major insight when struck by Te Shan. Te Shan's contemporary Lin Chi was equally famous for his shouting, and the "staff of Te Shan and the shout of Lin Chi" is a standard Ch'an expression to be met frequently in *The Blue Cliff Record*.

With the proliferation of Ch'an teaching throughout China, sincere Ch'an students usually made extensive journeys to call on various enlightened masters; some continued their travels after enlightment, to deepen their experience, test their realization and that of established teachers, and familiarize themselves with methods currently in use. Aside from encounter with living examples of enlightenment, travel also was a means of learning to reduce needs to a minimum, live as efficiently as possible with nothing fixed to rely on, and become immersed in the contemplation of impermanence. In this way, Ch'an monks came to be called "foot travelers"; emulating the ancient Buddhists as poor wayfarers, they were also known as "patchrobed monks."

By the end of the T'ang dynasty, Ch'an was the major form of Buddhism in China, but was beginning to become rigid with age and formality. Far more is recorded of the words of distinguished masters of the Sung dynasties (960–1276) than of those of T'ang, especially as they were often teaching in large official public monasteries. Ch'an teaching became more geographically concentrated, generally speaking, in Sung times, and many enlightened Ch'an adepts stayed for years as functionaries in the public monasteries without forming communities of their own, assisting the work of teaching masters among large groups of students.

The practice of reciting and recording sayings and stories had been in evidence since early T'ang, and a number of large collections of anecdotes of many generations of Ch'an masters were made in Sung times. Students sometimes carried a puzzling remark with them on their travels seeking resolution, or recorded and studied sayings or conversations of teachers they had met or had heard of. From the early masters of the five houses we have not only original sayings, but remarks, replies, and alternative sayings for stories of other masters conveyed by traveling students. Yun Men Wen Yen, patriarch of the Yun Men house, and Fen Yang Shan Chao (947–1024), a master influential in the revival of Lin Chi Ch'an, were among the first to use quotations extensively in their teaching, giving replies and posing questions about the sayings of the old masters. Eventually it became an established practice to use old sayings to test students' insight, and for students to focus their attention on some sayings during still and active meditation.

Ch'an is based on the actual experience of enlightenment, and though Ch'an students generally still studied major great vehicle Buddhist scriptures, the sayings and doings of enlightened Ch'an masters came to supplant the Indian Buddhist scriptures as guides, indications and inspiration for their conduct, meditation, and knowledge. The production of such books as *The Blue Cliff Record* was an outgrowth of the "recollections of the Buddhas" which was part of the practice of Ch'an. Although it seems from the sayings of Yuan Wu that many students wasted Ch'an literature by remaining in conceptual or aesthetic views, it seems that the use of "public cases" of the ancients was instrumental in revivifying the inspiration of Ch'an practice, especially as contact between teacher and disciple became more ritualized. In later Ch'an literature there are many stories of people awakening under the impact of a phrase or event, a sight or a sound, after becoming engrossed in a story or saying through contemplation and observation.

The practice of observation of sayings seems to have been applied with great effect by some masters in Sung times, and the literature which grew up around it concentrated the rich legacy of the highly original T'ang and Five Dynasties (906–960) masters and provided "grammars," as it were, of Ch'an idiom, and methods of describing Ch'an history and meditation states. Eventually traditional modes of expression and transformation became widely used as a medium for question and discussion of Ch'an, though there is a virtually endless variety of detail. A good deal of Zen literature of medieval Japan also consists of recorded sayings and poems in terse symbolic style like the Sung masters who founded several streams of Ch'an in Japan; part of the reason for this was the need to communicate in writing between Chinese teachers and Japanese students. Japanese masters inherited this style somewhat, and continued to write in Chinese for over five hundred years, but also produced a parallel literature in Japanese which came to be quite different in style from the Chinese.

Hsueh Tou Ch'ung Hsien, fourth patriarch and reviver of the Yun Men school, visited the lecturing halls after his ordination and was unmatched in the study of the Buddhist scriptures and treatises; he was considered a "vessel of the Dharma" by his teachers and urged to study Ch'an. When he met Chih Men

Kuang Tso, the outstanding Yun Men master of the time, he asked, "When one does not produce a single thought, how can there be any fault?" Chih Men called him closer: as Hsueh Tou approached, Chih Men hit him on the mouth with his whisk; as Hsueh Tou was about to open his mouth, Chih Men hit him again, whereupon Hsueh Tou awoke. Hsueh Tou became a great teacher, and is said to have had eighty-four enlightened successors; through his living heirs and his great literary ability his brilliance shone and reached many people.

Yuan Wu K'e Ch'in was a master in the tenth generation of the Lin Chi succession, descendent of Fen Yang Shan Chao and Yang Ch'i Fang Hui. He studied with teachers of the Yun Men and Ts'ao-Tung as well as both branches of the Lin Chi school before he finally succeeded to Wu Tsu Fa Yen (d. 1104). Yuan Wu, "Perfect Enlightenment," was one of the titles bestowed on him by the Sung emperor Hui Tsung; he served as abbot and teaching master in several major temples by imperial request, and is said to have had seventy-five enlightened disciples. Besides *The Blue Cliff Record*, there are extensive records of Yuan Wu's sayings, as well as a large collection of letters, many to his enlightened disciples. All of the Rinzai Zen schools in modern Japan are descended from Yuan Wu.

Hsueh Tou and Yuan Wu were from the schools of Ch'an which seem to have most emphasized work with *kung an*; as is usual in the doings of Ch'an teachers, there were different ways of using the stories and sayings of the ancients. In general it may be said that contemplation and gradual application as well as complete concentration without thought were used, and we have both discursive and abrupt comments on the cases from various masters. The method of concentration without thinking, used to stop mind wandering without letting it sink into oblivion, generally focused on a word or phrase, called a *hua tou*, and was used a lot by later Lin Chi masters. *The Blue Cliff Record* gives excellent insight into what the stories point to, and advice on how to apply them in life.

The Blue Cliff Record gained great popularity in a short time, so much so that Ta Hui, an influential successor of Yuan Wu sometimes called the second coming of Lin Chi, destroyed the printing blocks because he observed that enthusiasm for eloquence and beauty of expression was hindering people from directly experiencing enlightenment on their own. In Ta Hui's time there were still numerous enlightened teachers, and a long tradition; Ta Hui wrote and spoke a great deal, especially denouncing repetitious imitation Ch'an without enlightenment. One of his techniques was to reject all answers to *kung an;* his dynamic methods were very effective in his time, and he produced over ninety enlightened disciples, but his lineage died out after a few generations.

We in the West are lacking even in information about Ch'an, and many of the accounts we have been given in the last fifty years or so are quite confused and confusing, engendering misconceptions about Ch'an, if not about reality. These *The Blue Cliff Record* seriously challenges and can help us to see through if we do not insist upon our customary habits of thought. There are at least four books on the same model as *The Blue Cliff Record* made by Ts'ao-Tung masters after Yuan Wu's time, and innumerable other books related to Buddhism from all ages: instructions on conduct and meditation, recorded sayings, collections of incidents, remarks, conversations, poetry, general and specific treatises in prose and poetry on various aspects of Ch'an history, symbolism, contemporary situations, psychology, practice and realization. Certain communities in the present may find particular books useful and ignore others, but for the common human heritage over a longer period of time, individual communities or scholars cannot canonize only certain aspects of Buddhism. The publication of *The Blue Cliff Record* in English will help to open new vistas in the study of Buddhism in the West, but is only part of a larger task. Though even one story in this volume can reveal infinite implications to those of profound insight, for a larger audience the dimensions of the impact of *The Blue Cliff Record* will expand through long contemplation facilitated by the mirrors of other Ch'an and Buddhist texts as they become available.

Ultimately, the appreciation and usefulness of this book is in the hands of the reader. Its literary expressiveness is so rich that it can hardly fail to make an impression, even though the book was not translated as a literary work. Even the manifest content of this work provides a certain sustenance: the universality of the message beckons us on, and its immediate challenge can inspire us to profounder levels of insight. Even Hakuin, considered the greatest Zen master in Japan in the last five hundred years, said that he still had new insights on certain sayings after having lectured on *The Blue Cliff Record* for thirty years. Ch'an masters tell us to look right where we stand and step: they ask what is there, is there anything, who are you and where do you come from, what did you see and hear when you were there?—in a hundred ways they try to make us wake up, clear our minds, and face reality directly. While people pursue various paths, the inexorable laws of cause and effect will be their inconceivable partner on every turn of every path, regardless of the conceptions we may have about what is going on. The effort of the student is an essential ingredient in Ch'an, so explanation is minimal.

The format of this translation of *The Blue Cliff Record* is as follows:

POINTER: introduction by Yuan Wu, missing in some cases.

CASE: the *kung an,* public case record from Ch'an tradition or Buddhist scripture.

NOTES: remarks by Yuan Wu at certain points in each case; in Chinese texts, notes are put right in the text, but we have separated them out and listed them in Western footnote style after each case, to preserve the continuity of the original story for ease of reading.

COMMENTARY: by Yuan Wu on each case.

VERSE: by Hsueh Tou, interspersed with remarks by Yuan Wu; the lines of the verses are more individual units in form and content than prose sections, so the notes, though visually distinguished, are left between the lines of verse. Cases and verses should be read both as wholes all at once, and with notes at every step.

COMMENTARY: by Yuan Wu, on verse and its relation to the case.

Volume one of this translation presents the first thirty-five cases of *The Blue Cliff Record:* following these are excerpts from classical biographies of the Ch'an masters who appear in the main cases of volume one, presented in order of their appearance.

Due to the burning of the book, some parts of the commentaries and remarks are thought to have been lost or replaced. Fortunately, this is not a presentation of a system, and while the happenings reflect on each other, they do so by their own coherence; southern Ch'an was known as the "abrupt school," and its expression tends to be concise and quintessential. It is said that if one thoroughly penetrates one phrase, one penetrates innumerable phrases at the same time.

Monks' names consist of two two-syllable names; a place name, epithet, or title, and an individual initiatory name. Exceptions to this custom are self-evident and do not need special treatment. Of famous monks, usually only the first name of two syllables (generally the place name—of the mountain, monastery, or city, etc., where the master lived and taught) is used, or, when already mentioned in the context, the second syllable of the first name. In the case of later monks teaching in the same places as famous ancient masters, the whole first name and the second name or second syllable of the second name are used. We have generally followed this custom. Diacritical marks are omitted from Sanskrit names as well as from Japanese names and terms. Translator's notes are marked by letters of the alphabet and listed after the end of each case.

NOTES TO INTRODUCTION

1. Japanese *Hekiganroku*; also called *Pi Yen Chi*, Japanese *Hekiganshu*.

2. The term "public cases" or "public records" *(kung an; koan)* likens the Ch'an stories to law cases, legal precedents, according to which a determination—here, the understanding of a student—is made.

3. According to the *Hsu Kao Seng Chuan* (ca. 645), Bodhidharma arrived in China during the Liu Sung dynasty (420–479); according to the *Ching Te Ch'uan Teng Lu* (1004), a Ch'an history, he arrived in 520.

4. "Seal of Faith in the Heart." The heart is the enlightened mind; faith is in the enlightened mind inherent in all sentient beings, the potential of Buddhahood; the seal is an impression or inscription, also a name of a form of poem.

5. This book is lost, but a good deal of material quite probably excerpted from it is to be found in the *Leng Chia Shih Tzu Chi*, "Record of Masters and Disciples of the Lankavatara," a short Ch'an history written by a member of the northern school.

The Highest Meaning of the Holy Truths

POINTER *intro by Queen Wu*

When you see smoke on the other side of a mountain, you already know there's a fire; when you see horns on the other side of a fence, right away you know there's an ox there. To understand three when one is raised, to judge precisely at a glance—this is the everyday food and drink of a patchrobed monk. Getting to where he cuts off the myriad streams, he is free to arise in the east and sink in the west, to go against or to go with, in any and all directions, free to give or to take away. But say, at just such a time, whose actions are these? Look into Hsueh Tou's trailing vines.

CASE *Kenjou*

Emperor Wu of Liang asked the great master Bodhidharma,[1] "What is the highest meaning of the holy truths?"[2] Bodhidharma said, "Empty, without holiness."[3] The Emperor said, "Who is facing me?"[4] Bodhidharma replied, "I don't know."[5] The Emperor did not understand.[6] After this Bodhidharma crossed the Yangtse River and came to the kingdom of Wei.[7]

Later the Emperor brought this up to Master Chih and asked him about it.[8] Master Chih asked, "Does your majesty know who this man is?"[9] The Emperor said, "I don't know."[10] Master Chih said, "He is the Mahasattva Avalokitesvara, transmitting the Buddha Mind Seal."[11] The Emperor felt regretful, so he wanted to send an emissary to go invite (Bodhidharma to return).[12] Master Chih told him, "Your majesty, don't say that you will send someone to fetch him back.[13] Even if everyone in the whole country were to go after him, he still wouldn't return."[14]

1

NOTES

1. This dull fellow speaks up.
2. What a donkey-tethering stake this is.
3. Wu considered this answer rather extraordinary. The arrow has flown past Korea. Very clear.
4. Wu is filled with embarrassment, forcing himself to be astute. As it turns out, he gropes without finding.
5. Bah! His second reply isn't worth half a cent.
6. Too bad! Still, he's gotten somewhere.
7. This wild fox spirit! He can't avoid embarrassment. He crosses from west to east, he crosses from east to west.
8. A poor man thinks about an old debt. The bystander has eyes.
9. Wu should chase Master Chih out of the country too; Chih should be given thirty blows. Bodhidharma has come.
10. After all this is Emperor Wu's understanding of Bodhidharma's public case.
11. Chih explains haphazardly. The elbow doesn't bend outwards.
12. After all, Bodhidharma couldn't be held. As I said before, Wu is dull.
13. When someone in the eastern house dies, someone of the western house joins in the mourning. Better they should be all driven out of the country at once.
14. Again Master Chih deserves thirty blows. He doesn't know that the great illumination shines forth from under his own feet.

COMMENTARY by Yuan Wu

From afar Bodhidharma saw that this country (China) had people capable of the Great Vehicle, so he came by sea, intent on his mission, purely to transmit the Mind Seal, to arouse and instruct those mired in delusion. Without establishing written words, he pointed directly to the human mind (for them) to see nature and fulfill Buddhahood. If you can see this way, then you will have your share of freedom. Never again will you be turned around pursuing words, and everything will be completely revealed. Thereafter you will be able to converse with Emperor Wu and you will naturally be able to see how the Second Patriarch's mind was pacified.[a] Without the mental defilements of judgement and comparison, everything is cut off, and you are free and at ease. What need is there to go on distinguishing right and wrong, or discriminating gain and loss? Even so, how many people are capable of this?

Emperor Wu had put on monk's robes and personally expounded the *Light-Emitting Wisdom Scripture*; he experienced heavenly flowers falling in profusion and the earth turning to gold. He studied the Path and humbly served the Buddha, issuing orders throughout his realm to build temples and ordain monks, and practicing in accordance with the Teaching. People called him the Buddha Heart Emperor.

When Bodhidharma first met Emperor Wu, the Emperor asked, "I have built temples and ordained monks; what merit is there in this?" Bodhidharma said, "There is no merit." He immediately doused the Emperor with dirty water. If you can penetrate this statement, "There is no merit," you can meet Bodhidharma personally. Now tell me, why is there no merit at all in building temples and ordaining monks? Where does the meaning of this lie?

Emperor Wu held discussions with Dharma Master Lou Yueh, with Mahasattva Fu, and with Prince Chao Ming about the two truths, the real and the conventional. As it says in the Teachings, by the real truth we understand that it is not existent; by the conventional truth we understand that it is not nonexistent. That the real truth and the conventional truth are not two is the highest meaning of the holy truths. This is the most esoteric, most abstruse point of the doctrinal schools. Hence the Emperor picked out this ultimate paradigm to ask Bodhidharma, "What is the highest meaning of the holy truths?" Bodhidharma answered, "Empty, without holiness." No monk in the world can leap clear of this. Bodhidharma gives them a single swordblow that cuts off everything. These days how people misunderstand! They go on giving play to their spirits, put a glare in their eyes and say, "Empty, without holiness!" Fortunately, this has nothing to do with it.

My late Master Wu Tsu once said, "If only you can penetrate 'empty, without holiness,' then you can return home and sit in peace." All this amounts to creating complications; still, it does not stop Bodhidharma from smashing the lacquer bucket[b] for others. Among all, Bodhidharma is most extraordinary. So it is said, "If you can penetrate a single phrase, at the same moment you will penetrate a thousand phrases, ten thousand

4 THE BLUE CLIFF RECORD

phrases." Then naturally you can cut off, you can hold still. An Ancient said, "Crushing your bones and dismembering your body would not be sufficient requital; when a single phrase is clearly understood, you leap over hundreds of millions."

Bodhidharma confronted the Emperor directly; how he indulged! The Emperor did not awaken; instead, because of his notions of self and others, he asked another question, "Who is facing me?" Bodhidharma's compassion was excessive; again he addressed him, saying, "I don't know." At this, Emperor Wu was taken aback; he did not know what Bodhidharma meant. When you get to this point, as to whether there is something or there isn't anything, pick and you fail.

Master Shou Tuan had a verse which said,

> Ordinarily a single arrow fells a single eagle;
> Another arrow is already too many.
> Bodhidharma goes right back to sit before Few
>   Houses Peak;
> O Lord of Liang, speak no more of going to summon
>   him.

He also said, "Who wants to summon him back?"

Since Emperor Wu did not understand, Bodhidharma secretly left the country; all this old fellow got was embarrassment. He crossed the Yangtse River into Wei; at the time, the Hsiao Ming Emperor of Wei was reigning there. This emperor belonged to a northern tribe named Toba, who were later to call themselves Chinese. When Bodhidharma arrived there, he did not appear for any more audiences, but went directly to Shao Lin Monastery, where he sat facing a wall for nine years, and met the Second Patriarch. People thereabouts called him "The Wall-Gazing Brahmin."

Emperor Wu of Liang later questioned Master Chih. Chih said, "Does your majesty know who this man is?" The Emperor said, "I don't know." Tell me, is this ("I don't know") the same as what Bodhidharma said, or is it different? In appearance it indeed seems the same, but in reality isn't. People often misunderstand and say, "Before, when Bodhidharma said 'I don't know' he was replying about Ch'an; later, when Emperor answered Master Chih, this referred to the 'knowledge' of mutual acquaintance." This is irrelevant. Tell me, when Master Chih questioned him, how could Wu have answered? Why didn't he strike Chih dead with a single blow and avoid being seen as a fool? Instead Emperor Wu answered Master Chih sincerely and said, "I don't know." Master Chih saw his chance and acted; he said, "This is the Mahasattva Avalokitesvara transmitting the Buddha Mind Seal." The Emperor felt regret and was going to send an emissary to bring Bodhidharma back. How stupid! When Chih said, "This is Mahasattva Avalokitesvara transmitting the Buddha Mind Seal," if Wu had driven him out of the country, this would have amounted to something.

According to tradition, Master Chih died in the year 514, while Bodhidharma came to Liang in 520; since there is a seven year discrepancy, why is it said that the two met? This must be a mistake in the tradition. As to what is recorded in tradition, I will not discuss this matter now. All that's important is to understand the gist of the matter. Tell me, Bodhidharma is Avalokitesvara, Master Chih is Avalokitesvara, but which is the true Avalokitesvara? Since it is Avalokitesvara, why are there two? But why only two? They are legion.

Later in Wei, Bodhidharma debated with the Vinaya Master Kuang T'ung and the canonical master Bodhiruci. The Master Bodhidharma eliminated formalism and pointed to mind; because of their biased judgments, (the other two) would not put up with this, and instead developed feelings of malevolence and tried to poison Bodhidharma several times. On the sixth attempt, since his mission was completed and he had found someone to succeed to the Dharma, Bodhidharma made no further attempt to save himself, but sat upright and passed on. He was buried at Tinglin Temple on Bear Ear Mountain. Afterwards, while Sung Yun of Wei was on a mission, he met the Master in the Ts'ung Ling Range (in Sinkiang), carrying one shoe in his hand, returning (to India).

Emperor Wu mourned Bodhidharma's death and personally wrote an inscription for his monument. It read, "Alas! I saw him without seeing him, I met him without meeting him, I encountered him without encountering him; now as before I regret this deeply." He further eulogized him by saying, "If your mind exists, you are stuck in the mundane for eternity; if your mind does not exist, you experience wondrous enlightenment instantly."

Tell me, where is Bodhidharma right now? You've stumbled past him without even realizing it.

VERSE *Hsueh Tou*

The holy truths are empty;
> ***The arrow has flown past Korea. Ha!**

How can you discern the point?
> ***Wrong. What is there that's hard to discern?**

"Who is facing me?"
> ***The second try isn't worth half a cent. So you too go on
> like this.**

Again he said, "I don't know."
> ***A third man, a fourth man hits the mark. Bah!**

Henceforth, he secretly crossed the river;
> ***He could not pierce another's nostrils, but his own
> nostrils have been pierced by someone else.c What a
> pity! He sure isn't a great man.**

How could he avoid the growth of a thicket of brambles?
> ***The brambles are already several yards deep beneath
> his feet.**

*Though everyone in the whole country goes after him, he will
> not return;*
> ***A double case. What's the use of pursuing him? Where
> is he? Where is the spirit of a great man?**

(Wu) goes on and on vainly reflecting back.
> ***He wrings his hands and beats his breast, addressing a
> plea to the sky.**

Give up recollection!
> ***What are you saying? You are making a living in a
> ghost cave.**

What limit is there to the pure wind circling the earth?
> ***After all, the great Hsueh Tou is rolling around in the
> weeds.**

*The Master Hsueh Tou looked around to the right and left and
> said,*

"Is there any patriarch here?"
> ***So you want to retract your statement? You still act
> like this?**

He answered himself, "There is."
 **Too much trouble.*

"Call him here to wash this old monk's feet."
 **Give him thirty more blows and drive him away—this
 wouldn't be more than he deserves. Though he acts
 like this, he still amounts to something.*

COMMENTARY   Yuan Wu .

Now as for Hsueh Tou's verse on this case, it is like skillfully
doing a sword dance; sure and relaxed in mid-air, he naturally
does not run afoul of the sharp point. If he lacked this kind of
ability, as soon as he picked it up we would see him run afoul
of the point and wound his hand. For those who have the eye to
see, Hsueh Tou offers, takes back, praises, and deprecates,
using only four lines to settle the entire public case.

Generally, eulogies of the Ancients express Ch'an in a
roundabout way, picking out the main principles of the old
story, settling the case on the basis of the facts, and that is all.
Hsueh Tou gives a thrust and says right off, "The holy truths
are empty—how can you discern the point?" Beneath that first
phrase, he adds this one, which is quite extraordinary. Tell me,
after all how will you discern the point? Even if you have an
iron eye or a copper eye, still you will search without finding.
When you get here, can you figure it out by means of emo-
tive consciousness? This is why Yun Men said, "It is like flint
struck sparks, like flashing lightening." This little bit does not
fall within the scope of mental activity, intellectual consciousness, or emotional conceptions. If you wait till you open
your mouth, what good will it do? As soon as judgement and
comparison arise, the falcon has flown past Korea.

Hsueh Tou says, "How will all you monks distinguish the
real point? Who is facing the Emperor?" He adds the line,
"Again he said, 'I don't know.' " This is where Hsueh Tou is
excessively doting, redoubling his efforts to help people. Now
tell me, are "empty" and "I don't know" the same or different?
If you are someone who has personally understood completely,
you will understand without anything being said. Someone

who has not understood completely will undoubtedly separate them into two. Everywhere everyone always says, "Hsueh Tou (merely) brings up (the case) again." They are far from knowing that (the first) four lines of the verse complete the case entirely.

For the sake of compassion, Hsueh Tou versifies what happened: "Henceforth (Bodhidharma) secretly crossed the river; how could he avoid the growth of a thicket of brambles?" Bodhidharma originally came to this country to melt the sticking points, untie the bonds, pull out the nails and draw out the pegs, to cut down brambles for people: why then say that he gave rise to a thicket of brambles? This is not confined to those times; today the brambles under everyone's feet are already several yards deep. "Though everyone in the whole country goes after him, he will not come back; (Wu) goes on and on vainly reflecting back." Obviously Wu is not a powerful man. Tell me, where is Bodhidharma? If you see Bodhidharma, then you see where Hsueh Tou helps people in the end.

Hsueh Tou feared that people would pursue intellectual views, so he swung open the gate and brought out his own understanding, saying, "Give up recollecting; what limit is there to the pure wind circling the earth?" Once you give up recollection, what will become of the affairs you busy yourselves with? Hsueh Tou says, here and now the pure wind is circling the earth. Throughout heaven and earth, what is there that is limited? Hsueh Tou picks up the numberless concerns of all ages and throws them down before you. This is not confined to Hsueh Tou's time. What limit is there? All of you people—what limit is there on your part?

Again Hsueh Tou feared that people would grab ahold at this point, so again he exposed his skill; in a loud voice he asked, "Is there any patriarch here?" And he answered himself, "There is." Hsueh Tou doesn't hesitate to bare his heart entirely here for the sake of others. Again he spoke up himself: "Call him here to wash this old monk's feet." He certainly diminishes the man's dignity, but at the same time he properly offers his own hands and feet as well. Tell me, where does Hsueh Tou's meaning lie? When you get here, can you call it an ass? Can you call it a horse? Can you call it a patriarch? How can it be named or depicted? The frequently expressed opinion that Hsueh Tou is employing the Patriarch fortunately has nothing to do with it. But tell me, after all what's going on here? "I only allow that the old barbarian knows; I don't allow that the old barbarian understands."

TRANSLATOR'S NOTES

a. Bodhidharma, the first Patriarch of Ch'an in China, was asked by Hui K'e (Shen Kuang), the future Second Patriarch, to pacify his mind for him; Bodhidharma said, "Bring me your mind and I will pacify it for you." Hui K'e said, "When I search for my mind, I cannot find it." Bodhidharma said, "I have pacified your mind for you." At this Hui K'e was enlightened.

b. A lacquer bucket, pitch black, is a Ch'an metaphor for ignorance; to have "the bottom fall out of the bucket" is to become suddenly enlightened. To smash the bucket means to become enlightened or to enlighten others.

c. To pierce someone's nostrils, as in putting a ring through a bull's nose, means to master, to take control, to seize the advantage and have the upper hand. When one's nostrils are in another's hands, it means that one has been "caught," even be it metaphysically, so to speak.

The Ultimate Path is Without Difficulty

POINTER

Heaven and earth are narrow; sun, moon, and stars all at once go dark. Even if blows of the staff fall like rain and shouts roll like thunder, you still haven't lived up to the task of the fundamental vehicle of transcendence. Even the Buddhas of the three times can only know it for themselves; the successive generations of patriarchs have not been able to bring it up in its entirety. The treasury of teachings of the whole age cannot explain it thoroughly; clear eyed patchrobed monks cannot save themselves completely. When you get here, how will you ask for more instruction? To say the word "Buddha" is trailing mud and dripping water; to say the word "Ch'an" is a face full of shame. Superior people who have studied for a long time do not wait for it to be said; latecoming beginners simply must investigate and apprehend it.

CASE

Chao Chou, teaching the assembly, said,[1] "The Ultimate Path is without difficulty;[2] just avoid picking and choosing.[3] As soon as there are words spoken, "this is picking and choosing," "this is clarity."[4] This old monk does not abide within clarity;[5] do you still preserve anything or not?"[6]

At that time a certain monk asked, "Since you do not abide within clarity, what do you preserve?"[7]

Chao Chou replied, "I don't know either."[8]

The monk said, "Since you don't know, Teacher, why do you nevertheless say that you do not abide within clarity?"[9]

Chao Chou said, "It is enough to ask about the matter; bow and withdraw."[10]

10

NOTES

1. What's the old fellow doing? Don't create complications!
2. Not hard, not easy.
3. What's in front of your eyes? The Third Patriarch is still alive.
4. Two heads, three faces. A little boasting. When a fish swims through, the water is muddied; when a bird flies by, feathers fall.
5. His thieving intent already shows; where is the old fellow going?
6. He's defeated. Still there's something, or a half.
7. The monk presses him well; his tongue is pressed against the roof of his mouth.
8. (The monk) crushed this old fellow dead; he has to fall back three thousand miles.
9. Look! Where is he going? He's chased him up a tree.
10. Lucky thing he has this move; the old thief!

COMMENTARY

Chao Chou always used to bring up this saying; that is, "Just avoid picking and choosing." This is from the Third Patriarch's *Seal of Faith in the Heart*, which says,

> The Ultimate Path is without difficulty;
> Just avoid picking and choosing.
> Just don't love or hate,
> And you'll be lucid and clear.

As soon as you have affirmation and negation, "this is picking and choosing," "this is clarity." As soon as you understand this way, you have already stumbled past. When you're riveted down or stuck in glue, what can you do? Chao Chou said, "This is picking and choosing, this is clarity." People these days who practice meditation and ask about the Path, if they do not remain within picking and choosing, then they settle down within clarity. "This old monk does not abide within clarity; do you still preserve anything or not?" All of you people tell me, since he is not within clarity, where is Chao Chou? And why does he still teach people to preserve?

My late master Wu Tsu often would say, "I reach my hand down to show you, but how do you understand?" But tell me, where does he reach down his hand? Perceive the meaning on the hook; don't stick by the zero point of the scale.

This monk coming forth was undeniably extraordinary; he got ahold of Chao Chou's gap and proceeded to press him: "Since you do not abide within clarity, what do you preserve?" Chao Chou never used the staff or the shout; he just said, "I don't know either." When being pressed by that (monk), anyone but this old fellow would time and again be at a loss. Fortunately this old fellow Chao Chou had freedom to turn himself around in, so he answered him like this. Many followers of Ch'an these days will also say when asked, "I don't know either; I don't understand." Nevertheless, though they are on the same road, they are not in the same groove.

There was something special about this monk; only thus could he ask, "Since you don't know, Teacher, why do you nevertheless say that you do not abide within clarity?" Another good rejoinder! If it had been someone other than Chao Chou, he never would have been able to explain. But Chao Chou is an adept; he just said to him, "It's enough to ask about the matter; bow and withdraw." As before, the monk had no way to cope with this old fellow; all he could do was suck in his breath and swallow his voice.

This is a very capable teacher of our clan; he does not discuss the abstruse or the mysterious, he does not speak of mentality or perspectives[a] with you—he always deals with people in terms of the fundamental matter. Thus he would have said, "When we're reviling each other, I let you clamp beaks with me; when we're spitting at each other, I let you spew me with slobber." It is hardly known that while Chao Chou ordinarily never used beating or shouting to deal with people, and only used ordinary speech, still no one in the world could handle him. It was all because he never had so many calculating judgements: he could pick up sideways and use upside-down, go against or go with, having attained great freedom. People today do not understand this, and just say that Chao Chou did not answer the question or explain it to the man. How little you realize that you've stumbled past it.

VERSE

The Ultimate Path is without difficulty:
  **A triple case. A mouthful of frost. What is he saying?*

The speech is to the point, the words are to the point.
> **When the fish swims through, the stream is muddied.
> A profusion of confusion; he smeared it.*

In one there are many kinds;
> **You should open it up; what end will there be in just
> one kind?*

In two there's no duality.
> **How could it sustain four, five, six, seven?
> Why create complications?*

On the horizon of the sky the sun rises and the moon sets;
> **It's presented right to your face; above the head
> and beneath the feet it extends boundlessly. Don't
> lift or lower your head.*

*Beyond the balustrade, the mountains deepen, the waters
> grow chill.*
> **Once dead, you don't return to life again. Do you feel
> the hairs on your body stand on end in a chill?*

*When the skull's consciousness is exhausted, how can joy re-
> main?*
> **He twinkles his eyes within his coffin. Workman Lu
> (Hui Neng, the Sixth Patriarch) is a fellow student of
> his.*

In a dead tree the dragon murmurs are not yet exhausted.
> **Bah! The dead tree blooms again. Bodhidharma
> travels through the eastern land.*

Difficult, difficult!
> **A false teaching is hard to uphold.
> An upside-down statement. What place
> is this here, to speak of difficulty or ease?*

Picking and choosing? Clarity? You see for yourself!
> **Blind! One might have thought it depended on some-
> one else, but luckily (he says) 'See for yourself.' It's
> none of my business.*

COMMENTARY

Hsueh Tou knows where Chao Chou comes down; therefore
he versifies like this: "The Ultimate Path has no difficulties."
Then immediately following this, he says, "The speech is to
the point, the words are to the point." He raises one corner, but

doesn't come back with the other three; when Hsueh Tou says, "In one there are many kinds; in two there's no duality," this is like three corners returning to one. But tell me, where is it that words are to the point, and speech is to the point? In one, why are nevertheless many kinds, yet in two there is no duality? If you don't have eyes, where will you seek?

If you can penetrate these two lines, this is the basis of the ancient saying, "Fused into one whole, as of old you see that mountains are mountains, rivers are rivers, long is long, short is short, sky is sky, and earth is earth." But sometimes we call sky earth and earth sky, sometimes we say that mountains are not mountains and rivers are not rivers. Ultimately, how to attain imperturbable tranquility? When the wind comes, the trees move; when the waves swell, the boats ride high. In spring it sprouts, in summer it matures, in fall it is harvested, in winter it is stored; with uniform equanimity, everything disappears of itself.

Thus this four-line verse abruptly cuts off; but Hsueh Tou has extra ability, so he opens up the closed bag and gives a summary account. As he said at first,

> The Ultimate Path is without difficulty;
> Speech is to the point, words are to the point.
> In one there are many kinds;
> In two there is no duality.

Though there aren't so many things, when the sun rises over the horizon the moon goes down, and when the mountains beyond the balustrade deepen, the waters grow cold. When you get here, speech is indeed to the point, words are indeed to the point, everything is the Path and all things are completely real. Isn't this where mind and objects are both forgotten, fused into one whole? At the beginning of the verse Hsueh Tou was too solitary and steep; at the end, though, he is quite indulgent. If you can bore right through and see and penetrate, naturally it will be like the excellent flavor of ghee. If you don't forget your emotional interpretations, then you'll see a profusion of confusion, and you definitely won't understand this kind of talk.

"When the skull's consciousness is exhausted, how can joy remain? In the dead tree, dragon murmurs are not yet ended." This is just a bit of combination. These are from public cases of ancient questions about the Path, which Hsueh Tou has drawn out, pierced through and strung on the same thread to use in versifying "The Ultimate Path is without difficulty; just avoid picking and choosing." People these days don't understand the Ancient's meaning, and only chew on the words and gnaw on the phrases; when will they ever be done? If you are an adept who is a master of technique, only then can you understand this kind of talk.

Haven't you read how a monk asked Hsiang Yen, "What is the Path?" Hsiang Yen said, "In a dead tree, dragon murmurings." The monk asked, "What is a man of the Path?" Hsiang Yen said, "Eyeballs in a skull." Later the monk asked Shih Shuang, "What are 'dragon murmurings in a dead tree'?" Shih Shuang said, "Still having joy." The monk asked, "What are eyeballs in a skull?" Shih Shuang said, "Still having consciousness." The monk also asked Ts'ao Shan, "What are 'dragon murmurings in a dead tree'?" Ts'ao Shan said, "The blood line is not cut off." The monk asked, "What are 'eyeballs in a skull'?" Ts'ao Shan said, "Not dried up." The monk asked, "Who can hear this?" Ts'ao Shan said, "In the whole world, there is no one who does not hear it." The monk asked, "What book is 'dragon murmurings' taken from?" Ts'ao Shan said, "I don't know what book it's from, but all who hear it die." He also had a verse which said,

> In a dead tree the dragon murmurs and truly sees
>   the Path;
> When the skull has no consciousness, only then are
>   the eyes clear.
> When joy and consciousness come to an end, all
>   happenings are ended;
> How can such a one discriminate the pure in the
>   midst of impurity?

Hsueh Tou can be said to possess great skill in combining all this at once in his verse. Though he has done this, there's been no duality at all.

Hsueh Tou had help for people at the end of the verse when he added "Difficult, difficult!" It's exactly this "difficult, difficult," that you must penetrate through in order to attain. Why? Pai Chang said, "All words and speech, mountains, rivers, and the great earth, each come back to oneself." Whatever Hsueh Tou offers and takes back must ultimately be returned to oneself. Tell me, how did Hsueh Tou help people when he said, "Picking and choosing? Clarity? See for yourself!"? He had already created this complicated verse; why then did he say "See for yourself"? Tell me, what was his true meaning? Don't say you can't understand. At this point, even I simply cannot understand either.

TRANSLATOR'S NOTES

a. *Chi* and *ching*, rendered in this instance as 'mentality and perspective,' are very common technical terms, to be met with many times in this book, used individually and as a pair. Both are used in referring to both subjective and objective phenomena; in Ch'an meditation they sometimes speak of 'forgetting' or 'merging' subject and object; likewise, as 'turning words' or 'pivotal words,' these terms produce, individually and together, an effect which cannot be rendered conveniently in a single English expression.

   Chi is used for 'potential' (as of a student, or a situation), 'capability,' or a 'device' used to illustrate a point or state; it also means mental activity or state in general. Sometimes the first, or primary *chi* is contrasted to the secondary *chi*; this is like 'cognition' followed by 'recognition.'

   Ching is a mental object, an object, a state, a realm or sphere, a perspective (or perception). A common question is what a master's *ching* is like (i.e. what does he 'see,' what is his sphere or state of realization), and what the person in that 'realm' is like. When Ch'an students experienced purity or bliss, or perceived Buddhas and bodhisattvas in their meditations, they were told these were merely *ching*, mental objects or 'states' which should not be acknowledged as desirable or approved as real attainments, lest one become intoxicated by one's state. Similarly, all kinds of hallucinations were called *mo ching* or 'demon states,' illusory objects or perceptions caused by 'demons' or 'devils' (whether these are inside or outside the mind is a pointless question here), obstructing the path of meditation.

   As examples of *chi-ching*, Japanese commentaries conventionally refer to such things as 'twinkling the eyes,' 'raising the eyebrows,' 'raising the staff, the whisk, or the gavel,' gestures frequently met with in Ch'an records as replies to questions, or teaching devices of the masters. *Chi-ching* thus means the mentality, or mental working, and the perspective, or object it embraces; an act and the state it manifests, a device and the object(ive) it intends to convey. Ultimately, it seems that these terms can refer to any action or speech and the implication or impression it presents or represents, especially the intentional gesture or remark of the teaching master.

Master Ma is Unwell

POINTER

One device, one object; one word, one phrase—the intent is that you'll have a place to enter; still this is gouging a wound in healthy flesh—it can become a nest or a den. The Great Function appears without abiding by fixed principles—the intent is that you'll realize there is something transcendental; it covers the sky and covers the earth, yet it cannot be grasped.

This way will do, not this way will do too—this is too diffuse. This way won't do, not this way won't do either—this is too cut off. Without treading these two paths, what would be right? Please test; I cite this for you to see:

CASE

Great Master Ma was unwell.[1] The temple superintendent asked him, "Teacher, how has your venerable health been in recent days?"[2] The Great Master said, "Sun Face Buddha, Moon Face Buddha."[3,a]

NOTES

1. This fellow has broken down quite a bit. He's dragging in other people.
2. Four hundred and four diseases break out all at once. They'll be lucky if they're not seeing off a dead monk in three days. (This question) is in the course of humanity and righteousness.
3. How fresh and new! Sustenance for his fledgeling.

COMMENTARY

The Great Master Ma was unwell, so the temple superintendent asked him, "Teacher, how has your venerable health been in recent days?" The Great Master replied, "Sun Face Buddha, Moon Face Buddha." If the patriarchal teachers had not dealt with others on the basis of the fundamental matter, how could we have the shining light of this Path? If you know what this public case comes down to, then you walk alone through the red sky; if you don't know where it comes down, time and again you'll lose the way before the withered tree cliff. If you are somebody in your own right, when you get here you must have the ability to drive off the plowman's ox and to snatch away the hungry man's food before you will see how Great Master Ma helps people.

These days many people say that Master Ma was teaching the superintendent; fortunately, this has no connection. Right now in this assembly there are many who misunderstand; they put a glare in their eyes and say, "It's here; the left eye is the Sun Face, and the right eye is the Moon Face." What relevance does this have? Even by the (non-existent) Year of the Ass, you won't have seen it even in a dream. You just stumble past, missing what the Ancient was about.

So when Master Ma spoke like this, where was his meaning? Some say (he meant) "Fix some stomach medicine and bring me a bowl of it." What grasp has this got on it? Having gotten to this point, how would you attain tranquility? This is why it is said, "The single road of transcendence has not been transmitted by a thousand sages; students trouble themselves with forms like monkeys grasping at reflections."

This "Sun Face Buddha, Moon Face Buddha" is extremely difficult to see; even Hsueh Tou finds it difficult to versify this. But since he has seen all the way through, he uses his life's work to the full to make his comment. Do you people want to see Hsueh Tou? Look at the text below.

VERSE

Sun Face Buddha, Moon Face Buddha;
  **When he opens his mouth you see his guts.
  (Ma and Hsueh Tou) are like two facing mirrors;
  in between there's no image or reflection.*

What kind of people were the Ancient Emperors?
  **Too lofty. Don't belittle them. They
  can be valued high or low.*

For twenty years I have suffered bitterly;
  **This is your own fall into the weeds—
  it's none of my business. Here's a mute
  eating a bitter melon.*

How many times I have gone down into the Blue Dragon's
    cave for you!
  **How was it worth this! Don't misuse your mind.
  Don't say there isn't anything extraordinary here.*

This distress
  **He saddens people to death.
  Sad man, don't speak to sad people.*

Is worth recounting;
  **To whom would you speak of it!
  If you speak of it to sad people,
  you will sadden them to death.*

Clear-eyed patchrobed monks should not take it lightly.
  **You must be even more thoroughgoing. Bah! Fall
  back three thousand miles.*

COMMENTARY

When (the Sung Emperor) Shen Tsung was on the throne (1068–1085) he thought that this verse ridiculed the state, so he wouldn't let it be included in the (Buddhist) canon.

First Hsueh Tou quotes: "Sun Face Buddha, Moon Face Buddha." Having brought this up, then he says, "What kind of people were the Ancient Emperors?" Tell me, what is his meaning? I just finished telling you a minute ago; Hsueh Tou is commenting directly (on Master Ma). So it is said, "Letting down his hook in the four seas, he only fishes for terrible dragons." This one line has already been completed (the verse); afterwards, Hsueh Tou versifies how he concentrated on study and search all his life.

"For twenty years I have suffered bitterly; how many times I've gone down into the Blue Dragon's cave for you!" What is he like? He's like a man going into the Blue Dragon's cave to seize the pearl. Afterwards he broke apart the lacquer bucket. Though this might be considered quite extraordinary, basically it just amounts to "What kind of people were the Ancient Emperors?" Tell me, what are Hsueh Tou's words getting at? You have to take a step back on your own and look before you will see where he's at.

So what kind of people were the Ancient Emperors anyway? People mostly do not see Hsueh Tou's meaning, but only say that he is ridiculing the state. To understand in this way is merely an emotional view. This (line) comes from Ch'an Yueh's poem on "The behavior of barons," which says,

> *Clothes in brocades and fine embroidery, with fal-*
> *cons on their wrists,*
> *They go about at leisure, their manner scornful.*
> *They know nothing of the difficulties of sowing and*
> *harvesting;*
> *What kind of people were the Ancient Emperors?*

Hsueh Tou says, "This distress is worth recounting; clear eyed patchrobed monks must not take it lightly." How many people make their livelihood within the Blue Dragon's cave? Even if you're a clear eyed patchrobed monk with an eye on your forehead and a talisman under your arm, shining through the four continents, when you get here you still must not take it lightly; you must be thoroughgoing.

TRANSLATOR'S NOTES

a.   According to the *Buddha Name Scripture,* a Sun Face Buddha lives in the world for eighteen hundred years, whereas a Moon Face Buddha enters extinction after a day and a night. Tenkei Denson says, "But is everyone's own Sun Face Buddha Moon Face Buddha something long or short?"

Te Shan Carrying His Bundle

POINTER

Under the blue sky, in the bright sunlight, you don't have to point out this and that anymore; but the causal conditions of time and season still require you to give the medicine in accordance with the disease. But tell me, is it better to let go, or is it better to hold still? To test, I cite this: look!

CASE

When Te Shan arrived at Kuei Shan,[1] he carried his bundle with him into the teaching hall,[2] where he crossed from east to west and from west to east.[3] He looked around and said, "There's nothing, no one." Then he went out.[4]

Hsueh Tou added the comment, "Completely exposed."[5] But when Te Shan got to the monastery gate, he said, "Still, I shouldn't be so coarse."[6] So he reentered (the hall) with full ceremony to meet (Kuei Shan).[7] As Kuei Shan sat there,[8] Te Shan held up his sitting mat and said, "Teacher!"[9] Kuei Shan reached for his whisk,[10] whereupon Te Shan shouted, shook out his sleeves, and left.[11]

Hsueh Tou added the comment, "Completely exposed."[12]

Te Shan turned his back on the teaching hall, put on his straw sandals, and departed.[13] That evening Kuei Shan asked the head monk, "Where is that newcomer who just came?"[14] The head monk answered, "At that time he turned his back on the teaching hall, put on his straw sandals, and departed."[15]

Kuei Shan said, "Hereafter that lad will go to the summit of a solitary peak, build himself a grass hut, and go on scolding the Buddhas and reviling the Patriarchs."[16]

Hsueh Tou added the comment, "He adds frost to snow."[17]

NOTES

1. The board-carrying fellow,ᵃ the wild fox spirit!ᵇ
2. Unavoidably he causes people to doubt. He has suffered defeat.
3. He has a lot of Ch'an, but what for?
4. He deserves thirty blows of the staff. Indeed his spirit reaches the heavens. A real lion cub can roar the lion's roar.
5. Wrong. After all. Check!
6. Letting go, gathering in. At first too high, in the end too low. When one realizes one's fault one should reform, but how many people can?
7. As before, he acts like this. It's already his second defeat. Danger!
8. (Kuei Shan) watches this fellow with cold eyes. It takes this kind of man to grab a tiger's whiskers.
9. He changes heads, switches faces; he stirs up waves where there's no wind.
10. Only that fellow could do this; he sets his strategy in motion from within his tent. Nothing can stop him from cutting off the tongues of everyone in the world.
11. This is the understanding of a wild fox spirit. This one shout contains both the provisional and the real, both the illumination and the function. They're all people who can grab the clouds and grasp the fog, but he is outstanding among them.
12. Wrong. After all. Check!
13. The scenery is lovely, but the case is not yet completed. (Te Shan) won the hat on his head but lost the shoes on his feet. He's already lost his body and his life.
14. He lost his interest in the east, and loses his principal in the west. His eyes look southeast, but his mind is in the northwest.
15. The sacred tortoise is dragging his tail;ᶜ he deserves thirty blows. How many blows to the back of the head would it take for this kind of fellow?
16. He draws his bow after the thief is gone. No patchrobed monk in the world can leap out of this.
17. Wrong. After all. Check!

COMMENTARY

Three times I added the word "check." Do all of you understand? Sometimes I take a blade of grass and use it as the sixteen-foot golden body (of Buddha); sometimes I take the sixteen-foot golden body and use it as a blade of grass.

Originally Te Shan was a lecturing monk, expounding the *Diamond Cutter Scripture* in western Shu (Szechuan). According to what it says in that teaching, in the process of the knowledge attained after diamond-like concentration, one studies the majestic conduct of Buddhas for a thousand aeons and studies the refined practices of Buddhas for ten thousand aeons before finally fulfilling Buddhahood. On the other hand, the "southern devils" at this time were saying "Mind itself is Buddha." Consequently Te Shan became very incensed and went travelling on foot, carrying some commentaries; he went straight to the South to destroy this crew of devils. You see from how aroused he got what a fierce keen fellow he was.

When he first got to Li Chou (in Hunan), he met an old woman selling fried cakes by the roadside; he put down his commentaries to buy some refreshment to lighten his mind. The old woman said, "What is that you're carrying?" Te Shan said, "Commentaries on the *Diamond Cutter Scripture*." The old woman said, "I have a question for you: if you can answer it I'll give you some fried cakes to refresh your mind; if you can't answer, you'll have to go somewhere else to buy." Te Shan said, "Just ask." The old woman said, "The *Diamond Cutter Scripture* says, 'Past mind can't be grasped, present mind can't be grasped, future mind can't be grasped': which mind does the learned monk desire to refresh?" Te Shan was speechless. The old woman directed him to go call on Lung T'an.

As soon as Te Shan crossed the threshold he said, "Long have I heard of Lung T'an ('Dragon Pond'), but now that I've arrived here, there's no pond to see and no dragon appears." Master Lung T'an came out from behind a screen and said, "You have really arrived at Lung T'an." Te Shan bowed and withdrew. During the night Te Shan entered Lung T'an's room and stood in attendance till late at night. Lung T'an said, "Why don't you go?" Te Shan bade farewell, lifted up the curtain, and went out; he saw that it was dark outside, so he turned around and said, "It's dark outside." Lung T'an lit a paper lantern and handed it to Te Shan; as soon as Te Shan took it, Lung T'an blew it out. Te Shan was vastly and greatly enlightened. Immediately he bowed to Lung T'an, who said, "What have you seen that you bow?" Te Shan answered, "From now on I will never again doubt what's on the tongues of the venerable teaching masters of the world."

The next day Lung T'an went up into the teaching hall and said, "There is one among you with teeth like a forest of swords and a mouth like a bowl of blood; even if you hit him with a staff, he wouldn't turn back. Another day he will ascend to the summit of a solitary peak and establish my path there." Then Te Shan took all his commentaries in front of the teaching hall and raised a torch over them, declaring, "Even to plumb all abstruse locutions is like a single hair in the great void; to exhaust the essential workings of the world is like a single drop of water cast into a vast valley." Then he burned the commentaries.

Later he heard that Kuei Shan's teaching was flourishing, so he traveled to Kuei Shan to meet him as an adept. Without even untying his bundle, he went straight to the teaching hall, where he walked back and forth from east to west and west to east, looked around, and said, "Nothing, no one." Then he went out. Tell me, what was his meaning? Wasn't he crazy? People misinterpret this as 'establishment,' but that is simply irrelevant. See how extraordinary that Te Shan was; this is why it is said, "To stand out from the crowd, you must be a brave spirited fellow; to defeat enemies is a matter for a lion's son. If you try to become Buddha without an eye like this, how will you ever do it, even in a thousand years?"

When you get here, you must be a thoroughly competent adept before you will be able to see. Why? In the Buddha Dharma there are not so many complications; where can you bring intellectual views to bear? This is the action of (Te Shan's) mind; where is there so much toil? This is why Hsuan Sha said, "Even if you're like the moon reflected in an autumn pond, which when striking the waves is not scattered, or like the sound of a bell on a quiet night, which when hit never fails to resound, this is still an affair on this shore of birth and death." When you arrive here there is no gain or loss, no affirmation or negation, nor is there anything extraordinary or mysterious. Since there is nothing extraordinary or mysterious, how will you understand (Te Shan's) going back and forth from east to west and west to east? Tell me, what was his meaning?

This old fellow Kuei Shan still was not taken in by that (Te

Shan); anyone but Kuei Shan would have been crushed by him. Look at how the old adept Kuei Shan meets him; he just sits there and observes the outcome. If he did not profoundly discern the 'oncoming wind,' how could he have been like this? Hsueh Tou adds the comment "Completely exposed." This is like an iron spike. In the assembly this is called an added comment: although it goes for both sides, it does not remain on either side. How will you understand his statement, "Completely exposed"? Where does the complete exposure take place? Tell me, is Te Shan completely exposed, or is it Kuei Shan who is completely exposed?

On his way out Te Shan got as far as the monastery gate, but then he said to himself, "Still, I shouldn't be so coarse." He wanted to bring out his guts, his innermost heart, in a Dharma battle with Kuei Shan; so he went back in with full ceremony to meet him. As Kuei Shan sat there, Te Shan lifted up his sitting mat and said, "Teacher!" Kuei Shan reached for his whisk; Te Shan then shouted, shook his sleeves, and left. How extraordinary!

Many in the assembly say that Kuei Shan was afraid of him. What has this got to do with it? Kuei Shan was not flustered at all. This is why it is said, "One whose wisdom surpasses a bird's can catch a bird, one whose wisdom surpasses an animal's can catch an animal, and one whose wisdom surpasses a man's can catch a man." When one is immersed in this kind of Ch'an, even if the multitude of appearances and myriad forms, heavens and hells, and all the plants, animals, and people, all were to shout at once, he still wouldn't be bothered; even if someone overthrew his meditation seat and scattered his congregation with shouts, he wouldn't give it any notice. It is as high as heaven, broad as earth. If Kuei Shan did not have the ability to cut off the tongues of everyone on earth, at that time it would have been very difficult for him to test Te Shan. If he weren't the enlightened teacher of fifteen hundred people, at this point he wouldn't have been able to explain anything. But Kuei Shan was setting strategy in motion from within his tent that would settle victory over a thousand miles.

Te Shan turned his back on the teaching hall, put on his straw sandals, and departed. Tell me, what was his meaning? You tell me, did Te Shan win or lose? Acting as he did, did Kuei

Shan win or lose? Hsueh Tou commented, "Completely exposed." Here he makes an effort and sees through the Ancients' ultimate riddle; only thus could he be so extraordinary. Hsueh Tou added "Completely exposed" twice, making a three part judgement; only then had he revealed this public case. He was like a bystander judging those two men.

Afterwards, this old fellow (Kuei Shan) was unhurried; when evening came he finally asked the head monk, "Where is that newcomer who just came?" The head monk replied, "At that time, he turned his back on the teaching hall, put on his straw sandals, and left." Kuei Shan said, "Hereafter that lad will go up to the summit of a solitary peak, build himself a grass hut, and go on scolding the Buddhas and reviling the Patriarchs." But say, what was his meaning? Old man Kuei Shan was not being good hearted; in the future Te Shan could scold the Buddhas and revile the Patriarchs, pummel the wind and beat the rain, yet he would still never get out of that cave. Te Shan's whole lifetime's methods have been seen through by this old fellow. Should we say that Kuei Shan has given him a prophecy here? Or should we say that when the marsh is wide it can hide a mountain, that reason[d] can subdue a leopard? Fortunately this has nothing to do with it.

Hsueh Tou knows what this public case comes down to, so he can dare to settle it for them by further saying, "He adds frost to snow." Once again he offers it up for people to see. If you do see, I'll allow that you're a fellow student of Kuei Shan, Te Shan, and Hsueh Tou. If you don't see, beware of vainly producing intellectual interpretations.

VERSE

One "completely exposed"
   The words are still in our ears. Gone.

A second "completely exposed"
   A double case.

"Adding frost to snow"–(Te Shan) has had a dangerous fall.
   The three stages are not the same. Where (did Te Shan fall)?

The General of the Flying Cavalry enters the enemy camp;
    **Danger! No need to trouble to slash again at the*
    *general of a defeated army. He loses his body and life.**

How many could regain their safety?
    (Te Shan) gained life in the midst of death.

(Te Shan) hurriedly runs past—
    **He acts like no one is around him.*
    Although you exhaust the thirty-six
    strategems of your supernatural powers,
    *what is the use?**

(But Kuei Shan) doesn't let him go.
    **The cat can subdue the leopard.*
    *(Kuei Shan) pierced his nostrils.**

On the summit of the solitary peak, he sits among the weeds;
    **After all. To pierce his nostrils isn't out of the*
    ordinary. But why is he (Te Shan) sitting among the
    *weeds?**

Bah!
    **Understand? Two blades cut each other.*
    Two by two, three by three, they walk the
    old road. Singing and clapping go together.
    *I strike!**

COMMENTARY

When Hsueh Tou composed verses on one hundred public cases, with each case he burned incense and offered it up; therefore (his verses) have circulated widely throughout the land. In addition he mastered literary composition. When he had penetrated the public cases and become easily conversant with them, only then could he set his brush to paper. Why so? It is easy to distinguish dragons from snakes; it is hard to fool a patchrobed monk. Since Hsueh Tou immersed himself in this case and penetrated through it, he puts down three comments at those impenetrable, misleading places, then picks them up to make his verse.

"Adding frost to snow"—almost a dangerous fall. What is Te Shan like? He is just like Li Kuang, by innate talent a skilled archer, whom the Emperor (Wu of Han) commissioned as the General of the Flying Cavalry (Imperial elite corps). Li Kuang penetrated deep into enemy territory, where he was captured alive by the King of the Huns. Kuang was weak from wounds; they tied him prone between two horses. Kuang played dead, but stealthily observed that there was a Hun near him riding a good mount. Kuang suddenly sprang up and leaped on the horse, throwing down the Hun rider and seizing his bow and arrows. Whipping the horse, he galloped off towards the South; drawing the bow and shooting back at the riders pursuing him, he thus made good his escape. This fellow had the ability to wrest life from the midst of death; Hsueh Tou alludes to this in the verse to make a comparison with Te Shan, who re-entered (the teaching hall) to meet (Kuei Shan), and was able to leap out again, as before.

Look at how that Ancient (Te Shan) sees all the way, speaks all the way, acts all the way, and functions all the way; he's undeniably a brave spirit. Only if you possess the ability to kill a man without blinking an eye can you then become Buddha right where you stand. Someone who can fulfill Buddhahood right where he stands naturally kills people without blinking an eye; thus he has his share of freedom and independence.

When some people these days are questioned, at first they seem to have the qualities of a patchrobed monk, but when they're pressed even slightly, their waists snap and their legs break; they come all to pieces. They totally lack the slightest continuity. That is why an Ancient said, "Continuity is indeed very difficult." Look at how Te Shan and Kuei Shan acted; were theirs stammering, halting views?

"How many could regain their safety? (Te Shan) hurriedly runs past." Te Shan shouted and left; this is just like Li Kuang's strategy after he was captured, seizing a bow to shoot and kill his guard, and making good his escape from enemy territory. Hsueh Tou's verse at this point has great effect.

Te Shan turned his back on the teaching hall, put on his straw sandals and left. Some say he gained the advantage; how far they are from realizing that this old fellow (Kuei Shan), as before, still doesn't allow (Te Shan) to appear. Hsueh Tou says, "He doesn't let him go." The same evening Kuei Shan asked the head monk, "Where is that newcomer who just came?" The head monk said, "Back then, he turned his back on the teaching hall, put on his straw sandals and left." Kuei Shan said, "Hereafter that lad will go up to the summit of a solitary peak, build himself a grass hut, and go on scolding the Buddhas and reviling the Patriarchs." When did he ever let him go? Nevertheless, he's outstanding.

At this point, why does Hsueh Tou say, "On the summit of the solitary peak, he sits among the weeds," and then add an exclamation? Tell me, what does this come down to? Study for thirty more years!

TRANSLATOR'S NOTES

a.   Someone carrying a board can only see one side, vision being obstructed by the burden.

b.   A wild fox spirit is usually an expression of blame, referring to someone who indulges in cleverness. According to an old story, someone once became a wild fox because he said that an accomplished yogi is not subject to cause and effect. However, like all 'turning words,' this expression also has a positive side, meaning one who has complete freedom of action.

c.   That is, he is leaving a trail. Some commentators explain the general metaphor by saying that when a tortoise lays eggs in the sand it covers them to hide them, but as it leaves its tail makes a track, after all revealing the whereabouts of the eggs. This expression is thus similar to the Ch'an saying about hiding the body but revealing the shadow.

d.   The alternate version of this saying is that "a cat can subdue a leopard," meaning that the weaker can subdue the stronger. Confusion arose from the similarity between the Chinese characters used for "cat" and for "reason."

Hsueh Feng's Grain of Rice

POINTER

Whoever would uphold the teaching of our school must be a brave spirited fellow; only with the ability to kill a man without blinking an eye can one become Buddha right where he stands. Therefore his illumination and function are simultaneous; wrapping up and opening out are equal in his preaching. Principle and phenomena are not two, and he practices both the provisional and the real. Letting go of the primary, he sets up the gate of the secondary meaning; if he were to cut off all complications straightaway, it would be impossible for late-coming students of elementary capabilities to find a resting place. It was this way yesterday; the matter couldn't be avoided. It is this way today too; faults and errors fill the skies. Still, if one is a clear eyed person, he can't be fooled one bit. Without clear eyes, lying in the mouth of a tiger, one cannot avoid losing one's body and life. As a test, I cite this; look!

CASE

Hsueh Feng, teaching his community, said,[1] "Pick up the whole great earth in your fingers, and it's as big as a grain of rice.[2] Throw it down before you:[3] if, like a lacquer bucket, you don't understand,[4] I'll beat the drum to call everyone to look."[5]

NOTES

1. One blind man leading a crowd of blind men. It's not beyond him.
2. What technique is this? I myself have never sported devil eyes.
3. I'm afraid it can't be thrown down. What skill do you have?
4. Hsueh Feng relies on his power to deceive people. Take what's coming to you and get out!
5. Blind! The beat of the drum is for the three armies.

31

COMMENTARY

Ch'ang Ch'ing asked Yun Men, "When Hsueh Feng spoke like this, was there any place where he wasn't able to appear?" Men answered, "There is." Ch'ing asked, "How so?" Men said, "One can't always be making wild fox spirit interpretations."

Yun Feng said, "Compared to above, not enough; compared to below, too much. I am making up more complications for you." He raised his staff and said, "Do you see Hsueh Feng? Where the King's rule is a little more strict, it's not permitted to plunder the open markets."

Che of Ta Kuei said, "I'll add more mud to dirt for you." He raised his staff and said, "Look! Look! Hsueh Feng has defecated right in front of you all. Come now, why don't you even recognize the smell of shit?"

Hsueh Feng, teaching his assembly, said, "Pick up the whole great earth in your fingers, and it's as big as a grain of rice." There was something extraordinary in the way this Ancient guided people and benefited beings. He was indefatigably rigorous; three times he climbed (Mount) T'ou Tzu, nine times he went to Tung Shan. Wherever he went, he would set up his lacquer tub and wooden spoon and serve as the rice steward, just for the sake of penetrating this matter.

When he arrived at Tung Shan, he served as the rice steward; one day Tung Shan asked Hsueh Feng, "What are you doing?" Hsueh Feng said, "Cleaning rice." Shan asked, "Are you washing the grit to get rid of the rice, or are you washing the rice to get rid of the grit?" Feng said, "Grit and rice are both removed at once." Shan said, "What will everybody eat?" Feng then overturned the basin. Shan said, "Your affinity lies with Te Shan," and he directed Feng to go see him.

As soon as he got there, Hsueh Feng asked, "Does this student have any share in this matter handed down from antiquity as the fundamental vehicle?" Te Shan struck him a blow and said, "What are you saying?" Because of this, Hsueh Feng had an insight.

Later Hsueh Feng was snowed in on Tortoise Mountain (in Hunan). He told Yen T'ou, "When Te Shan hit me, it was like the bottom falling out of a bucket." Yen T'ou shouted and said, "Haven't you heard it said that what comes in through the gate isn't the family treasure? You must let it flow out from your own breast to cover heaven and earth; then you'll have some small portion of realization." Suddenly Hsueh Feng was greatly enlightened; he bowed and said to Yen T'ou, "Elder brother, today on Tortoise Mountain I have finally attained the Path."

People these days only say that the Ancient (Hsueh Feng) made something up specially to teach people of the future fixed precepts that they can rely on. To say this is just slandering that ancient master; this is called "spilling Buddha's blood." The Ancients weren't like people today with their spurious shallow talk; otherwise, how could they have used a single word or half a phrase for a whole lifetime? Therefore, when it came to supporting the teaching of the school and continuing the life of the Buddhas, they would spit out a word or half a phrase which would spontaneously cut off the tongues of everyone on earth. There's no place for you to produce a train of thought, to make intellectual interpretations, or to grapple with principles. See how Hsueh Feng taught his community; since he had seen adepts, he had the hammer and tongs of an adept. Whenever he utters a word or half a phrase, he's not making his livelihood within the ghost caves of mental activity, ideational consciousness and calculating thought. He just surpasses the multitudes and stands out from the crowd; he settles past and present and leaves no room for uncertainty. His actions were all like this.

One day Hsueh Feng said to his community, "On South Mountain there's a turtle-nosed snake; all of you should take a good look at it." Thereupon Wayfarer Leng (Ch'ang Ch'ing) came forward from the assembly and said, "If so, then there are a lot of people in this hall today who lose their bodies and lives."

On another occasion Hsueh Feng said, "The whole great earth is the single eye of a monk; where will you people go to defecate?" Another time he said, "I have met with you at Wang Chou Pavilion; I have also met with you in the Black Rock Range, and I have also met with you in front of the monks' hall." At the time Pao Fu asked E Hu, "Leaving aside 'in front of the monks' hall,' what about the meetings at Wang Chou Pavilion and Black Rock Range?" E Hu hurried back to his room. Hsueh Feng was always bringing up this kind of talk to instruct his community.

As for "Pick up the whole great earth in your fingers, and it's as big as a grain of rice"—tell me, at this juncture, can you figure it out by means of intellectual discrimination? Here you must smash through the net, at once abandon gain and loss, affirmation and negation, to be completely free and at ease; you naturally pass through his snare, and then you will see what he's doing. Tell me, where is Hsueh Feng's meaning?

People often make up intellectual interpretations and say, "Mind is the master of myriad things; the whole great earth is all at once in my hand." Fortunately, this has no connection. Here you must be a true and genuine fellow, who penetrates the bone through to the marrow, and sees all the way through as soon as he hears it brought up, yet without falling into emotional considerations or conceptual thinking. If you are a genuine foot-traveling patchrobed monk, you will see that in acting this way, Hsueh Feng was already indulging to help others.

Look at Hsueh Tou's verse, which says,

VERSE

An ox head disappears,
    **Like a flash of lightening.
    You've already stumbled past it.*
A horse head emerges.
    **Like sparks struck from flint.*
In the mirror of Ts'ao Ch'i,ᵃ absolutely no dust.
    **Come smash the mirror and I will meet with
    you; you must first smash it.*
He beats the drum for you to come look, but you don't see:
    **He pierces your eyes. Don't take it lightly. In the
    lacquer bucket, where is it hard to see?*
When spring arrives, for whom do the hundred flowers bloom?
    **Things don't overlap. What a mess! He sticks his head
    out from within a cave of tangled vines.*

COMMENTARY

Naturally Hsueh Tou sees that other Ancient; he only needs to go to his lifeline, and in one spurt produces a verse for him.

"An ox head disappears, a horse head emerges." Tell me, what is he saying? If you see all the way through to the bottom, it is like eating gruel early in the morning and eating rice at midday—just this ordinary. Out of compassion, Hsueh Tou shatters (everything) with one hammer blow at the outset, and settles (everything) with a single phrase. He is just undeniably solitary and steep, like a flint-struck spark or a flash of lightning. He doesn't reveal his sword point; there's no place for you to linger over. Tell me, can you search it out in your intellectual faculty? These first two lines have said it all.

In the third line, instead Hsueh Tou opens a pathway and displays a little bit of formal style—already he has fallen into the weeds. If you produce words on top of words, phrases on top of phrases, ideas on top of ideas, making up explanations and interpretations, you will not only get me bogged down, but you'll also turn your backs on Hsueh Tou. Although old man Hsueh Tou's verse is this way, his intention is not like this. He has never made up principles to bind people.

"In the mirror of Ts'ao Ch'i, absolutely no dust." Quite a few people say that a stilled mind is the mirror itself. Fortunately, this has nothing to do with it; if you're only concerned with judging and comparing principles, what end will there be to it? Hsueh Tou has spoken clearly; it's just that people do not see. Therefore Hsueh Tou, being such a dotard, says in verse, "He beats the drum for you to come look, but you don't see." Do ignorant people see? He says more to you: "When spring arrives, for whom do the hundred flowers bloom?" One could say he's opening the doors and windows, throwing them wide open all at once for you. When spring comes, in the hidden valleys and wild ravines, in places where there are no people, a hundred flowers burst forth in profusion. Tell me, who else do they bloom for?

TRANSLATOR'S NOTES

a. Ts'ao Ch'i was the abode of the great Sixth Patriarch of Chinese Ch'an, Hui Neng (also known as 'workman Lu'), and is used to refer to him, as well as to his inspiration and lineage. According to tradition, when the Fifth Patriarch Hung Jen wanted to appoint a successor, he told his students to each compose a verse expressing his understanding. All deferred to the senior disciple, Shen Hsiu, a man of great learning and accomplishment in discipline and meditation. Shen Hsiu wrote,

The body is the tree of enlightenment,
The mind like a bright mirror-stand;
Time and again polish it diligently,
Do not let there be any dust.

Hui Neng, however, then a workman in the temple, composed the following verse:

Enlightenment is basically not a tree,
And the mind-mirror not a stand;
Originally there is not a single thing—
What is the use of wiping away dust?

An alternate version has the last line, "Where is there any dust?" Hung Jen accepted Hui Neng as his successor.

Yun Men's Every Day is a Good Day

CASE

Yun Men said, "I don't ask you about before the fifteenth day;[1] try to say something about after the fifteenth day."[2]

Yun Men himself answered for everyone, "Every day is a good day."[3]

NOTES

1. Half south of the river, half north of the river. We don't keep old calendar dates here.
2. Inevitably it will go from dawn to sunset; just don't say that the next day is the sixteenth. Days and months seem to flow by.
3. He's gathered it up. Though the frog jumps, he can't get out of the basket. Whose house has no bright moon and pure wind? But do you know it? The sea god knows its value, he doesn't know its price.

COMMENTARY

Yun Men first called on Mu Chou. Mu Chou spun devices that turned like lightning, so it was difficult to approach and linger. Whenever he received someone, he would grab him as soon as he crossed the threshold and say, "Speak! Speak!" If he couldn't attempt a reply, he would push him out, saying, "Antique drill turning in a rut!"

When Yun Men went to see Mu Chou, on the third time, as soon as he knocked on the door, Mu Chou said, "Who's there?" Yun Men answered, "(Me,) Wen Yen."[a] As soon as (Mu Chou) opened the door a little, (Yun Men) immediately bounded in; Mu Chou held him fast and said, "Speak! Speak!" Yun Men hesitated, and was pushed out; he still had one foot inside when Mu Chou slammed the door, breaking Yun Men's leg. As Yun Men cried out in pain, he was suddenly greatly enlightened. Subsequently, the trend of his words in dealing with people, his whole style, emerged from Mu Chou. After this, Yun Men stayed for three years in the home of the ministry president Ch'en Ts'ao.[b]

Mu Chou directed Yun Men to go to Hsueh Feng; when he arrived there, he came forth from the assembly and said, "What is Buddha?" Hsueh Feng said, "Don't talk in your sleep." Yun Men then bowed. He dwelt there for three years. One day Hsueh Feng asked him, "What is your perception?" Yun Men said, "My view doesn't differ in the slightest from that of all the sages since antiquity."

For twenty years Ling Shu did not appoint a head monk. He used to say, "My head monk is born," and "My head monk is tending oxen," and he would say, "My head monk is traveling on foot." Suddenly one day he ordered the bell to be struck (for everyone to assemble) to receive the head monk at the gate. The congregation was dubious about this, but Yun Men actually arrived. Ling Shu immediately invited him into the head monk's quarters to unpack his bundle. People called Ling Shu the Knowing Sage Ch'an Master, since he knew of all past and future events in advance.

Once King Liu, the Lord of Kuang (-tung), was going to mobilize his army; he intended to go to the monastery personally to ask the master (Ling Shu) to determine whether conditions were auspicious or not. Ling Shu, knowing of this beforehand, sat down and peacefully passed away. The Lord of Kuang said angrily, "Since when was the master sick?" The attendant answered, "The master hadn't been sick. He had just entrusted a box (to me), which he ordered me to present to your majesty when you arrived." The Lord of Kuang opened the box and took out a card which said, "The Eye of Humans and Gods (a living Buddha) is the head monk in the hall." Having understood Ling Shu's inner meaning, the Lord of Kuang thereupon dismissed his soldiers and invited Yun Men to appear in the world at Ling Shu Monastery. Only later did he dwell at Yun Men.

As the master was expounding the Dharma, the royal attendant Ju posed a question; "Is the fruit of Ling Shu ('Spiritual

Tree') ripe yet, or not?" Yun Men said, "When have you ever heard it said that it was unripe?"

One day King Liu summoned the master to spend the summer in the palace. Together with several other venerable abbots, he was to receive the questions of the courtiers and expound the Dharma. Only one man, the master Yun Men, did not speak, and there was no one on familiar terms with him. One of the palace functionaries wrote a verse and posted it in the Green Jade Hall:

> *Cultivation of the great wisdom—only that is Ch'an;*
> *Silence, not clamor, is in order for the Ch'an school.*
> *Ten thousand kinds of clever talk—how can they be as good as reality?*
> *They lose to Yun Men's total not speaking.*

Yun Men usually liked to teach three word Ch'an:ᶜ observing, "Reflect!" "Ha!" He also taught one word Ch'an: a monk asked, "When you kill your father and mother, you repent before the Buddha; when you kill the Buddha and Patriarchs, where do you turn to repent?" Yun Men said, "Exposed." Again a monk asked, "What is the treasury of the eye of the true Dharma?" Yun Men said, "Universal." It just doesn't allow any attempts to explain. In ordinary situations, even, Yun Men would still revile people. When he uttered a phrase, it was like an iron spike.

Later Yun Men produced the Four Sages: Tung Shan Shou Ch'u, Chih Men Shih Kuan, Te Shan Yuan Mi, and Hsiang Lin Teng Yuan. They all were great masters of the school. Hsiang Lin served as Yun Men's attendant for eighteen years; whenever Yun Men dealt with him, he would just call out, "Attendant Yuan!" Yuan would answer, "Yes?" Yun Men would say, "What is it?" It went on like this for eighteen years, when one day Hsiang Lin finally awakened. Yun Men told him, "From now on I won't call you any more."

In Yun Men's usual dealings with people, he would often use the methods of Mu Chou; though it was hard to approach him, he had the hammer and tongs to pull out nails and wrench out pegs. Hsueh Tou said of him, "I like the fresh devices of Shao Yang;ᵈ he spent his life pulling out nails and pegs for people."

Yun Men set down a question to instruct his community, "I

don't ask you about before the fifteenth day; try to say something about after the fifteenth day." He cuts off the thousand distinctions, and doesn't let either ordinary or holy pass. He himself answered for everyone, "Every day is a good day." The words "before the fifteenth day" already cut off the thousand distinctions; the words "after the fifteenth day" also cut off the thousand distinctions. The fact is that Yun Men did not say that the next day is the sixteenth day. People coming after him merely followed his words to produce interpretations; but what relevance has this? Yun Men established a protean style; he surely had a way to benefit people. Having spoken some words, he then answered himself in everyone's behalf: "Every day is a good day." These words pervade past and present, from before until after, and settle everything at once.

I too am following his words to produce interpretations when I talk like this. Killing others is not as good as killing yourself. As soon as you make a principle, you fall into a pit. Three phrases are inherent in every one phrase of Yun Men; since the source inspiration of his family is like this, when Yun Men utters a phrase, it must be returned to the source. Anything but this will always be phony. The affair has no multitude of arguments and propositions, though those who have not yet penetrated want (me as commentator) to go on like this. If you do penetrate, then you will immediately see the essential meaning of the Ancient.

Take a look at the complications Hsueh Tou creates:

VERSE

He throws away one,
     **Seven openings, eight holes.
     Where has it gone? He lets up
     a little.*

Picks up seven.
     **He can't pick them up, yet
     he doesn't let them go.*

Above, below, and in the four directions, there is no comparison.
     **What's it like? Above is the sky, below is the earth.

East, west, south, north; what comparison is there?
*Nevertheless, the staff is in my hand.**

Placidly walking along, he treads down the sound of the flow-
ing stream;
   **Don't ask what's right under your feet. It's difficult to*
investigate it thoroughly. He's gone into the nest of en-
*tangling vines.**

His relaxed gaze descries the tracks of flying birds.
   **In the eye, there is no such happening. A wild*
fox spirit view; as before, he's just inside the
*same old den.**

The grasses grow thick,
   **He pulls the arrow out of the back*
of his head. What's going on here?
*He is fallen into equanimity.**

The mists overhang.
   **He hasn't come out of this nest yet.*
*Beneath his feet clouds arise.**

'Round Subhuti's cliff, the flowers make a mess;
   **Where is he? The stupid fellow! He's*
*been completely exposed.**

I snap my fingers;[e] *how lamentable is Shunyata!*
   **The four quarters and eight directions,*
the whole cosmos; inside Shunyata's nostrils,
*try to say something. Where is (Shunyata)?**

Don't make a move!
   **How come your previous words?*
*When you move, then what?**

If you move, thirty blows!
   **Take what's coming to you*
*and get out. I strike!**

COMMENTARY

Hsueh Tou's eulogies of the Ancients were always accomplished like this: at first he takes the jewel sword of the
Diamond King and brings it down at once; then afterwards he

reveals a little bit of formal style. Although it's like this, ultimately there are not two understandings.

"He throws away one, picks up seven." People often make
an understanding based on the numbers and say, "'He throws
away one' refers to 'before the fifteenth day'." Having abruptly
put down two lines and sealed it up, Hsueh Tou then instead
reveals it to let people see; "He throws away one, picks up
seven." You must avoid turning to the words for your subsistence. Why? What moisture is there in unleavened bread?
People often fall back into conceptual consciousness. You
must obtain your understanding before the words arise; then
the great function will become manifest and you will naturally
see it.

This is why after old man Shakyamuni had attained the Path
in the land of Magadha, he spent three weeks contemplating
this matter: "The nature of all things being quiescent extinction cannot be conveyed by words; I would rather not preach
the Dharma, but quickly enter nirvana." When he got to this
point, even Shakyamuni couldn't find any way to open his
mouth. But by virtue of his power of skill in technique, after he
had preached to the five mendicants, he went to three hundred
and sixty assemblies and expounded the teachings for his age.
All these were just expedients. For this reason he had taken off
his bejewelled regal garments and put on rough dirty clothing.
He could not but turn towards the shallows within the gate of
the secondary meaning in order to lead in his various disciples.
If we had him face upwards and bring it all up at once, there
would hardly be anyone in the whole world (who could understand).

But tell me, what is the supreme word? At this point Hsueh
Tou reveals a little of the meaning to let people see. Just don't
see that there are any buddhas above, don't see that there are
sentient beings below; don't see that there are mountains, rivers, and earth without, and don't see that there are seeing,
hearing, discernment, or knowledge within: then you will be
like one who has died the great death and then returned to life.
With long and short, good and evil, fused into one whole,
though you bring them up one by one, you'll no longer see
them as different. After that, you'll be able to function respon-
sively without losing balance. Then you will see the meaning
of his saying, "He throws away one, picks up seven; above,

below, and in the four directions, there is no comparison." If you pass through at these lines, then and there above, below, and in the four directions, there is no comparison. The myriad forms and multitude of appearances—plants, animals, and people—everything everywhere completely manifests the way of your own house. Thus it was said,

> Within myriad forms, only one body is revealed;
> Only when one is sure for himself will he then be near.
> In past years I mistakenly turned to the road to search;
> Now I look upon it like ice within fire.

"In the heavens and on earth, I alone am the honored one." Many people pursue the branches and don't seek the root. First get the root right, then naturally when the wind blows the grass bends down, naturally where water flows a stream forms.

"Placidly walking along, he treads down the sound of the flowing stream." As he goes along placidly, he can tread down and cut off even the roar of a vast swelling torrent. "His relaxed gaze descries the tracks of flying birds." Even if it's the tracks of flying birds, allow the eye one look, and it is like tracing them out. When you get here, you will not consider it difficult to blow out the fires under the cauldrons of hell, or to shatter sword forests and knife mountains with a shout.

Because of his compassion, at this point Hsueh Tou feared that people would settle down within the realm of unconcern, so he went on to say, "The grasses grow thick, the mists overhang." But tell me, whose world is this? Can it be called "Every day is a good day"? Fortunately, there's no connection. In fact, "Placidly walking along, he treads down the sound of the flowing stream" isn't it; "His relaxed gaze descries the tracks of flying birds" isn't it either; nor is "The grasses grow thick," nor "The mists overhang." But even something entirely different would just be "'Round Subhuti's cliff, the flowers make a mess." It is still necessary to turn beyond That Side. Haven't you read how as Subhuti was sitting in silent meditation in a cliffside cave, the gods showered down flowers to praise him. The venerable Subhuti said, "Flowers are showering down from the sky in praise; whose doing is this?" A god said, "I am Indra, king of the gods." Venerable Subhuti asked, "Why are you offering praise?" Indra said, "I esteem the Venerable One's skill in expounding the transcendence of wisdom." Subhuti said, "I have never spoken a single word about wisdom; why are you offering praise?" Indra said, "You have never spoken and I have never heard. No speaking, no hearing—this is true wisdom." And again he caused the earth to tremble, and showered down flowers.

Hsueh Tou once made up another verse about this:

> The rain has passed, the clouds are shrinking, dawn
>   has halfway broken through;
> The multiple peaks are like a drawing of blue-green
>   rocky crags.
> Subhuti did not know how to sit upon a cliff;
> He brought on the heavenly flowers and the shaking
>   of the earth.

When the king of gods is shaking the earth and raining down flowers, at this point where else will you go to hide? Hsueh Tou also said,

> I fear Subhuti won't be able to escape him;
> Even beyond the cosmos all is filled to the brim.
> What end will he know to his frantic turmoil?
> From all sides the pure wind tugs at his clothes.

Though you be clean and naked, bare and purified, totally without fault or worry, this is still not the ultimate. In the end though, what is? Look carefully at this quote; "I snap my fingers; how lamentable is Shunyata!" The Sanskrit word "Shunyata" in our language means the spirit of emptiness. Empty space is her body; she has no physical body to be conscious of contact. When the Buddha's brilliance shines forth, then she manifests her body. When you get to be like Shunyata, then Hsueh Tou will rightly snap his fingers in lament.

Again Hsueh Tou says, "Don't make a move!" What's it like when you move? (Like) sleeping with your eyes open under the bright sun in the blue sky.

TRANSLATOR'S NOTES

a.   Wen Yen was Yun Men's personal initiatory name: see the biographical supplement.

b. Ch'en Ts'ao was an enlightened disciple of Mu Chou and lived in the same area.

c. When Yun Men encountered someone, he would look at him and say, "Reflect!" and "Ha!" (a laugh of derision or scorn); later the word describing Yun Men's action was included by a compiler as one of the "three words" he is supposed to have used.

d. Shao Yang is the name of the region where Yun Men monastery was located, and so according to the custom of referring to Ch'an masters by the name of their abode, this is another name for Yun Men.

e. Snapping the fingers is used for alerting, warning, and for warding off filth or taboo. Abiding in subjective emptiness is referred to as intoxication in Ch'an, considered onesided, incomplete, and narrow-minded; hence it is taboo.

Hui Ch'ao Asks about Buddha

POINTER

The thousand sages have not transmitted the single word before sound; if you have never seen it personally, it's as if it were worlds away. Even if you discern it before sound and cut off the tongues of everyone in the world, you're still not a sharp fellow. Therefore it is said, "The sky can't cover it; the earth can't support it; empty space can't contain it; sun and moon can't illumine it." Where there is no Buddha and you alone are called the Honored One, for the first time you've amounted to something. Otherwise, if you are not yet this way, penetrate through on the tip of a hair and release the great shining illumination; then in all directions you will be independent and free in the midst of phenomena; whatever you pick up, there is nothing that's not it. But tell me, what is attained that is so extraordinary?

Does everyone understand? No one knows about the sweating horses of the past; they only want to emphasize the achievement that crowns the age. Leaving this matter aside for the moment, what about Hsueh Tou's public case? Look into what's written below.

CASE

A monk (named Hui Ch'ao) asked Fa Yen,[1] "Hui Ch'ao asks the Teacher, what is Buddha?"[2]

Fa Yen said, "You are Hui Ch'ao."[3]

NOTES

1. What is he saying? He's wearing stocks, giving evidence of his crime.
2. What is he saying? His eyeballs pop out.

46

3. He comes out with this according to his pattern. Iron scrap stuffing. He goes right up to him and takes him.

COMMENTARY

Ch'an Master Fa Yen had this ability of breaking in and crashing out at the same time,ᵃ and also the use of this ability; thus he could answer like this. This is what is called passing beyond sound and form, achieving the great freedom, letting go or taking back as the occasion requires, where killing or bringing life rests with oneself. He is undeniably extraordinary. Nevertheless, people from all over who deliberate over this public case are many, and those who make intellectual interpretations to understand it are not few. They do not realize that whenever the Ancients handed down a word or half a phrase, it was like sparks struck from flint, like a flash of lightning, directly opening up a single straight path.

People of later times just went to the words to make up interpretations. Some say, "Hui Ch'ao is himself Buddha; that is why Fa Yen answered as he did." Some say, "It's much like riding an ox searching for an ox." Some say "The asking is it." What relevance has any of this? If you go on understanding in this fashion, not only do you turn against yourself, but you seriously demean that man of old.

If you want to see the whole of (Fa Yen's) device, you must be a fellow who doesn't turn his head when struck, a fellow with teeth like sword trees and a mouth like a blood bowl, who knows outside the words what they refer to; then you will have a small portion of realization. If one by one they make intellectual interpretations, everyone on earth would be an exterminator of the Buddha's race. As for Ch'an traveller Hui Ch'ao's awakening here, he was constantly engrossed in penetrating investigation; therefore under the impact of one word, it was as if the bottom fell out of his bucket.

It's like Superintendent Tse: he had been staying in Fa Yen's congregation, but had never asked to enter (Fa Yen's) room (for special instruction). One day Fa Yen asked him, "Why haven't you come to enter my room?" Tse replied, "Didn't you know, Teacher, when I was at Ch'ing Lin's place, I had an entry." Fa Yen said, "Try to recall it for me." Tse said, "I asked, 'What is

Buddha?' Lin said, 'The Fire God comes looking for fire.'" Fa
Yen said, "Good words, but I'm afraid you misunderstood. Can
you say something more for me?" Tse said, "The Fire God is in
the province of fire; he is seeking fire with fire. Likewise, I am
Buddha, yet I went on searching for Buddha." Fa Yen said,
"Sure enough, the Superintendent has misunderstood." Containing his anger, Tse left the monastery and went off across
the river. Fa Yen said, "This man can be saved if he comes
back; if he doesn't return, he can't be saved." Out on the road,
Tse thought to himself, "He is the teacher of five hundred
people; how could he deceive me?" So he turned back and
again called on Fa Yen, who told him, "Just ask me and I'll
answer you." Thereupon Tse asked, "What is Buddha?" Fa Yen
said, "The Fire God comes looking for fire." At these words Tse
was greatly enlightened.

These days there are those who just put a glare in their eyes
and interpret that as understanding. As it is said, "Since this
has no wounds, don't wound it."[b] With this kind of public case,
those who have practiced for a long time know where it comes
down as soon as it's brought up. In the Fa Yen succession this is
called "arrowpoints meeting."[c] They don't employ the five
positions of prince and minister,[d] or the four propositions;[e]
they simply talk of arrowpoints meeting. The style of Fa Yen's
family is like this; one word falls and you see and immediately
directly penetrate. But if you ponder over the words, to the end
you will search without finding.

Fa Yen appeared in the world and had a congregation of five
hundred. At this time the Buddha Dharma flourished greatly.
At this time the (future) National Teacher Te Shao had spent a
long time with Su Shan, and he considered himself to have
attained Su Shan's meaning. So he had gathered together the
writings made by Su Shan in the course of his lifetime, and
a portrait of him (to symbolize his succession to Su Shan), and
led a band of followers travelling on foot. When they got to Fa
Yen's community, he himself did not go to enter the Master's
room, but just ordered his followers to go along with the others
to enter the room.

One day when Fa Yen had ascended his seat, there was a
monk who asked, "What is one drop from the fount of Ts'ao
Ch'i?" Fa Yen said, "It's one drop from the fount of Ts'ao Ch'i."
The monk was dumbfounded and withdrew; Shao, who was in

the assembly, was suddenly greatly enlightened when he heard this. Later he appeared in the world as one of Fa Yen's successors. Shao had a verse which he presented, saying,

> *The summit of the peak of the mystic crossing*
> *Is not the human world;*
> *Outside the mind there are no things—*
> *Blue mountains fill the eyes.*

Fa Yen gave his seal of approval and said, "This one verse alone can perpetuate my school. In the future kings and lords will honor you. I am not equal to you."

Look at those Ancients; when they awaken like this, what truth is this? It won't do just to have me tell you; you yourself must tune your spirit all day long. If you can attain fulfillment the way these people did, then someday you will let down your hand for people in the crossroads, and won't consider it a difficult thing, either.

Thus, when the monk asked Fa Yen, "What is Buddha?" Fa Yen said, "You are Hui Ch'ao." Is there any contradiction here? Haven't you read what Yun Men said—"When it is brought up, if you don't take heed, then you'll miss it; if you try to assess it by thinking, in what aeon will you awaken?" Hsueh Tou subsequently versified it with unmistakable clarity. I'll bring it up: Look!

VERSE

In the river country the spring wind isn't blowing;
> ***Where in the world do you find this scene?*
> *The pattern is already showing.**

Deep within the flowers partridges are calling.
> ***What's the use of this chatter? He is*
> *blown by the wind into a different tune.*
> *How can there be such a thing?**

At the three-tiered Dragon Gate, where the waves are high,
> *fish become dragons,*
> ***Traverse this one road. Don't fool the great congregation. Tread upon the dragon's head.**

Yet fools still go on scooping out the evening pond water.
    **Leaning on a fence, groping along a wall;*[f]* next to the
    gate, standing by the door;*[g]* what use is this for a patch-
    robed monk? This is standing by a stump waiting for a
    rabbit.*[h]**

COMMENTARY

Hsueh Tou is an adept: where the Ancients are hard to gnaw on
and hard to chew, hard to penetrate and hard to see, an impenetrable riddle, he produces it in verse to let people see. He is
indeed extraordinary. Hsueh Tou knew Fa Yen's key device,
and he also knew where Hui Ch'ao was at. Still, he feared that
people in the future would turn to Fa Yen's words and mistakenly conceive an understanding, so he came out with this
verse.

This monk's asking like this, Fa Yen's answering like
this—this is "In the river country the spring wind isn't blowing; deep within the flowers partridges are calling." These two
lines are just one line. But say, where is Hsueh Tou's meaning?

In Kiangsi and Chiangnan many people make a two-part
interpretation; they say that "In the river country the spring
wind isn't blowing" is used to versify "You are Hui Ch'ao."
(They say that) this scene—even if the spring wind doesn't
blow in the river country, still "deep within the flowers partridges are calling"—is used to compare the endless haggling
over these words everywhere to the partridges crying deep in
the flowers. But what relevance has this? How far they are from
knowing that these two lines of Hsueh Tou's are but a single
line. Do you want to have no seam or gap? Clearly I tell you,
his speech is to the point, his words are to the point; they cover
heaven and earth.

(Hui Ch'ao) asked, "What is Buddha?" Fa Yen answered,
"You are Hui Ch'ao." Hsueh Tou says, "In the river country
the spring wind isn't blowing; deep within the flowers partridges call." If you can make the grade here, you will be able to
walk alone through the red skies; if you make intellectual interpretations, (you'll go on through) past, present, and future
lives for sixty aeons.

Hsueh Tou is extremely compassionate in the third and

fourth lines; all at once he explains completely for people. Ch'an Master Ch'ao's great awakening is likened to fish becoming dragons where the waves are high at the three-tiered Dragon Gate, while fools still go on dragging through evening pond water. (The Dragon Gate is a gorge through which the Yellow River passes at the border of Shensi and Shansi; according to tradition,) King Yu cut it (through the mountains) forming a three-level (passage for the river). Nowadays, on the third day of the third month, when the peach blossoms bloom, and heaven and earth are ready, if there is a fish that can get through the Dragon Gate, horns sprout on his head, he raises his bristling tail, catches hold of a cloud, and flies away. Those who cannot leap through fail and fall back.[i] Fools who gnaw on the words are like scooping out the evening pond water looking for fish; how little they realize that the fish have already turned into dragons! Old Master Tuan had a verse which said,

> *A copper of bright money*
> *Buys a fried cake;*
> *He gobbles it down into his belly,*
> *And from then on no longer feels hunger.*

This verse is very good, only it's too crude. Hsueh Tou's verse is very clever, and he doesn't cut his hand on its sharp point.

In the old days Librarian Ch'ing liked to ask people, "What is 'Fish turn into dragons at three-tiered Dragon Gate where the waves are high'?" For me, it's not necessary, but now I'm asking you: having turned into a dragon, where is he now?

TRANSLATOR'S NOTES

a. Breaking in and crashing out at the same time symbolizes the action of the teacher and student encounter: the student is likened to a chick still inside the shell of his ego, trying to crash its way out, while the teacher, as the 'parent,' breaks through from the outside to help the chick out. See the sixteenth case.

b. This saying is taken from the *Vimalakirtinirdesa* scripture, in which context it should be read, "Since they have no wounds, don't wound them," meaning that the lesser vehicle of revulsion should not be taught to those who have the capacity for the greater vehicle of tolerance. We have not used "they" because of the preceding sentence in the context; "they" would cause confusion here. Yuan Wu's intent seems to be don't impute any flaw to the flawless Buddha-essence by intellectual, emotional interpretations. Tenkei Denson says, "Fa Yen's answer 'You're Hui Ch'ao,' breaking in and crashing out at the same time, has no gap or flaw, so don't you people ruin it with intellectual judgements."

c.   This represents question and answer meeting, like two arrows meeting head on in midair, stopping each other at once; the meeting of minds.

d.   This was an illustrative device of the Ts'ao-Tung tradition of Ch'an: the Prince, or Lord, symbolizes emptiness, while the Minister, or Vassal, symbolizes the world of matter, or form. The five positions are: minister turning towards prince (emptiness within matter), prince looking at minister (matter within emptiness), prince alone (emptiness as such), minister alone (matter as such), and prince and minister in harmony (simultaneous interidentification of emptiness and matter).

e.   This was a device of the Lin Chi tradition of Ch'an: the four propositions involve conceding or taking away person and/or environment, taking away the person but not the environment, taking away the environment but not the person, taking away both, and leaving both. See the appendix on teaching devices.

f.   This depicts the blind groping their way along.

g.   This means not yet having entered.

h.   This refers to a story of a man who saw a running rabbit happen to collide with a tree stump and die; the man took the rabbit for food, and, thinking to obtain another rabbit, he foolishly stood by the stump, waiting for it to 'catch' another rabbit for him. This is used to describe those who cling to words or images, thinking them to be a source of enlightenment.

i.   This simile of passing through the Dragon Gate was also used to refer to the Chinese civil service examinations; those who passed could become government officials.

Ts'ui Yen's Eyebrows

POINTER

If you understand, you can make use of it on the road, like a dragon reaching the water, like a tiger in the mountains. If you don't understand, then the worldly truth will prevail, and you will be like a ram caught in a fence, like (a fool) watching over a stump waiting for a rabbit. Sometimes a single phrase is like a lion crouching on the ground; sometimes a phrase is like the Diamond King's jewel sword. Sometimes a phrase cuts off the tongues of everyone on earth, and sometimes a phrase follows the waves and pursues the currents.

If you make use of it on the road, when you meet with a man of knowledge you distinguish what's appropriate to the occasion, you know what's right and what's wrong, and together you witness each other's illumination. Where the worldly truth prevails, one who has the single eye can cut off everything in the ten directions and stand like a mile high wall. Therefore it is said, "When the great function appears it does not keep to any fixed standards." Sometimes we take a blade of grass and use it as the sixteen foot golden body (of Buddha); sometimes we take the sixteen foot golden body and use it as a blade of grass. But tell me, what principle does this depend upon? Do you really know? To test, I cite this; Look!

CASE

At the end of the summer retreat Ts'ui Yen said to the community, "All summer long I've been talking to you, brothers;[1] look and see if my eyebrows are still there."[2,a]
    Pao Fu said, "The thief's heart is cowardly."[3]
    Ch'ang Ch'ing said, "Grown."[4]
    Yun Men said, "A barrier."[5]

NOTES

1. If you open your mouth, how can you know it to be so?
2. All he's achieved is that his eyes have fallen out too, along with his nostrils, which he's already lost. He enters hell fast as an arrow shot.
3. Obviously. This is a thief recognizing a thief.
4. His tongue falls to the ground; he adds error to error. After all.
5. Where is there to run to? No patchrobed monk in the world can leap out. He's defeated.

COMMENTARY

The Ancients had morning study and evening inquiry; at the end of the summer retreat Ts'ui Yen turned around and spoke to the community like this, and he was undeniably solitary and steep—nothing could stop him from startling the heavens and shaking the earth. But tell me, in the whole great treasury of teachings, in the five thousand and forty-eight volumes of the canon, whether they talk of mind or nature, whether they preach the sudden or the gradual, has there ever been this happening? They're all this kind of occasion, but among them Ts'ui Yen is outstanding. Look at the way he talks; tell me, where is his true meaning?

When the Ancients let down a hook, it was never an empty manoeuvre; they invariably had some truth to benefit people. Many people misunderstand and say, "Under the bright sun in the blue sky, Ts'ui Yen spoke aimless talk producing concern where there was none; at the end of the summer he spoke of his own faults and examined himself first to avoid others criticizing him." Fortunately this has nothing to do with it. Such views are called exterminators of the Buddha's race. The appearance in the world of the successive generations of teaching masters would have been entirely without benefit if they hadn't reached down to instruct people. What would have been the purpose? When you get here, if you can see all the way through, then you will know that the Ancients had the method to drive off a plowman's ox and to snatch away a hungry man's food.

People today, when questioned, immediately turn to the words to chew on them, making a living on Ts'ui Yen's eyebrows. Look at how the people of his house naturally know where he is operating: through a thousand changes and ten thousand transformations, amidst impenetrable complications, everywhere they have ways to show themselves; hence they are able to chime in with him like this in response. If there is nothing extraordinary about these words of Ts'ui Yen's, why then would these three men, Yun Men, Pao Fu, and Ch'ang Ch'ing, have replied to him so profusely?

Pao Fu said, "The thief's heart is cowardly." How much intellectual interpretation these words have provoked lately! But say, what about Pao Fu's meaning? You must avoid searching for that Ancient in his words. If you give rise to feelings and arouse your thoughts, then he'll snatch your eyeballs away. Above all, people don't realize that when Pao Fu utters one turning word, he cuts off Ts'ui Yen's footsteps.

Ch'ang Ch'ing said, "Grown." Many people say, "Ch'ang Ch'ing turns along following Ts'ui Yen's footsteps, therefore he says (that Ts'ui Yen's eyebrows have) grown." But this has nothing to do with it. They don't know that Ch'ang Ch'ing brings out his own view when he says, "Grown." Each has a place to appear in person, but I ask you, where is the growth?

It's just like being face to face with an adept brandishing the Diamond King's jewel sword. If you can smash the views of the ordinary current and cut off gain and loss, affirmation and negation, then you will see where Ch'ang Ch'ing responded to Ts'ui Yen.

Yun Men said, "A barrier." This is undeniably outstanding, but hard to penetrate. The great master Yun Men often taught people with one word Ch'an, though in the one word the three phrases were always present. Look how this Ancient replied to suit the occasion; naturally he was far removed from the people of this day and age. This then is the way to utter a phrase. Although Yun Men spoke like this, his meaning is definitely not here. Since the meaning is not here, tell me, where is it? If you are a clear eyed man with the ability to illumine heaven and earth, just be crystal clear in every respect. For his single word "barrier" and the words of the other three, Hsueh Tou has strung them together in one verse:

VERSE

Ts'ui Yen teaches the followers;
　　**The old thief! He's corrupting
　　other people's children.*

For a thousand ages, there is no reply.
　　**In a thousand or ten thousand,
　　still there's one or a half. He
　　divides a tally.*

The word "barrier" answers him back;
　　**Didn't you believe what I said?
　　He is undeniably extraordinary.
　　Only if you're such a person can
　　you understand such talk.*

He loses his money and suffers punishment.ᵇ
　　**He gulps down his breath and swallows
　　his voice. Hsueh Tou too has done quite
　　a bit of this. I'd strike while he's still
　　talking.*

Decrepit old Pao Fu—
　　**You're fellow travelers on
　　the same path; and still you
　　act this way. Two, three.*

Censure or praise are impossible to apply.
　　**Letting go, holding still. Who is born
　　the same and dies the same? Don't slander
　　him. Luckily there's no connection.*

Talkative Ts'ui Yen
　　**Wild fox spirit!
　　Shut your mouth!*

Is clearly a thief.
　　**So it may be said. He's been caught!*

The clear jewel has no flaws;
　　**Can you tell? No one in the world knows its price.*

Who can distinguish true from false?
　　**Many are just false. I myself have never had the eye
　　(for this); (what about) the blue-eyed foreign monk
　　(Bodhidharma)?*

Ch'ang Ch'ing knows him well;
   **This is a spirit recognizing a spirit; only*
   he could do this. Yet he still hasn't gotten
   *(the other) half.**

His eyebrows are grown.
   **Where? From head to foot there isn't a single blade of*
   *grass.**

COMMENTARY

How could Hsueh Tou be called a Good Friend if he hadn't
been this compassionate, making a verse to enable people to
see? When the Ancients acted like this, it was all something
they couldn't but do. Because later students become attached
to their words and more and more give rise to intellectual
interpretations, therefore they do not see the Ancients' message. If someone suddenly came forward right now to overturn
the meditation seat and scatter the great assembly with shouts,
we shouldn't be amazed at him. Though someone acted like
this, you yourself would still have to really arrive in this realm
in order to attain this.

When Hsueh Tou says, "For a thousand ages there is no
reply," he is just telling you to see if Ts'ui Yen's eyebrows are
there What's so extraordinary that there is no reply for a
thousand ages? You must realize that when the Ancients spat
out a word or half a phrase, it wasn't blurted out; one must
have the eye to judge heaven and earth before this is possible.

When Hsueh Tou writes a word or half a phrase it's like the
Diamond King's jewel sword, like a lion crouching on the
ground, like sparks struck from stone, like the brilliance of a
lightning flash. If he didn't have the eye on his forehead, how
could he have seen where that man of old (Ts'ui Yen) comes
down? This lesson that Ts'ui Yen gave the people was such
that "for a thousand ages there is no reply." It goes beyond Te
Shan's staff and Lin Chi's shout. But say, where is Hsueh Tou's
meaning for us? And how will you understand his statement,
"For a thousand ages there is no reply"?

"The word 'barrier' answers him back; he loses his money
and suffers punishment." What is the meaning of this? Even if

you have the eye to pass through the barrier, when you get here you still must be most thoroughgoing before you are done. Tell me, is it Ts'ui Yen who loses his money and suffers punishment, or is it Hsueh Tou, or is it Yun Men? If you can penetrate this, I'll allow that you have the eye.

"Decrepit old Pao Fu; censure or praise are impossible to apply." Does he censure himself? Does he praise the Ancients? Tell me, where does Pao Fu censure? Where does Pao Fu praise?

"Talkative Ts'ui Yen is clearly a thief." Tell me, what has he stolen, that Hsueh Tou says he's a thief? You must avoid being whirled around following after the stream of his words; when you get here you must have your own accomplishment before you'll understand.

"The clear jewel has no flaws." Hsueh Tou says that Ts'ui Yen is like a clear jewel without any flaws or cloudy patches. "Who can distinguish true from false?" It can be said that rarely is there anyone who can make this distinction.

Hsueh Tou has great talent, so he can string together the whole case from beginning to end on the single thread of this verse. Only at the very end does he then say, "Ch'ang Ch'ing knows him well; his eyebrows are grown." Tell me, where are they growing? Hurry up, take a look!

TRANSLATOR'S NOTES

a.   Teaching is said to be an act of 'facing downwards' since the transcendental cannot be spoken of directly; hence it is said in Ch'an that if one speaks too much, tries to explain too much, his eyebrows may fall out. Similarly, when one has, so to speak, 'Said everything,' it is said that he isn't anxious for, or does not spare, his eyebrows.

b.   That is to say, he loses the bribe money he has offered, and suffers the punishment he was due anyway. This is a common phrase in Ch'an.

Chao Chou's Four Gates^a

POINTER

When the bright mirror is on its stand, beauty and ugliness are distinguished by themselves. With a sharp sword in his hand, one can kill or bring life to fit the occasion. A foreigner goes and a native comes; a foreigner comes and a native goes. In the midst of death he finds life; in the midst of life he finds death. But tell me, when you get to this point, then what? If you don't have the eye to penetrate barriers, if you don't have any place to turn yourself around in, at this point obviously you won't know what to do. Tell me, what is the eye that penetrates barriers, what is a place to turn around in? To test, I cite this; look!

CASE

A monk asked Chao Chou, "What is Chao Chou?"[1]
   Chao Chou replied, "East gate, west gate, south gate, north gate."[2]

NOTES

1. North of the river, south of the river, no one can say. There are thorns in the soft mud. If it's not south of the river, then it's north of the river.
2. They're open. "When we're reviling each other, I let you lock lips with me; when we're spitting at each other, I let you spew me with slobber." The public case is obviously complete; but do you see? I strike!

COMMENTARY

When you immerse yourself in meditation and inquire about the Path, it is in order to clearly understand yourself; just avoid picking and choosing among verbal formulations. Why? Haven't you read what Chao Chou said—"The ultimate path has no difficulties; just avoid picking and choosing." And haven't you read what Yun Men said—"These days whenever followers of Ch'an gather in threes and fives their mouths chatter on and on; they say 'these are words of high ability, those are words uttered in reference to the self.'" They don't realize that within the gate of expedient means the Ancients couldn't help but establish expedient verbal formulae for latecoming students of elementary capacities who had not yet clarified their mind ground nor seen their fundamental nature. In the Patriarch's coming from the West for the sole transmission of the mind seal, directly pointing to the human mind for the perception of nature and fulfillment of Buddhahood, where were there any such complications? It is necessary to cut off words, to see the truth outside of any pattern. When you penetrate through to liberation, this can be compared to a dragon reaching the water or a tiger at home in the mountains.

To have seen but not yet penetrated, or to have penetrated but not yet become illumined—among the worthies of the past who investigated for so long, this was called seeking more instruction. To ask for more instruction when you have seen and penetrated, you then must still turn round and round on the words so there will be no doubtful sticking points. When one who has investigated for a long time asked for more instruction, this would be giving a ladder to a thief. In reality this matter does not lie in words; that is why Yun Men said, "If this matter were in words, are there no words in the twelve part canon of the three vehicles? What need would there have been for Bodhidharma's coming from the West?"

Within Fen Yang's eighteen categories of questions,[b] this question (in the case) is called a question to examine the host; it's also called a seeking out question. The monk posing this question is undeniably extraordinary; anyone but Chao Chou would have found it hard to reply to him. The monk asked, "What is Chao Chou?" Chao Chou is an adept in his own right, so he immediately replied, "East gate, west gate, south gate, north gate." The monk said, "I wasn't asking about that Chao Chou." Chao Chou said, "What Chao Chou were you asking about?"

Later people said this was "no-nothing Ch'an" cheating quite a few people. What was their reason? When the monk asked about Chao Chou, Chao Chou answered, "East gate, west gate, south gate, north gate"; therefore (these people say) he was just answering about the other Chao Chou (i.e. the city). If you understand in this fashion, then any rustic from a village of three families understands more about the Buddha Dharma than you do. Such an interpretation destroys the Buddha Dharma. It's like comparing a fish eye to a bright pearl; in appearance they are alike, but actually they are not the same. As I said, if it's not south of the river, then it's north of the river. But say, is there something or is there nothing? This does indeed require you to be thoroughgoing before you understand.

Yuan "The Jurist"[c] said, "The very last word finally reaches the closed barrier; the inner essence of pointing out the Way is not in words and explanations:

> *In ten days, one breeze;*
> *In five days, one rain.*
> *In the peaceful countryside enjoying their tasks,*
> *Drumming their full bellies and singing hallelujah."*

This is called the season of great peace. When I call this having no concerns, it is not a matter of covering your eyes with your hands and saying "I have no concerns." You must penetrate through the barrier, emerge from the forest of brambles, clean and naked, bare and untrammelled: as before you will resemble any ordinary person, but now it's all right whether there is anything of concern or there is nothing; it's up to you. Free in all directions, you will never cling to nothingness and establish it as something.

Some people say, "Fundamentally there isn't the slightest bit of anything, but when we have tea we drink tea, and when we have rice we eat rice." This is big vain talk; I call this claiming attainment without having attained, claiming realization without having realized. Basically since they haven't bored in and penetrated through, when they hear people speaking of mind or nature, of the mysterious or the abstruse, they say, "This is just mad talk; fundamentally there isn't anything to be concerned with." This could be called one blind man leading many blind men. They are far from knowing that before the Patriarch came, people scarcely called the sky earth, or called mountains rivers; why did the Patriarch still come from the West? Everyplace where they "go up into the hall"ᵈ and "enter the room"ᵉ what do they speak of? It is all judgements of intellectual consciousness; when the feelings of judgements of intellectual consciousness are ended, only then can you see through. And when you see through, then as of old sky is sky, earth is earth, mountains are mountains, rivers are rivers.

An Ancient said, "Mind is the sense faculty, things are the objects; both elements are like flaws on a mirror." When you get to this realm you will naturally be clean and naked, bare and untrammelled. Even the ultimate principle of theory is not yet the place of peace and security. People often misunderstand this point; they stay within the realm of unconcern and neither pay homage to the Buddhas nor burn incense. They do indeed seem to be right, but in spite of that they're totally wrong. When questioned, their replies do resemble the ultimate principle, but as soon as they are pressed, they're shattered, confused; they sit there with an empty belly and a proud heart, but when they get to their last day they'll wring their hands and beat their breasts, but it'll already be too late.

This monk asked this way, Chao Chou answered this way; tell me, how will you look for them? This way won't do, not this way won't do either; ultimately, how is it? This bit is a hard one, so Hsueh Tou has brought it out in front of you to show you people.

One day while Chao Chou was sitting, his attendant reported to him, "The great king has come." Chao Chou looked surprised and said, "Myriad felicitations, O great king!" The attendant said, "He has not yet come to you, Master." Chao Chou said, "And you said he's come." He penetrated this far, he saw this far; undeniably extraordinary. Ch'an Master Hui Nan of Huang Lung commented on this, saying,

> *The attendant only knew how to announce a guest,*
> *He did not know that he himself was in the imperial city.*

*Chao Chou went into the weeds to look for the
    man,
Heedless of getting his whole body soaked in
    muddy water.*

Do all of you people know the truth of this? Look into Hsueh
Tou's verse:

VERSE

In their words they show their ability in direct confrontation:
    **Echoing. When fish swim through, the water is mud-
    died.
    Better not slander Chao Chou.**

The Adamantine Eye is completely void of dust.
    **Scattering sand, scattering dirt: don't
    drag Chao Chou into this. Why search the
    sky and grope over the earth?**

East, West, South, North—the gates face each other;
    **They're open. Where are there so many gates!
    If you turn your back on Chao Chou city, where
    will you go?**

An endless series of hammer blows can't smash them open.
    Your revolving hammer won't reach. They are open.

COMMENTARY

Chao Chou faces situations just like the Diamond King's jewel
sword: hesitate, and immediately he cuts your head off; time
and time again he will go on and snatch your eyeballs right
away. Nevertheless, this monk dares to grab the tiger's whiskers and pose a question. It's like giving rise to something
where there's nothing; yet nevertheless in his words there is
ability. Once the monk had shown his ability, Chao Chou did
not turn his back on his question; thus he too showed his
ability in answering. It wasn't that he acted like this out of
whimsy; because he was a man who had penetrated through,

naturally he fit in the same groove with the monk, as if it were all arranged.

Haven't you heard? There was an outsider who came to question the World Honored One holding a sparrow in his hand. He said, "Tell me, is this sparrow in my hand dead or alive?" The World Honored One then went and straddled the threshold and said, "You tell me, am I going out or coming in?" (One version has it that the World Honored One raised his fist and asked, "Open or closed?") The outsider was speechless; then he bowed in homage. This story is just like the main case; ever since then the bloodline of the Ancients has been unbroken. Thus it is said, "The question is where the answer is, the answer is where the question is."

Since Hsueh Tou can see through things like this, he says, "In their words they show their ability in direct confrontation." There is skill in the monk's words, which seem to bear two meanings; he seems to ask about the man and he also seems to ask about the place. Without stirring a single hairsbreadth Chao Chou immediately replies to him, "East gate, west gate, south gate, north gate."

"The Adamantine Eye is completely void of dust." This praises Chao Chou snatching away both person and environment, and in his words showing his ability, giving him an answer. This is called having ability, having perspective. The moment the monk turns around, Chao Chou sees through his innermost heart. If he couldn't do this, it would have been difficult for Chao Chou to parry the monk's question. Chakra^f Eye is a Sanskrit expression that means an adamantine eye, a diamond eye, which illumines and sees everywhere without obstruction. Not only can it clearly make out a tiny hair a thousand miles away, but also it can determine what's false and decide what's true, distinguish gain and loss, discern what's appropriate to the occasion, and recognize right and wrong.

Hsueh Tou says, "East, west, south, north—the gates face each other; an endless series of hammer blows can't smash them open." Since the hammer blows continue without limit, why can't they smash the gates open? It's that Hsueh Tou's vision is like this. How will all of you people get these gates open? Please examine this thoroughly.

TRANSLATOR'S NOTES

a. Chao Chou was the name of the city and the province where the Ch'an master Ts'ung Shen lived, and is hence the name by which he is usually known, according to Ch'an custom.

b. Fen Yang Shan Ch'ao (947-1024), a great master of the Lin Chi sect, commented on many of the devices of earlier Ch'an masters and attempted to synthesize the teachings of the various Ch'an sects; for an enumeration of his 'eighteen questions,' see the appendix on the Lin Chi sect.

c. Fu Shan Fa Yuan (10-11c.) was accredited by several masters, including Fen Yang; his nickname 'The Jurist' was on account of his great knowledge of history and legal cases, which he once had to display to free himself and his traveling companions from the clutches of a corrupt magistrate in western China.

d. This refers to masters addressing students in the teaching hall.

e. This refers to masters interviewing disciples in the master's room.

f. Chakra in Sanskrit actually means wheel or disc, whence it means a disc-shaped weapon, especially that of Vishnu, the maintainer in Hindu cosmology. The sense of adamantine, or diamond-like, in which it is used here, is a common Ch'an metaphor for wisdom which cuts through all obscurity and confusion, like 'the jewel sword of the Diamond King.' As the destroyer of all opinion and doubt, the image of the weapon cutting through fits in with this usage. The diamond is also used in classical Buddhist metaphor to symbolize the ultimate meditative concentration, which nothing can destroy, whence emerges the sharp wisdom whose function cuts off all afflictions, removes all obstacles to knowledge of things as they are.

Mu Chou's Thieving Phoney

POINTER

So, so; not so, not so. In battle, each occupies a pivotal position. That is why it is said, "If you turn upwards, then even Shakyamuni, Maitreya, Manjusri, Samantabhadra, and the myriad sages, together with all the masters in the world, all suck in their breath and swallow their voices: if you turn downwards, worms and maggots and everything that crawls, all sentient beings, each and every one emits great shining light, each and every one towers like a wall miles high." If, on the other hand, you neither face upwards nor downwards, how would you deal? If there is a principle, go by the principle; if there is no principle, go by the example. To test, I cite this; look!

CASE

Mu Chou asked a monk, "Where have you just come from?"[1] The monk immediately shouted.[2] Mu Chou said, "I've been shouted at by you once."[3] Again the monk shouted.[4] Mu Chou said, "After three or four shouts, then what?"[5] The monk had nothing to say.[6] Mu Chou then hit him and said,[7] "What a thieving phoney you are!"[8]

NOTES

1. A probing pole; a reed shade.
2. An adept Ch'an traveller! But don't pretend to be enlightened. Still, he does know how to act like this.
3. A trap to fell a tiger. Why is he making a monkey of the man?
4. Look for the horns on his head: he seems to be (a real 'dragon'), but actually isn't yet. I'm afraid he has a dragon's head but a snake's tail.

5. A wave against the current. There's never been anyone who could stick his head out (in front of Mu Chou). Where will (the monk) go?
6. After all, he searched without finding.
7. If we let Mu Chou carry out his mandate to the full, then all the plants and trees on earth would be cut into three pieces.
8. He lets go the first move and falls back into the secondary.

COMMENTARY

Whoever would uphold and establish the teaching of our school must have the eye of a true master of our school, and must have the functional ability of a true master of our school. Mu Chou's mental acuity is like a flash of lightening. He liked to put lecturers[a] to the test; he would usually utter a word or half a phrase like a thicket of brambles that can't be stepped on or touched. As soon as he saw a monk coming, he would say, "The case is complete; I let you have thirty blows of the staff." Or he would see a monk and call out "Elder!" If the monk turned his head, Mu Chou would say, "You board-carrying fellow!" Again, when he was teaching his community, he would say, "If you don't have a place to enter,[b] you must find a place to enter; once you have gained entry, you still must not turn your backs on me." Mu Chou's efforts for people were mostly like this.

This monk was also well polished and prepared, but nevertheless he had a dragon's head but a snake's tail. At the time anyone but Mu Chou would have been thrown into confusion by this monk. Like when Mu Chou asked him, "Where have you just come from?" and the monk immediately shouted: tell me, what was his meaning? The old fellow wasn't at all flustered; calmly he replied, "I've been shouted at by you once." He seems to take that shout and put it to one side, and he also seems to test him; he leans over to see how he is. Again the monk shouted; he seems to be right, but isn't yet really right—his nostrils were pierced by the old fellow, who immediately asked, "After three or four shouts, then what?" After all, this monk was speechless. Mu Chou then hit him and said, "What a thieving phoney you are!"

The aim of testing people is to know them intimately the

minute they open their mouths. Too bad this monk was speechless, provoking Mu Chou to call him a thieving phoney. If it had been any of you people who had been asked by Mu Chou, "After three or four shouts, then what?" how should you have replied in order to avoid his calling you a thieving phoney? Here if you can discern survival and destruction and distinguish right and wrong, if your feet tread the ground of reality, then who is concerned with "After three or four shouts, then what?"? But since this monk was speechless, his case was decided by old Mu Chou on the basis of the facts.

Listen to Hsueh Tou's verse:

VERSE

Two shouts and a third shout:ᶜ
  **The sound of thunder is tremendous,
  but there isn't even a drop of rain.
  From ancient times up till now, there's
  rarely been anyone like this.*

Adepts recognize the opportune moment to change.
  **If he weren't an adept, how could (Mu Chou)
  have tested (the monk)? I'm just afraid that
  you aren't this way.*

If you call that riding the tiger's head,
  **Unh! Blind man! How can you ride
  a tiger's head? Quite a few people
  have understood in this way, and there
  are still people who entertain this view.*

The two of them would both turn out to be blind men.
  **An intimate comment from the mouth of an intimate.
  Why only two? Take what's coming to you and get out!*

Who is a blind man?
  **Who would you have decide?
  Fortunately there is a last word:
  (Hsueh Tou) is on the verge of
  cheating people completely.*

I bring it out for everyone to see.
  **When you look, it's not that it's

not there, but if you stare at it,
you'll go blind. If you set your eyes
to look, then you are grabbing empty space
with both hands. When you bring it up this
way, what level of activity is it? *

COMMENTARY

Nothing can prevent Hsueh Tou from being able to help people. If he weren't an adept, he would just be shouting wildly at random. Therefore it is said, "Sometimes a shout isn't used as a shout; then again, sometimes a shout is used as a shout. Sometimes a shout is like a lion crouching on the ground; sometimes a shout is like the Diamond King's jewel sword."

Hsing Hua said, "I see all of you shouting in the east hall and shouting in the west hall. Don't shout at random. Even if you shout me up to the heavens, break me to pieces, and I fall back down again without even a trace of breath left in me, wait for me to revive and I'll tell you it's still not enough. Why? I have never set out real pearls for you inside the Purple Curtains. As for all of you here, what are you doing when you just go on with wild random shouting?"

Lin Chi said, "I've heard all of you imitate my shouting. But I ask you, if a monk comes from the east hall and another monk comes from the west hall, and they both shout at once, which one is the guest and which one is the host? If you can't distinguish host and guest, then you must not imitate me any more after this."

Therefore Hsueh Tou says in his verse, "Adepts recognize the opportune moment to change." Although the monk in the case was taken in by Mu Chou, still he could perceive the opportune moment to change. Tell me, where did he do this? Ch'an Master Chih of the Deer Gate graded this monk by saying, "One who knows the Law fears it." Yen T'ou said, "In battle, each man occupies a pivotal position." Master Hsin of Huang Lung said, "When you reach an impasse, change; having changed, then you get through." This is where the patriarchs cut off the tongues of everyone in the world. If you recognize the opportune moment to change, then when something is raised, you immediately know what it comes down to.

Some people say, "Why worry about Mu Chou saying, 'After three or four shouts, then what?'?" and just go on shouting. Let them give twenty or thirty shouts, even go on shouting until Maitreya (the future Buddha) comes down to be born, and call this riding the tiger's head: if you understand in this fashion, it's because you don't know Mu Chou. Even if you want to see the monk, you're still too far away. To ride a tiger's head one must have a sword in his hand and versatility too before he can succeed.

Hsueh Tou says, if you call this riding the tiger's head, "The two of them would both turn out to be blind men." Hsueh Tou is like a long sword leaning against the sky, stern and awesome in full majesty. If you understand Hsueh Tou's meaning, you will naturally understand everything at once. Then you will see that the latter part of Hsueh Tou's verse is just making footnotes.

Hsueh Tou goes on to say "Who is a blind man?" Tell me, is it the guest who's blind, or is it the host who's blind? Aren't guest and host both blind at the same time? "I bring it out for everyone to see." This is the living place, where Hsueh Tou finishes the verse all at once. Yet why does he say, "I bring it out for everyone to see"? Tell me, how will you see it? Open your eyes and you can; shut your eyes and you can too. Is there anyone who can avoid it?

TRANSLATOR'S NOTES

a. These were professor-monks of the scholastic schools, specializing in various Buddhist texts and philosophies and expounding them in temples devoted to the study of the written teachings. They are sometimes derided in Ch'an literature for being too attached to doctrines and theories, or full of self-importance and pride in their learning, but without real accomplishment.

b. A place to enter the Path; this is the true initiation, disentanglement from the bonds of egoism. Beyond this is the phase of 'getting oneself out' or 'showing onself,' which means to transcend the state of quiescence and nothingness, so to speak, to go beyond the point of entry and absorption into the Path, and bring out the active function of illumination. As an Ancient said, "A sage has no self, but there is nothing that is not his self." Although the phase of getting out or showing has attributes and is personal in the sense that the nirvana of the Great Vehicle is personal, it is beyond the concept of ego and personal possession, and is like the revelation of the adamantine being spoken of in esoteric Buddhism.

c. "Two shouts" refers to the monk; "a third shout" refers to Mu Chou.

Huang Po's Gobblers of Dregs

POINTER

The great capacity of Buddhas and Patriarchs is completely within his control; the lifeline of humans and gods is entirely subject to his direction. With a casual word or phrase he astounds the crowd and stirs the masses; with one device, one object, he smashes chains and knocks off fetters. Meeting transcendental potential, he brings up transcendental matters. But tell me, who has ever come on like this? Are there any who know where he is at? To test, I cite this: look!

CASE

Huang Po, instructing the community, said,[1] "All of you people are gobblers of dregs; if you go on travelling around this way,[2] where will you have Today?[3] Do you know that there are no teachers of Ch'an in all of China?"[4]

At that time a monk came forward and said, "Then what about those in various places who order followers and lead communities?"[5]

Huang Po said, "I do not say that there is no Ch'an; it's just that there are no teachers."[6]

NOTES

1. Drawing water, he's limited by (the size of) the bowl. He swallows all in one gulp. No patchrobed monk in the world can leap clear.
2. He's said it. You'll wear out your straw sandals.
3. What's the use of Today? Nothing can stop him from astounding the crowd and stirring up the community.
4. I hadn't realized. He swallows all in one gulp. He too is a cloud-dwelling saint.

5. He too gives a good thrust; confronting the situation, he couldn't but do so.
6. He just can't explain. The tiles are scattered, the ice melts. He's a fellow with a dragon's head but a snake's tail.

COMMENTARY

Huang Po was seven feet tall; on his forehead there was (a lump like) a round pearl. He understood Ch'an by nature. It's also said that he once travelled in the company of a saint: once when the master was travelling to Mount T'ien T'ai, he met a monk on the way. They talked and laughed together like old acquaintances. Huang Po looked him over carefully; the light in his eyes pierced people, and his appearance was extremely unusual. As they thus travelled along together, when they came to a swollen valley stream, Huang Po planted his staff (in the ground), took off his hat, and stopped there. The other monk tried to take the master across with him, but the master said, "Please cross over yourself." The other one then gathered up his robes and walked upon the waves as though treading on level ground. He looked back and said, "Come across! Come across!" The master upbraided him, saying, "You self-perfected fellow! If I had known you would concoct wonders, I would have broken your legs!" The other monk sighed in admiration and said, "You are a true vessel of the teaching of the Great Vehicle." As his words ended, he disappeared.

When Huang Po first met Pai Chang, Pai Chang said, "Magnificent! Imposing! Where have you come from?" Huang Po said, "Magnificent and imposing, I've come from the mountains." Pai Chang asked, "What have you come for?" Huang Po said, "Not for anything else." Pai Chang esteemed him deeply as a vessel (of Dharma).

The next day he took leave of Pai Chang. Pai Chang asked, "Where are you going?" Huang Po replied, "To Kiangsi to pay my respects to the Great Master Ma." Pai Chang said, "The Great Master Ma has already passed on." Huang Po asked, "What did he have to say when he was alive?" Pai Chang then related the circumstances of his second encounter with Ma Tsu:

"When Ma Tsu saw me approach, he raised his whisk. I asked, 'Do you identify with this action or detach from this action?' Ma Tsu then hung the whisk on the corner of the meditation seat. There was a long silence; then Ma Tsu asked me, 'Later on, when you're flapping your lips, how will you help people?' I took the whisk and held it up. Ma Tsu said, 'Do you identify with this action or detach from this action?' I took the whisk and hung it back on the corner of the meditation seat. Ma Tsu drew himself up and gave a shout that left me deaf for three days."

Huang Po unconsciously stuck out his tongue in awe. Pai Chang said, "After this, won't you be a successor of the Great Master Ma?" Huang Po said, "No. Today, because of the master's recital, I've gotten to see the Great Master Ma's great capacity and its great function; but if I were to succeed to Master Ma, in the future I would be bereft of descendants." Pai Chang said, "It is so, it is so. If your view equals your teacher, you have less than half your teacher's virtue; only when your wisdom goes beyond your teacher are you worthy to pass on the transmission. As your view is right now, it seems that you have ability which transcends any teacher." You must see for yourself how father and son act in that house before you begin to understand.

Again one day Huang Po asked Pai Chang, "How has the vehicle of the school that comes down from ancient times been demonstrated and taught?" Pai Chang was silent for a long time; Huang Po said, "You shouldn't let posterity be cut off." Pai Chang said, "I thought you were the man." Then he got up and went into his abbot's quarters.

Huang Po was an informal friend of prime minister P'ei Hsiu; he explained the essence of mind[a] to him. When P'ei was commander of Wan Ling, he invited the master to come to the district capital. He showed the master a book (expressing) his understanding. The master took the book and put it down on the seat without even opening it to look through it. After a long silence, the master asked, "Do you understand?" P'ei said, "I don't understand." Huang Po said, "If you had understood this way, you still would have gotten somewhere; if you're still trying to describe it with paper and ink, where would there still be room for my school?" At this P'ei offered a verse of praise:

From the great man he has inherited the mind seal;
There's a round jewel on his forehead, his body is
seven feet tall.
He hung up his staff and stayed ten years by the
River Shu;
Today his floating coracle has crossed to the banks
of the Chang.
Eight thousand dragons and elephants follow his
giant strides;
Over ten thousand miles fragrant flowers join in his
excellent cause.
I hope to serve the master as his disciple;
I do not know to whom he will entrust his teaching.

The master made no sign of being pleased, but said,[b]

My mind is like the boundlessness of the great
ocean;
My mouth spews red lotuses to nurse a sick body.
I myself have a pair of hands with nothing to do;
I have never received an idle man.

After Huang Po was dwelling (in a temple as a teacher), his active edge was sharp and dangerous. When Lin Chi was in his community, Mu Chou was the head monk. (Mu Chou) asked (Lin Chi), "How long have you been here? Why don't you go ask (Huang Po) a question?" Chi said, "What would you have me ask?" The head monk said, "Why don't you go ask what is the essential meaning of the Buddha Dharma?" Chi then went and asked (Huang Po); three times he was beaten and driven out. He took leave of the head monk, saying, "I have been bidden to ask the question three times by you, and have been beaten and driven out. Perhaps my affinity is not here; for now I will leave the mountain." The head monk said, "If you're going, you should bid farewell to the master (Huang Po) first." The head monk went beforehand and said to Huang Po, "The questioning monk is a very rare one; why don't you work on him to make him into a tree to provide cool shade for people of later times?" Huang Po said, "I already know."

When Chi came to take leave, Po said, "You don't need to go anyplace else; just go to the riverbank at Ta An and see Ta Yu."

When Chi got to Ta Yu, he related the preceding story and said, "I do not know where my fault was." Ta Yu said, "Huang Po was so kind, he exerted himself to the utmost for you; why do you go on speaking of fault or no fault?" Chi was suddenly greatly enlightened: he said, "There's not much to Huang Po's Buddha Dharma." Ta Yu grabbed and held him and said, "You just said you were at fault; now instead you say there's not much to the Buddha Dharma." Chi hit Ta Yu in the side three times with his fist; Yu pushed him away and said, "Your teacher is Huang Po; it has nothing to do with me."

One day Huang Po, instructing his community, said, "The Great Master Fa Jung of Ox Head Mountainᶜ spoke horizontally and spoke vertically, but he still didn't know the key of transcendence. These days the Ch'an followers after Shih T'ou and Ma Tsu speak of Ch'an and speak of the Way most voluminously." But why did Huang Po talk this way? It was because of this that he taught the community by saying, "All of you are gobblers of dregs; if you travel around like this, you'll get laughed at by people. As soon as you hear of a place with eight hundred or a thousand people, you immediately go there. It won't do just to seek out the hubbub; if you always take things this easy here, then where else would there be this matter of Today?"

In T'ang times they liked to revile people by calling them "gobblers of dregs," so many people say that Huang Po was reviling the people. Those with eyes see for themselves what he was getting at. The whole idea is to let down a hook to fish out people's questions. In the assembly there was a Ch'an man who didn't fear for his body or life, so he could come forth this way from the crowd to question Huang Po, saying, "Then what about those in various places who order followers and lead communities?" And he makes a good point, too. After all the old fellow Huang Po couldn't explain, so instead he broke down and said, "I don't say there is no Ch'an, just that there are no teachers." But tell me, where does his meaning lie?

That essence of the school that has come down from ancient times—sometimes holding, sometimes letting go, sometimes killing, sometimes giving life, sometimes releasing, sometimes gathering up—I dare to ask all of you, what would be a teacher of Ch'an? As soon as I speak this way, I've already lost my head. People, where are your nostrils? (A pause) They've been pierced through!

VERSE

His cold severe solitary mien does not take pride in itself;
    **He himself doesn't know he has it. He too is a cloud-
    dwelling saint. *

Solemnly dwelling in the sea of the world, he distinguishes
        dragons and snakes.
    **It is still necessary to distinguish initiate and unin-
    itiate, and it is also necessary that black and white be
    clearly distinguished. *

Ta Chung the Son of Heaven has been lightly handled;
    **What Ta Chung the Son of Heaven are you talking
    about? However great, he too must get up from the
    ground; and even higher, there's still the sky—what
    about that? *

Three times he personally felt those claws and fangs at work.
    **A dead frog. Why so talkative? It's not yet anything
    extraordinary; it's still a minor skill. When his great
    capacity and great function become manifest, then the
    whole world in all ten directions, the mountains and
    rivers and the great earth, all are at Huang Po's place
    begging for their lives. *

COMMENTARY

This verse by Hsueh Tou seems just like praise on a portrait of
Huang Po, yet you people mustn't understand it as "praise on a
portrait." Right in his words there's a place to get oneself out.[d]
Hsueh Tou clearly says, "His cold severe solitary mien does
not take pride in itself." When Huang Po instructed the community this way, he wasn't contesting others or asserting
himself, displaying himself or boasting of himself. If you understand what happened here, you are free in all directions:
sometimes you stand alone on a solitary peak, sometimes you
stretch out in the bustling market place. How could you one-
sidedly hold fast to a single corner? The more you abandon, the
more you aren't at rest; the more you seek, the more you don't
see; the more you take on, the more you sink down. An Ancient said, "Without wings, fly through the sky; with fame,
become known throughout the world." Wholeheartedly dis-

card the marvelous wonders of the principle of Buddha Dharma; let it all go at once, and then you will after all have gotten somewhere, and wherever you are it will naturally become manifest.

Hsueh Tou says, "Solemnly dwelling in the sea of the world, he distinguishes dragons and snakes." Is it a dragon or is it a snake? As soon as anyone comes in through the door, he puts him to the test; this is called the eye to distinguish dragons and snakes, the ability to capture tigers and rhinos. Hsueh Tou also said, "Judging dragons and snakes—how is that eye correct? Capturing tigers and rhinos—that skill is not complete."

Hsueh Tou also says, "Ta Chung the Son of Heaven has been lightly handled; three times he personally felt those claws and fangs at work." Huang Po is not just acting bad right here (in this case); he's always been like this. As for Ta Chung the Son of Heaven (Emperor), it is recorded in the *Continued Biographies of the Hsien T'ung Era* that the T'ang Emperor Hsien Tsung (r. 806–820) had two sons, one called Mu Tsung and the other called Hsuan Tsung. This Hsuan Tsung (r. 847–860) was the Ta Chung Emperor.

When Hsuan Tsung was thirteen years old, though still young, he was keen and clever, and always liked to sit in the lotus posture. During the reign of Mu Tsung (821–824), one time when the morning audience was over, Hsuan Tsung playfully mounted the (Imperial) Dragon Throne and went through the motions of saluting the assembled officials. One of the great ministers saw this and thought that Hsuan Tsung was demented, so he reported this to Mu Tsung. When Mu Tsung saw Hsuan Tsung, he rubbed his head and sighed, saying, "My younger brother is indeed a valiant son of my clan."

Mu Tsung died in 824, leaving three sons, called Ching Tsung, Wen Tsung, and Wu Tsung. Ching Tsung succeeded to his father's throne and reigned for two years until the inner court plotted against him and removed him. Wen Tsung succeeded to the throne and reigned for fourteen years. When Wu Tsung came to the throne, he always spoke of Hsuan Tsung as an imbecile. One day, filled with hatred for Hsuan Tsung because long ago he had playfully climbed up on his father's throne, he finally had Hsuan Tsung beaten almost to death, thrown out into the back gardens, and drenched with filthy water to revive him.

After this Hsuan Tsung went into hiding in the community of the Master Chih Hsien of Hsiang Yen. Later he had his head shaved as a novice, but had not yet received full ordination. He travelled around with Chih Hsien; when they got to Mount Lu, Chih Hsien made up a poem about a waterfall:

> *Piercing the clouds, penetrating rock, never declin-*
> *ing the work;*
> *When the land is distant, you know how high is the*
> *place it appears.*

Having intoned these two lines, Chih Hsien remained a long time in thought; he wanted to draw out a stream of words from Hsuan Tsung to see what he was like. Hsuan Tsung continued the verse, saying,

> *How can the mountain torrent be held back?*
> *Eventually it must return to the great ocean to be-*
> *come waves.*

At this Chih Hsien knew that Hsuan Tsung was no ordinary man, and he silently acknowledged him.

Later Hsuan Tsung went into the community at Yen Kuan, where he was asked to be the temple scribe. Huang Po was there serving as head monk. One day as Huang Po was paying respects to (an image of a) Buddha, Hsuan Tsung saw him and asked, "If you don't seek from Buddha, don't seek from Dharma, and don't seek from the Sangha, then what are you seeking by bowing in respect?" Huang Po replied, "I don't seek from Buddha, I don't seek from the Dharma, and I don't seek from the Sangha; I always pay my respects this way." Hsuan Tsung said, "What's the use of paying respect?" Immediately Huang Po slapped him. Hsuan Tsung said, "Too coarse." Huang Po said, "What place is this to talk of coarse and fine?" and slapped him again. Later, when Hsuan Tsung succeeded to the throne of the nation, he bestowed on Huang Po the title, "Coarse-acting Ascetic." When prime minister P'ei was at court later, he proposed that Huang Po be given the title Tuan Chi Ch'an Shih, "Boundless Ch'an Master."

Hsueh Tou knew where his bloodline appeared, so he could use it cleverly. Right now is there anyone to use his claws and fangs? If so, then I'll strike!

TRANSLATOR'S NOTES

a.   This refers to the *Ch'uan Hsin Fa Yao*, the "Essential Method of the Transmission of Mind," a collection of Huang Po's sermons for P'ei Hsiu.

b.   According to Tenkei Denson, the following verse is probably not really Huang Po's; it does not appear in the version of this story given in the *Ching Te Ch'uan Teng Lu*. Tenkei also says that the following story of Lin Chi's enlightenment also has no particular use in this commentary, and is probably a later insertion.

c.   593–657; he was later claimed to be a successor of Tao Hsin, the Fourth Patriarch of Ch'an after Bodhidharma. A distinguished meditation master, Fa Jung is known as the first patriarch of the so-called Ox Head sect of Ch'an, which continued for ten generations and produced numerous distinguished masters. Although historically of independent origin, this sect later developed close relations with the streams of the Ts'ao Ch'i succession.

d.   This means a place which reveals Huang Po's state, and the way a student must go to realize his sphere of attainment. To 'get oneself out' has the meaning of 'appearing in the world' (though this latter expression usually has the specific meaning of accepting leadership of a community as the spiritual guide, it can have the more inclusive meaning of actively revealing enlightened knowledge and conduct). The Zen master Dogen, in his *Fukanzazengi*, says, 'Although one may roam freely in the realm of entry, one may lack a living road to get himself out on.'

Tung Shan's Three Pounds of Hemp

POINTER

The sword that kills people, the sword that brings people to life: this is the standard way of high antiquity and the essential pivot for today as well. If you discuss killing, you don't harm a single hair; if you discuss giving life, you lose your body and life. Therefore it is said, "The thousand sages have not transmitted the single transcendental path; students toil over appearances like monkeys grasping at reflections." Tell me, since it is not transmitted, why then so many complicated public cases? Let those with eyes try to explain.

CASE

A monk asked Tung Shan, "What is Buddha?"[1]
Tung Shan said, "Three pounds of hemp."[2]

NOTES

1. Iron brambles; no patchrobed monk on earth can leap clear.
2. Clearly. Worn out straw sandals. He points to a pagoda tree to scold a willow tree.

COMMENTARY

So many people misunderstand this public case. It really is hard to chew on, since there's no place for you to sink your teeth into. What is the reason? Because it's bland and flavorless. The Ancients had quite a few answers to the question "What is Buddha?" One said, "The one in the shrine." One said, "The thirty-two auspicious marks." One said, "A bamboo whip on a mountain covered with a forest grown from a staff."

81

And so on, to Tung Shan, who said, "Three pounds of hemp." He couldn't be stopped from cutting off the tongues of the Ancients.

Many people base their understanding on the words and say that Tung Shan was in the storehouse at the time weighing out hemp when the monk questioned him, and therefore he answered in this way. Some say that when Tung Shan is asked about the east he answers about the west. Some say that since you are Buddha and yet you still go to ask about Buddha, Tung Shan answers this in a roundabout way. And there's yet another type of dead men who say that the three pounds of hemp is itself Buddha. But these interpretations are irrelevant. If you seek from Tung Shan's words this way, you can search until Maitreya Buddha is born down here and still never see it even in a dream.

What's the reason? Words and speech are just vessels to convey the Path. Far from realizing the intent of the Ancients, people just search in their words; what grasp can they get on it? Haven't you seen how an Ancient said, "Originally the Path is wordless; with words we illustrate the Path. Once you see the Path, the words are immediately forgotten." To get to this point, you must first go back to your own original state. Just this three pounds of hemp is like the single track of the great road to the Capital; as you raise your feet and put them down, there's nothing that is not this. This story is the same as Yun Men's saying "Cake"[a] but it's unavoidably difficult to understand. My late teacher Wu Tsu made a verse about it:

> The cheap-selling board-carrying fellow
> Weighs it out, three pounds of hemp.
> With a hundred thousand years of unsold goods,
> He has no place to put it all.

You must clean it all up; when your defiling feelings, conceptual thinking, and comparative judgements of gain and loss and right and wrong are all cleared away at once, then you will spontaneously understand.

VERSE

The Golden Raven[b] hurries;
  **In the left eye, half a pound.

The swift sparrowhawk can't overtake it.
*Lay the body down in flames of fire.**

The Jade Rabbit[c] *is swift.*

***In the right eye, eight ounces.*
*He makes his nest in the palace of Heng O, the Moon Lady.**

Has there ever been carelessness in a good response?

***As the bell when struck, as the valley embracing the echo.**

To see Tung Shan as laying out facts in accordance with the situation

***Mistakenly sticking by the zero point of the scale; it's just Your Reverence who sees things this way.**

Is like a lame tortoise and a blind turtle entering an empty valley.

***Take what's coming to you and get out. In the same pit, there's no different dirt. Who killed your sparrowhawk?**

Flowering groves, multicolored forests;

***A double case; he handles all crimes with the same indictment. As before, they're the same.**

Bamboo of the South, wood of the North.

***A quadruple case. He puts a head on top of his head.**

So I think of Ch'ang Ch'ing and Officer Lu:

***A leper drags his companions along with him.*
*I am this way, and Hsueh Tou is this way too.**

He knew how to say he should laugh, not cry.

***Ha ha. By day and by night he adds to the suffering.**

Ha!

***Bah! What is this? I strike!**

COMMENTARY

Hsueh Tou can see all the way through, so he immediately says, "The Golden Raven hurries; the Jade Rabbit is swift." This is of the same kind as Tung Shan's reply "Three pounds of hemp." The sun rises, the moon sets; every day it's like this. People often make up intellectual interpretations and just say,

"The Golden Raven is the left eye and the Jade Rabbit is the right eye." As soon as they're questioned, they put a glare in their eyes and say, "They're here!" What connection is there? If you understand in this way, the whole school of Bodhidharma would be wiped off the face of the earth. That is why it is said,

> Letting down the hook in the four seas
> Just to fish out terrible dragons;
> The mysterious device outside conventions
> Is for seeking out those who know the self.

Hsueh Tou is a man who has left the heaps and elements;[d] how could he make up this sort of interpretation? Hsueh Tou easily goes to where the barriers are broken and the hinges are smashed to reveal a little something to let you see; there he adds a footnote, saying, "Has there ever been carelessness in a good response?" Tung Shan does not reply lightly to this monk; he is like a bell when struck, like a valley embracing an echo. Great or small, he responds accordingly, never daring to make a careless impression. At once Hsueh Tou has brought out his guts and presented them to all of you. Hsueh Tou had a verse on being tranquil but responding well:

> Presented face to face, it's not a matter of multiplicity;
> Dragons and snakes are easily distinguished, but a patchrobed monk is hard to deceive.
> The golden hammer's shadow moves, the jewel sword's light is cold;
> They strike directly; hurry up and take a look!

When Tung Shan first saw Yun Men, Yun Men asked him, "Where have you just come from?" Tung Shan said, "From Cha Tu." Yun Men said, "Where did you spend the summer retreat?" Tung Shan said, "In Hunan, at Pao Tz'u." Yun Men asked, "When did you leave there?" Tung Shan said, "August twenty-fifth." Yun Men said, "I should let you have three score blows of the staff; go meditate in the hall."

That evening Tung Shan entered Yun Men's room; drawing near, he asked, "Where was my fault?" Yun Men said, "You rice bag! From Kiangsi to Hunan, and still you go on this way." At these words Tung Shan was vastly and greatly awakened. After a while he said, "Another day I'll go to a place where

there are no human hearths and build myself a hut; I won't
store even a single grain of rice or plant any vegetables. There
I'll receive and wait upon the great sages coming and going
from the ten directions; I'll pull out all the nails and pegs for
them, I'll pull off their greasy caps and strip them of their
stinking shirts. I'll make them all clean and free, so they can be
unconcerned people." Yun Men said, "Your body is the size of
a coconut, but you can open such a big mouth."

Tung Shan then took his leave and departed. His enlightenment at the time was a direct complete breakthrough; how
could it have anything in common with small petty views?
Later when he appeared in the world to respond to people's
various potentialities, the words "Three pounds of hemp" were
understood everywhere merely as a reply to the question about
Buddha; they just make their reasoning in terms of Buddha.
Hsueh Tou says that to understand Tung Shan's reply as expressing facts in accordance with the situation is like a lame
tortoise or a blind turtle going into an empty valley; when will
they ever find a way out?

"Flowering groves, multicolored forests." When a monk
asked Master Hsien of Fu Teh,ᵉ "What is the mind of the Buddhas of antiquity?" The master replied, "Flowering groves,
multicolored forests." The monk also asked Ming Chiao,
"What is the inner meaning of 'three pounds of hemp'?" Ming
Chiao said, "Bamboo of the South, wood of the North." The
monk came back and recounted this to Tung Shan, who said, "I
won't explain this just for you, but I will explain it to the whole
community." Later he went into the hall and said, "Words do
not express facts, speech does not accord with the situation.
Those who accept words are lost, and those who linger over
phrases are deluded."

To smash people's intellectual views, Hsueh Tou purposely
draws these together on a single thread to produce his verse.
Yet people of later times still give rise to even more intellectual views and say, " 'Three pounds of hemp' is the robe of
mourning; bamboo is the staff of mourning: that's why he said,
'Bamboo of the South, wood of the North.' 'Flowering groves,
multicolored forests' is the flowers and plants painted on the
coffin." Do these people realize their disgrace? How far are
they from realizing that "bamboo of the South, wood of the
North" and "three pounds of hemp" are just like "daddy" and

"poppa." When the Ancients answered with a turn of words, their intention was definitely not like these (interpretations). It's just like Hsueh Tou's saying, "The Golden Raven hurries; the Jade Rabbit is swift"—it's just as broad. It's just that real gold and fool's gold are hard to tell apart; similar written characters are not the same.

Hsueh Tou has the kind heart of an old woman; he wants to break up your feelings of doubt, so he brings in more dead men. "So I think of Ch'ang Ch'ing and Officer Lu; he knew how to say he should laugh, not cry." To discuss the verse itself, the first three lines by themselves have already completed the verse. But I ask you, since the whole universe is just this three pounds of hemp, why does Hsueh Tou still have so many complications? It's just that his compassion is excessive, therefore he is like this.

When Officer Lu Hsuan was Inspector of Hsuan Chou, he studied with Nan Ch'uan. When Nan Ch'uan passed on, Lu heard the (sound of) mourning so he entered the temple for the funeral. He laughed aloud a great laugh. The temple director said to him, "The late master and you were teacher and disciple; why aren't you crying?" Officer Lu said, "If you can say something, I'll cry." The temple director was speechless. Lu gave a loud lament; "Alas! Alas! Our late master is long gone." Later Ch'ang Ch'ing heard of this and said, "The officer should have laughed, not cried."

Hsueh Tou borrows the essence of this meaning to say that if you make up these kinds of intellectual interpretations, this calls for laughter, not crying. This is so, but at the very end there's a single word which is unavoidably easy to misunderstand, when he goes on to say "Ha!" Has Hsueh Tou washed himself clean?

TRANSLATOR'S NOTES

a. Asked, "What is talk that goes beyond buddhas and patriarchs?" Yun Men said, "Cake."
b. The Golden Raven is the sun.
c. The Jade Rabbit is the moon.
d. The heaps (Sanskrit *skandha*) are form (matter), sensation, perception, synergies, and consciousness; the elements (Sanskrit

dhatu) are the six sense faculties (eye, ear, nose, tongue, body, and mind), the six sense fields (form, sound, smell, taste, feeling, and entity), and the six associated consciousnesses. While the five heaps are often used to refer specifically to the human being, in which context the synergies include all sorts of mental activities such as emotion and volition, functional relations not connected with mind are also classified as synergies. It is obvious in this context that to leave the five heaps and eighteen elements does not mean annihilation, but refers to being free from attachment to them, having died the esoteric death, sloughed off the claims of egoism, under whose sway emotion and intellect, thought and habit, had been in fact inseparable.

e.   The names of Chien and Ming Chiao are used after the critical edition of Ito Yuten, in accord with the One Night Book, which also accords with tradition from other sources; the Chang version has it that both these questions were posed to Chih Men, Hsueh Tou's teacher, but this poses a contradiction in time.

Pa Ling's Snow in a Silver Bowl

POINTER

Clouds are frozen over the great plains, but the whole world is not hidden. When snow covers the white flowers, it's hard to distinguish the outlines. Its coldness is as cold as snow and ice; it fineness is as fine as rice powder. Its depths are hard for even a Buddha's eye to peer into; its secrets are impossible for demons and outsiders to fathom. Leaving aside "understanding three when one is raised" for the moment, still he cuts off the tongues of everyone on earth. Tell me, whose business is this? To test, I cite this: look!

CASE

A monk asked Pa Ling, "What is the school of Kanadeva?"[1] Pa Ling said, "Piling up snow in a silver bowl."[2]

NOTES

1.   A white horse enters the white flowers. What are you saying? Check!
2.   He blocks off your throat. A profuse outburst![a]

COMMENTARY

People often misunderstand and say this is a heretical school. What does this have to do with it? The fifteenth Patriarch, the honorable Kanadeva, was indeed (at one time) numbered among the outsiders; but when he met the fourteenth Patriarch, the honorable Nagarjuna (who presented a bowl of water to him), he put a needle into the bowl: Nagarjuna esteemed his capacity, transmitted the Buddha Mind School to him, and invested him as the fifteenth Patriarch.

In doctrinal disputes in India the winner holds a red flag in his hand, while the loser turns his clothes inside out and departs through a side door. Those who wanted to hold doctrinal disputes in India were required to obtain royal permission. Bells and drums would be sounded in the great temples and afterwards the debates could begin. In Kanadeva's day the heretics impounded the bell and drum in the (Buddhist) community temple in a purge. At this time the honorable Kanadeva knew that the Buddhist Teaching was in trouble, so he made use of his supernatural powers to ascend the bell tower and ring the bell, for he wanted to drive out the heretics.

Soon one of the heretics called out, "Who is up in the tower ringing the bell?" Kanadeva said, "A deva." The heretic asked, "Who is the deva?" Kanadeva said, "I." The heretic said "Who is 'I'?" Kanadeva said, " 'You' is a dog." The heretic asked, "Who is the dog?" Kanadeva said, "The dog is you." After seven go-rounds like this, the heretic realized he was beaten, so he submitted and himself opened the door of the bell tower, whereupon Kanadeva came down from the tower holding a red flag. The heretic said, "Why do you not follow?" Kanadeva said, "Why do you not precede?" The heretic said, "You're a knave." Kanadeva said, "You're a freeman."

Over and over Kanadeva would respond to questions like this, using his unobstructed powers of argument to overcome heretics, who would therefore submit. At such times the honorable Kanadeva would hold a red flag in his hand, and the one who had been defeated would stand beneath the flag. Among the heretics, to have their hands cut was generally the punishment to expiate the fault (or defeat in argument), but at this time Kanadeva put a stop to this; he only required his defeated adversaries to shave off their hair and enter the Buddhist path. Therefore the school of Kanadeva flourished greatly. Later on Hsueh Tou uses these facts to versify this.

Ma Tsu said, "The *Lankavatara* scripture says that Buddha's words have mind as their source and the gate of nothingness as the gate of the Dharma." Ma Tsu also said, "Whenever there are words and phrases, this is the Kanadeva school; just this he considered to be principal."

All of you are guests in the school of the patchrobed monks; have you ever thoroughly comprehended the school of Kanadeva as well? If you have thoroughly comprehended it, then the ninety-six kinds of heretics are all vanquished by you all at once. If you have not been able to comprehend it thoroughly, then you can't avoid going off with your clothes on inside out. Tell me, what about this? If you say words are it, this has no connection; if you say words are not it, this has no connection either. Tell me, where does Great Master Ma's meaning lie?

Later Yun Men said, "Great Master Ma spoke good words, but no one asks about it." Thereupon a monk asked, "What is the school of Kanadeva?" Yun Men said, "Of the ninety-six kinds of heretics, you are the lowest."

Formerly there was a monk who was taking leave of Ta Sui. Ta Sui asked, "Where are you going?" The monk said, "To do homage to Samantabhadra." Ta Sui raised his whisk and said, "Manjusri and Samantabhadra are both here." The monk drew a circle and pushed it towards Ta Sui with his hand; then he threw it behind him. Ta Sui said, "Attendant, bring a spot of tea for this monk."

Yun Men also said, "In India they cut off heads and arms; here you take what's coming to you and get out." He also said, "The red flag is in my hand."

In the community (of Yun Men) Pa Ling was called Mouthy Chien. When he was travelling around he always sewed sitting mats.[b] He had attained deeply into the great matter upon which Yun Men tread: thus he was outstanding. Later he appeared in the world as a Dharma successor to Yun Men. Formerly he dwelt at Pa Ling in Yueh Chou (in Hunan). He didn't compose any document of succession to the teaching, but just took three turning words to offer up to Yun Men: "What is the Path? A clear eyed man falls into a well." "What is the sword (so sharp it cuts) a hair blown (against it)? Each branch of coral upholds the moon." "What is the school of Kanadeva? Piling up snow in a silver bowl." Yun Men said, "Later on, on the anniversary of my death, just recite these three turning words, and you will have repaid my kindness in full." Thereafter, as it turned out, he did not hold ceremonial feasts on the anniversaries of his death, but followed Yun Men's will and just brought up these turning words.

Although people from all over have given answers to this question ("What is the school of Kanadeva?"), mostly they have turned to events to make up their answers; there is only Pa Ling who speaks as he does—he's extremely lofty and unique, unavoidably difficult to understand. Then too, without revealing a trace of his sharp point, he takes on enemies on all sides, and blow by blow finds a way to get himself out. He has the skill to fell tigers; he strips off human emotional views. As for the matter of One Form,[c] to get here you must have penetrated all the way through on your own, but after all you must meet another (enlightened) person before you are done. Therefore it is said, "When Tao Wu brandished his sceptre, one who was his equal would understand;[d] when Shih Kung bent his bow, an adept would tacitly comprehend."[e] For this truth, if you have no master to seal and instruct you, what teaching can you use to carry on the esoteric conversation?

Afterwards Hsueh Tou picked things out and brought them up for people in this verse:

VERSE

Old Hsin K'ai
    ***A thousand soldiers are easy to get, but one general is hard to find. Talkative teacher!**
Is truly something else:
    ***What truth is this? Have you ever felt his single knock on your head, even in a dream?**
He knows how to say, "Piling up snow in a silver bowl."
    ***The frog can't leap out of the basket. A double case. Quite a few people will lose their bodies and lives.**
The ninety-six each must know for themselves;
    ***You're included too; but do you know, Reverend? All are buried in the same pit.**
If you don't know, then ask the moon in the sky.
    ***It's farther than far. Take what's coming to you and get out. Address your plea to the sky.**
The school of Kanadeva, Kanadeva's school;
    ***What are you saying? I'm here. A mouthful of frost.**
Beneath the red flag, arouse the pure wind.
    ***Shattered in a hundred fragments. Having struck, I'll say I've already hit it. Just cut off your heads and arms, and I'll speak a phrase for you.**

COMMENTARY

"Old Hsin K'ai." Hsin K'ai is the name of a monastery (in Pa Ling, Hunan, where the master Pa Ling stayed, hence a name for him). "Is truly something else." Hsueh Tou has ample praise for him. But tell me, how is Pa Ling special? "All words are the Buddha Dharma." When I talk like this, what's the reason for it? Hsueh Tou subtly reveals a little of his meaning when he says it's just that Pa Ling is truly something else.ᶠ Afterwards he opens up and says, "He can say, 'Piling up snow in a silver bowl.'"

Hsueh Tou goes on to provide you with further footnotes: "The ninety-six must each know for themselves." Before they can do so, they must acknowledge defeat. If you don't know, ask the moon in the sky. The Ancient used to give this answer, "Ask the moon in the sky."

Hsueh Tou's eulogy being finished, at the end there must be a living road, a phrase where the lion rears. He raises it higher for you and says, "The school of Kanadeva, the Kanadeva school; beneath the red flag, arouse the pure wind." Pa Ling said he piled up snow in a silver bowl; why then does Hsueh Tou say he roused the pure wind beneath the red flag? Do you know that Hsueh Tou kills people without using a sword?

TRANSLATOR'S NOTES

a. This obscure phrase is interpreted by commentators (hence translated) in various ways. It means the question is cracked and shattered, the answer is piercing and penetrating. Hence it can mean profusion, confusion, or it can mean opened up, clearly distinct (this latter includes the manifold, that everything is revealed in all its multiplicity). One commentator says that in this case it refers to the profuse discourse of the Kanadeva school, represented by Pa Ling's answer. Tenkei says that it means here burst open, clear and distinct, not hard to see.

b. This is interpreted in two ways; one, that Pa Ling travelled around with his sitting mat folded up, meaning that he did not prostrate himself before the teachers he visited (one rolls out one's mat to bow in full prostration). It is also interpreted to mean that he used to sew others' sitting mats for them.

c. Or, 'One Color'; unity, or equanimity. In Tung Shan Liang Chieh's *Pao Ching San Mei Ke*, 'Song of the Jewel Mirror Concentration' (9th century), it says 'Piling up snow in a silver bowl, hiding a heron in the bright moonlight; when you array them they are not the same, when you mix them you know where they are.' Silver and snow, moonlight and the white heron, are all white, but when associated, they are not identically the same; this symbolizes the sameness within difference, the difference within sameness. Sameness and difference correspond to the 'heart of nirvana' (equanimity) and the 'knowledge of differentiation,' sometimes referred to as successive stages on the Ch'an path. It is this latter that is in the sphere of 'meeting another.'

d. Kuan Nan Tao Wu, while on his foot travels, once heard a shamaness in a village spirit shrine take up her sceptre and intone her pledge to the spirit; at one point she said, 'Do you know the spirit or not?' whereupon Tao Wu was greatly enlightened. After travelling around to various places, he came to Kuan Nan Tao Ch'ang; to show his realization, Tao Wu flourished a sceptre, whereupon Tao Ch'ang recognized his enlightenment.

e. Shih Kung, a successor of Ma Tsu, was formerly a hunter. Later, he used to draw his bow on those who came to ask about Ch'an. When San P'ing came to him, he drew his bow; San P'ing bared his breast and said, 'Is this a killing arrow or a life-giving arrow?' Shih Kung threw away his bow and said that after thirty years he had finally managed to shoot half a sage.

f. This phrase also conveys the sense, 'his real point is distinct.'

Yun Men's Appropriate Statement

CASE

A monk asked Yun Men, "What are the teachings of a whole lifetime?"[1]

Yun Men said, "An appropriate statement."[2]

NOTES

1. Even up till now they're not finished with. The lecturer does not understand; he's in the cave of entangling complications.
2. An iron hammerhead with no handle-hole. A profuse outburst. A rat gnawing on raw ginger.

COMMENTARY

Members of the Ch'an family, if you want to know the meaning of Buddha-nature, you must observe times and seasons, causes and conditions. This is called the special transmission outside the (written) teachings, the sole transmission of the mind seal, directly pointing to the human mind for the perception of nature and realization of Buddhahood.

For forty-nine years old Shakyamuni stayed in the world; at three hundred and sixty assemblies he expounded the sudden and the gradual, the temporary and the true. These are what is called the teachings of a whole lifetime.[a] The monk (in this case) picked this out to ask, "What are the teachings of a whole lifetime?" Why didn't Yun Men explain for him in full detail, but instead said to him, "An appropriate statement"?

As usual, within one sentence of Yun Men three sentences are bound to be present. These are called the sentence that encloses heaven and earth, the sentence that follows the waves, and the sentence that cuts off the myriad streams. He lets go and gathers up; he's naturally extraordinary, like cut-

94

ting nails or shearing through iron. He makes people unable to comprehend him or figure him out. The whole great treasure-house of the teachings just comes down to three words ("An appropriate statement"); there is no facet or aspect in which you can rationalize this.

People often misunderstand and say, "Buddha's preaching was appropriate to the conditions of one time." Or they say, "The multitude of appearances and myriad forms are all the impressions of a single truth,"[b] and call this "an appropriate statement." Then there are those who say, "It's just talking about that one truth." What connection is there? Not only do they not understand, they also enter hell as fast as an arrow flies. They are far from knowing that the meaning of that man of old is not like this.

Therefore it is said, "Shattering one's bones and crushing one's body is still not sufficient recompense; when a single phrase is understood, you transcend ten billion." Undeniably extraordinary: "What are the teachings of a whole lifetime?" just boils down to his saying, "An appropriate statement." If you can grasp this immediately, then you can return home and sit in peace. If you can't get it, then listen humbly to the verdict:

VERSE

An appropriate statement;
>   ***Leaping with life.*
>   *The words are still in our ears.*
>   *Undeniably unique and lofty.* *

How utterly unique!
>   ***The onlooker has some part in it.*
>   *Why only stand like a mile high wall?*
>   *Is there any such thing?* *

He wedges a stake into the iron hammerhead with no hole.
>   ***He misunderstands the words. Old Yun Men too is*
>   *washing a lump of dirt in the mud; Hsueh Tou also*
>   *is just pasting on ornaments.* *

Under the Jambu Tree I'm laughing; ha, ha!
>   ***This fellow has never been seen anywhere.*

Only those on the same path would know.
*How many people could there be who know?**

Last night the black dragon had his horn wrenched off:
    ***It's not just the black dragon who gets twisted*
    and broken. Has anyone seen? Do you have proof?
    *Dumb!**

Exceptional, exceptional—
    ***Ample praise; it takes Hsueh Tou to do this.*
    *Where is he exceptional?**

The old man of Shao Yang got one horn.^c
    ***Where is it? To whom is the other*
    horn given? Te Shan and Lin Chi too
    must fall back three thousand miles.
    *Again, what about that other horn? I strike!**

COMMENTARY

"An appropriate statement; how utterly unique!" Hsueh Tou cannot praise him enough. These words of Yun Men are independent and free, unique and lofty, prior to light and after annihilation. They are like an overhanging cliff ten thousand fathoms high. Then, too, they are like a million man battle line; there is no place for you to get in. It's just that it's too solitary and perilous.

An Ancient said, "If you want to attain intimacy, don't use a question to ask a question; the question is in the answer and the answer is in the point of the question." Of course it's solitary and steep, but tell me, where is it that it's solitary and steep? No one on earth can do anything about it.

This monk (in the case) was also an adept, and that is why he could question like this. And Yun Men too answered this way, much like "wedging a stake into the iron hammerhead with no hole." Hsueh Tou employs literary language so artfully! "Under the Jambu Tree I'm laughing; ha, ha!" In the *Scripture on the Creation of the World* it says, "On the south side of Sumeru a crystal tree shines over the continent of Jambu, making all in between a clear blue color. This continent takes its name from this great tree; hence it is called Jambudvipa. This tree is seven thousand leagues high; beneath it are the golden mounds of the Jambu altar, which is twenty leagues high. Since gold is produced from beneath the tree, it is called the Jambu tree."

Thus Hsueh Tou says of himself that he is under the Jambu tree laughing out loud. But tell me, what is he laughing at? He's laughing at the black dragon who last night got his horn wrenched off. He's just looking up respectfully; he can only praise Yun Men. When Yun Men says, "An appropriate statement," what's it like? It's like breaking off one of the black dragon's horns. At this point, if there were no such thing, how could he have spoken as he did?

Hsueh Tou has finished his verse all at once, but he still has something to say at the very end: "Exceptional, exceptional—the old man of Shao Yang got one horn." Why doesn't Hsueh Tou say he got them both? How is it that he just got one horn? Tell me, where is the other horn?

TRANSLATOR'S NOTES

a. According to the analysis of Chih I, founder of the T'ien T'ai school of Chinese Buddhism, Buddha's teaching was divided into five periods: first, the period of the Hua Yen (Avatamsaka) scripture, where the Buddha directly expressed his own realization under the tree of enlightenment. Second, since no one at the time could understand the first, he expounded the Agamas for twelve years to suit elementary capacities. Third, he preached a transitional stage from this lesser to the greater vehicle, known as the extensive, or universally equal scriptures. Fourth, he preached the transcendence of wisdom. Fifth, he preached the Lotus of Truth (Saddharmapundarika) and Great Decease (Mahaparinirvana) scriptures. The teaching is divided by the Hua Yen school into the lesser vehicle, the elementary greater vehicle, the final greater vehicle, the sudden teaching, and the round, or complete teaching.

b. This saying comes from the *Dhammapada*; Yun Men's reply can be read as 'teaching in reference to one.'

c. The old man of Shao Yang is Yun Men. The horn is the stake driven into the holeless hammerhead. A hammerhead without a hole is an image used for something into which the 'handle' of logic and reason cannot be fit.

Yun Men's Upside-Down Statement

POINTER

The single-edged sword that kills people, the double-edged sword that brings people to life; the customary rule of high antiquity is still the pivotal essential for today. But tell me, right now, which is the sword that kills people, which is the sword that brings people to life? To test, I cite this; look!

CASE

A monk asked Yun Men, "When it's not the present intellect and it's not the present phenomena, what is it?"[1,a]

Yun Men said, "An upside-down statement."[2]

NOTES

1. Why the leaping about? Fall back three thousand miles.
2. They come out even. Truth comes out of the convict's mouth; he can't be let go. He stretches out his body in the wild weeds.

COMMENTARY

This monk is unquestionably an adept, to know how to pose questions like this. The question by the monk in the previous case is called "asking for more instruction"; in the present case it is a question to demonstrate understanding, and it can also be called a question with a concealed barb. For anyone but Yun Men, there would have been no way to cope with this monk. Yun Men possesses such ability that he cannot but reply once the question is raised. Why? An expert teaching master is like a bright mirror on its stand; if a foreigner comes a foreigner is reflected, and if a native comes a native is reflected.

An Ancient said, "If you want to attain intimate understanding, don't use a question to ask a question. Why? Because
the answer is where the question is." Since when have the
sages from past times ever had anything to give to people?
Where is there Ch'an or Tao that can be given to you? If you
don't do hellish deeds, naturally you will not bring on hellish
results. If you don't create heavenly conditions, naturally you
won't receive heavenly rewards. All circumstances of activity
are self-made and self-received. The Ancient Yun Men clearly
tells you, "When we discuss this affair, it's not in the words
and phrases. If it were in words and phrases, doesn't the twelve
part canon of the three vehicles have words and phrases? Then
what further use would there be for the Patriarch's coming
from the West?"

In the previous case Yun Men said, "An appropriate statement." Here, on the other hand, he says, "An upside-down
statement." Since there's only a difference of a single word,
why then are there a thousand differences, ten thousand distinctions? Tell me, where is the confusion? This is why it is
said, "The Teaching is carried out according to facts; the banner of the Teaching is set up according to the situation."

"When it's not the present intellect and it's not the present
phenomena, what is it?" is just worth a nod of agreement.
Since Yun Men is a fellow with eyes, he can't be fooled one
little bit. Since the point of the question was abstruse and
misleading, the answer too had to be this way. In fact Yun Men
is riding the thief's horse in pursuit of the thief.

Some people mistakenly say, "Basically these are words of a
host, but it was a guest who spoke them; therefore Yun Men
said, 'An upside-down statement.'" What relevance does this
have?

This monk asked well; "When it's not the present intellect
and it's not the present phenomena, what is it?" Why didn't
Yun Men answer him with some other words? Why instead did
he just say to him, "An upside-down statement"? Yun Men at
once demolished him utterly. Still, to say "an upside-down
statement" at this point is to gouge out a wound in healthy
flesh. Why? "The emergence of tracks of words is the source
from which divergent opinions are born." Suppose there never
were words and phrases; have this pillar and lamp right here
ever had any words or phrases? Do you understand? If you don't

understand at this point, you still need to turn over before you will know where the ultimate point of this is.

VERSE

An upside-down statement:
     **Can't let it go. Mixed up. He wraps up all five
     thousand and forty-eight volumes of the canon.*
Dividing one token,
     **Part on your side, part on my side.
     Half south of the river, half north of the river.
     Walking together holding hands.*
Dying with you, being born with you, to give you certainty.
     **Washing a lump of dirt in the mud. For what reason?
     He won't let you go.*
The eighty-four thousand disciples of Buddha were not
          phoenix feathers;
     **They looked like feathers. He diminishes these
     people's grandeur too much. Lacquer buckets are as
     plentiful as hemp and millet.*
Thirty-three men entered the tiger's den.
     **Only I can know. A single general is hard to find.
     A band of wild fox spirits.*
Distinctly outstanding—
     **How is it exceptional? A little boasting. Skip and leap
     as you will.*
The moon in the churning rushing water.
     **Under the blue sky and bright sun, he mistakes the
     reflection for the head. Why so busy?*

COMMENTARY

Hsueh Tou too is undeniably an adept. Right under the first line he immediately says, "Dividing one token." Clearly he lets go of the ultimate and joins hands with Yun Men to walk along together with him. Hsueh Tou has always had the technique of letting go; he dares to enter the mud and water for your sake, to die and be born together with you. This is the reason Hsueh Tou praises Yun Men this way. In reality he has no other purpose than to melt the glue and untie the bonds for you, to pull out the nails and wrench out the pegs.

These days, however, people base themselves on his words to spin out intellectual interpretations. Just as Yen T'ou said, "Although Hsueh Feng was born of the same lineage as me, he does not die of the same lineage as me." If Yun Men were not someone whose whole capacity had penetrated through to liberation, how could he die with you and be born with you? Why can he do this? Because he is free from the many leaking points of gain and loss, of is and is not.

Thus Tung Shan said, "If you would judge whether one going beyond is genuine or false, there are three kinds of leakage: emotional leakage, leakage of views, and verbal leakage. If there is leakage of views, the intellect does not stir from its fixed position and falls into the poisonous sea. If feelings leak, knowing always turns towards and against, and one's view is biased. Verbal leakage embodies the marvel but loses the fundamental; the intellect confuses beginning and end. You should know these three leaks for yourself."

There are also three mysteries; the mystery within the essence, the mystery within the phrase, and the mystery within the mystery.[b] When the Ancients came into this realm, their whole capacity was fully used: if you happened to be born, they would be born together with you; if you happened to die, they would die with you. They stretched out their bodies in the tiger's mouth; letting go their hands and feet, they would follow your lead for a thousand miles, for ten thousand miles. Why? You must go back with them to get this one realization before you'll understand.

As for "Eighty-four thousand disciples of Buddha were not phoenix feathers," this is the assembly of eighty-four thousand holy people on Vulture Peak of Spirit Mountain—they were not phoenix feathers.[c] The *Southern History* relates that in Sung times (420-479) there lived Hsieh Ch'ao-tsung ("surpassing his clan"), a man of Yang Hsia in Ch'en prefecture, the son of Hsieh Feng ("phoenix"). He had studied widely and his literary talent was superlative. At court there was no one to equal him; his contemporaries considered him unique. Since he was skilled in the written word, he served as permanent attendant at the capital. For the funeral ceremonies of the king's mother Yinshu, Ch'ao-tsung composed a eulogy and presented it at

102 THE BLUE CLIFF RECORD

court. Emperor Wu saw what he had written and praised him
highly, saying, "Ch'ao-tsung does indeed have phoenix feathers!" An old poem says,

> Audiences over, the incense smoke fills his billow-
>   ing sleeves;
> In the perfection of a poem, the perfect jewel lies in
>   the stroke of his brushtip.
> If you want to know the excellence of the hereditary
>   managers of Imperial decrees,
> On the pond right now there's a phoenix feather
>   floating.

In ancient times, at the assembly on Spirit Mountain, the
four groups (monks, nuns, men and women devotees) had
gathered like clouds. The World Honored One held up a flower;
Kashyapa alone changed his expression with a smile. The others did not know his meaning. Taking this, Hsueh Tou says,
"The eighty-four thousand were not phoenix feathers; thirty-
three men entered the tiger's den."
Ananda asked Kashyapa, "The World Honored One be-
queathed to you his golden robe; what special teaching did he
transmit besides?" Kashyapa called out "Ananda!" Ananda responded. Then Kashyapa said, "Take down the banner pole in
front of the gate."[d] Thereafter it was handed on from patriarch
to patriarch, in India and this country, through thirty-three
men. All had the ability to enter the tiger's den. The Ancients
said, "If you don't enter the tiger's den, how can you catch a
tiger cub?" Yun Men is this kind of man, well able to accompany people through birth and death. To help people, a teacher
of our school must get to be like this, to sit in the carved wood
seat of the teachers; abandoned, he makes you break open and
lets you grab the tiger's whiskers. He must have reached such a
realm to be able to teach. He has the seven things[e] always with
him, so he can accompany (beings) through life and death. The
high he presses down, the low he uplifts; to those who lack he
gives. Those on the solitary peak he rescues and sends them
into the wild weeds; if they have fallen into the wild weeds, he
rescues them and puts them on the solitary peak. "If you enter
a molten cauldron or a fiery furnace, I too will enter the molten
cauldron and the fiery furnace." In reality there is no other
purpose, just to melt the sticking points and release the bonds
for you, to pull out nails and draw out pegs, to strip off the

blinders, to unload the saddle bags. Master P'ing T'ien had a most excellent verse:

> *Spiritual light undimmed,*
> *Ages of good advice.*
> *Once it comes through this door,*
> *Don't keep any intellectual understanding.*

"Distinctly outstanding—the moon in the churning rushing water." Hsueh Tou unfailingly has a way to show himself, and also the skill to bring people to life. Hsueh Tou has picked this out to get people to go themselves to awaken their living potential. Don't follow another's words; if you follow them, that indeed would be the moon in the churning rushing water. Right now, how will you find peace and security? Let go!

TRANSLATOR'S NOTES

a. The monk in this case is supposed to be the same as in the fourteenth; the teachings of the age are devised and established according to the state of the intellect and total capacity of the hearers, in terms of the phenomenal situation. In an immediate sense, the present intellect and phenomena mean perceiver and perceived; according to Tenkei, the monk had seen that there is nothing outside of mind, and that all things are empty.

b. Also translated as three profundities, this was a classification of the Lin Chi school, interpreted variously through the ages. The mystery within the essence corresponds to the phrase that encloses heaven and earth; the mystery within the phrase corresponds to the phrase that follows the waves; the mystery within the mystery corresponds to the phrase that cuts off myriad streams. Yun Men's replies are said to contain all three of these aspects.

c. Phoenix feather is a metaphor for someone of outstanding talent, and also for a worthy successor.

d. The banner in front of a monastery in India signaled that teaching and debate were going on therein (see the commentary to case 13).

e. The seven items of a teacher are 1) great capacity and great function 2) swiftness of intellect 3) wondrous spirituality of speech 4) the active edge to kill or give life 5) wide learning and broad experience 6) clarity of mirroring awareness 7) freedom to appear and disappear.

Ching Ch'ing's Man in the Weeds

POINTER

The Path has no byroads; one who stands upon it is solitary and dangerous.ᵃ The truth is not seeing or hearing; words and thoughts are far removed from it. If you can penetrate through the forest of thorns and untie the bonds of Buddhahood and Patriarchy, you attain the land of inner peace, where all the gods have no way to offer flowers, where outsiders have no gate to spy through. Then you work all day without ever working, talk all day without ever talking; then you can unfold the device of 'breaking in and breaking out' and use the double-edged sword that kills and brings to life, with freedom and independence.

Even if you are this way, you must also know that within the gate of provisional expedients, there is 'one hand uplifting, one hand pressing down'; yet this still only amounts to a little bit: as for the fundamental matter, this has nothing to do with it. What about the fundamental matter? To test, I cite this; look!

CASE

A monk asked Ching Ch'ing, "I am breaking out; I ask the Teacher to break in."[1]

Ching Ch'ing said, "Can you live or not?"[2]

The monk said, "If I weren't alive, I'd be laughed at by people."[3]

Ching Ch'ing said, "You too are a man in the weeds."[4]

NOTES

1. Why raise waves where there's no wind? What do you want with so many views?

2. A jab. He buys the hat to fit the head. He adds error to error. Everyone can't be this way.
3. He drags others into it. He's holding up the sky and supporting the earth; the board-carrying fellow!
4. After all. Take what's coming to you and get out. He can't be let go.

COMMENTARY

Ching Ch'ing was a successor of Hsueh Feng, and a contemporary of the likes of Pen Jen, Hsuan Sha, Su Shan, and Fu of T'ai Yuan. First he met Hsueh Feng and understood his message. Thereafter he always used 'breaking in and breaking out' devices to instruct later students. He was well able to expound the teaching according to the potentialities of his listeners.

Once Ching Ch'ing taught the community saying, "In general, foot-travelers must have the 'simultaneous breaking in and breaking out' eye and must have the 'simultaneous breaking in and breaking out' function; only then can they be called patchrobed monks. It's like when the mother hen wants to break in, the chick must break out, and when the chick wants to break out, the mother hen must break in."

Thereupon a monk came forward and asked, "When the mother hen breaks in and the chick breaks out, from the standpoint of the teacher, what does this amount to?" Ching Ch'ing said, "Good news." The monk asked, "When the chick breaks out and the mother hen breaks in, from the standpoint of the student, what does this amount to?" Ching Ch'ing said, "Revealing his face." From this we see that they did have the device of 'simultaneous breaking in and breaking out' in Ching Ch'ing's school.

This monk (in the case) was also a guest of his house, and understood (Ching Ch'ing's) household affairs; therefore he questioned like this: "I am breaking out; I ask the Teacher to break in." Within the Ts'ao-Tung tradition this is called using phenomena to illustrate one's condition. How so? When the chick breaks out and the mother breaks in, naturally they are perfectly simultaneous.

Ching Ch'ing too does well; we could say his fists and feet are coordinated, his mind and eye illumine each other. He answered immediately by saying, "Can you live or not?" The monk too does well; he also knows how to change with the circumstances. In this one sentence of Ching Ch'ing's there is guest and there is host, there is illumination and there is function, there is killing and there is giving life.

The monk said, "If I weren't alive, I'd be laughed at by people." Ching Ch'ing said, "You too are a man in the weeds." He's first class at going into the mud and water, but nothing stops his wicked hands and feet. Since the monk understood enough to question in this way, why did Ching Ch'ing nevertheless say, "You too are a man in the weeds"? Because the eye of an adept must be this way, like sparks struck from stone, like flashing lightning. Whether you can reach it or not, you won't avoid losing your body and life. If you are this way, then you see Ching Ch'ing calling him a man in the weeds.

Therefore Nan Yuan taught his assembly saying, "In the various places they only have the eye of simultaneous breaking in and breaking out, but they don't have the function of simultaneous breaking in and breaking out." A monk came forward and asked, "What is the function of simultaneous breaking in and breaking out?" Nan Yuan said, "An adept does not break in and break out; breaking in and breaking out are both at once error." The monk said, "This is still doubtful to me." Nan Yuan said, "What are you in doubt about?" The monk said, "Error." Thereupon Nan Yuan struck him; the monk did not agree, so Nan Yuan drove him out.

Later this monk went to Yun Men's community, where he brought up the previous conversation. There was a monk who said, "Did Nan Yuan's staff break?" The first monk was greatly awakened. But tell me, where is the meaning? This monk returned to see Nan Yuan, but since Nan Yuan had already passed on, he saw Feng Hsueh instead. As soon as he bowed, Feng Hsueh asked, "Aren't you the monk who was asking our late teacher about the simultaneous breaking in and breaking out?" The monk said, "That's right." Feng Hsueh asked, "What was your understanding at that time?" The monk said, "At first it was as if I were walking in the light of a lamp." Feng Hsueh said, "You've understood." But say, what principle is this? This monk came and just said, "At first it was as if I were walking in the light of a lamp." Why did Feng Hsueh immediately tell him, "You've understood"?

Later Ts'ui Yen commented, "Although Nan Yuan puts his

plans into operation from within his tent, nevertheless the
country is vast, the people are few, and sympathizers are rare."
Feng Hsueh commented, "At the time Nan Yuan should have
hit him right across the back the moment he opened his
mouth, to see what he would do." If you see this public case,
then you see where the monk and Ching Ch'ing met each
other. How will all of you avoid Ching Ch'ing calling you a
man in the weeds? For this reason Hsueh Tou likes his saying
"man in the weeds," so he presents it in verse:

VERSE

The Ancient Buddhas had a family style;
> **The words are still in our ears. The model for all time.
> Don't slander old Shakyamuni.*

Responsive preaching comes to scornful detraction
> **Why are your nostrils in my hand? Eight blows pays for
> thirteen. What about you? He lets the initiative go, so I'll
> strike.*

Chick and mother hen do not know each other;
> **Since they don't know each other, why then
> do they naturally break in and break out?*

Who is it that breaks in and breaks out together?
> **Shattered in a hundred fragments. (Hsueh Tou) has the
> kindness of an old granny; but don't misunderstand.*

A peck, and he awakens;
> **What are you saying? You've fallen into the second-
> ary.*

But he's still in the shell.
> **Why doesn't he stick his head out?*

Once again he receives a blow;
> **Wrong! I strike! A double case; triple, quadruple.*

*All the patchrobed monks in the world name and describe it
> in vain.*
> **He has let go; he needn't bring it up. Is there anyone
> who can name or describe it? If there is, he too is a
> man in the weeds. From remote antiquity, the dark-
> ness is vast and boundless; it fills the channels and
> clogs the gullies. No one understands.*

COMMENTARY

With the one line "The Ancient buddhas had a family style," Hsueh Tou has completed his verse. Whoever sticks his head out simply won't be able to approach. If you do approach, you'll fall off a cliff ten thousand miles high. As soon as you come out, you've fallen into the weeds. Even if you can go freely in all directions, it wouldn't be worth a pinch.

Hsueh Tou says, "The Ancient buddhas had a family style." It's not just right now that this is so; when old Shakyamuni was first born, he pointed to the sky with one hand and to the earth with the other hand, scanned the four directions and said, "In the heavens and on earth, I alone am the Honored One." Yun Men said, "If I had seen him then, I would have struck him dead with one blow and fed him to the dogs, hoping that there would be peace in the world." Only by being like this can one reply appropriately. Thus, devices of breaking in and breaking out are all in the family tradition of the Ancient Buddhas.

If you can attain to this Path, then you'll be able to knock down a mountain fortress with one blow of your fist, you'll be able to topple a cliff-top temple with a single kick. It's like a great mass of fire; approach it, and it will burn off your face. It's like the T'ai Ya Sword; fool around with it and you lose your body and life. For this one, only those who have penetrated through and gained the great liberation will be able to act like this. Otherwise, if you miss the source and get stuck in the words, you definitely won't be able to grasp this kind of talk.

"Responsive preaching comes to scornful detraction." This then is 'one guest, one host, one question, one answer.' Right in the asking and answering, there's the scornful detraction. It's called "responsive preaching comes to scornful detraction." Hsueh Tou has deep knowledge of this matter, so he can complete his verse in only two lines.

At the end it's just Hsueh Tou going down into the weeds to explain things thoroughly for you. "Chick and mother hen do not know each other; who is it that breaks in and breaks out together?" Although the mother hen breaks in, she cannot cause the chick to break out; although the chick breaks out, he cannot cause the mother hen to break in. Neither is aware of the other. At the moment of breaking in and breaking out, who is it that breaks in and breaks out together?

If you understand this way, you still haven't been able to get beyond Hsueh Tou's final line. Why? Haven't you heard Hsiang Yen's saying,

> *The chick breaks out, the mother hen breaks in—*
> *When the chick awakens, there is no shell.*
> *Chick and hen both forgotten,*
> *Response to circumstance is unerring.*
> *On the same path, chanting in harmony,*
> *Through the marvelous mystery, walking alone.*

Nevertheless Hsueh Tou comes down into the weeds and creates entangling complications by saying, "A peck." This one word praises Ching Ch'ing's answer, "Can you live or not?" "He awakens" praises the monk's reply, "If I weren't alive, I'd be laughed at by people." Whey then does Hsueh Tou go ahead and say, "He's still in the shell"? Hsueh Tou can distinguish initiated from uninitiated in the light of a stone-struck spark; he can discern the clue to the whole thing in the flash of a lightening bolt.

Ching Ch'ing said, "You too are a man in the weeds." Hsueh Tou says, "Once again he receives a blow." This difficult part is correct. Ching Ch'ing said, "You too are a man in the weeds." Can this be called snatching the man's eyeballs away? Doesn't this line mean he's still in the shell? But this has nothing to do with it. How so? If you don't understand, you can travel on foot all over the world and still not be able to requite your debt. When I talk like this, I too am a man in the weeds.

"All the patchrobed monks in the world name and describe it in vain." Who doesn't name and describe? At this point, Hsueh Tou himself cannot name or describe it, yet he drags in others, the patchrobed monks of the world. But tell me, how did Ching Ch'ing help this monk? No patchrobed monk in the world can leap out.

TRANSLATOR'S NOTES

a.   Expressions such as 'solitary and steep,' 'solitary and dangerous (high)' are used to describe the method of an adept who is bringing up 'the true imperative,' likened to a steep and precipitous mountain peak which is unapproachable, offering no hand or foot hold, nothing to grasp. It is dangerous because if you approach you may lose your life.

Hsiang Lin's Meaning of the Coming from the West

POINTER

Cut through nails and shear through iron, then you can be a genuine master of our school. If you run away from arrows and avoid swords, how could you possibly be a competent adept? The place where even a needle cannot enter, I leave aside for now; but tell me, what's it like when the foamy waves are flooding the skies? To test, I cite this; look!

CASE

A monk asked Hsiang Lin, "What is the meaning of the Patriarch's coming from the West?"[1]

Hsiang Lin said, "Sitting for a long time becomes toilsome."[2,a]

NOTES

1. There have been many people with doubts about this; there is still news of this around.
2. When a fish swims through, the water is muddied; when a bird flies by, feathers drop down. Better shut that dog's mouth. The eye of an adept. A saw cutting apart a scale beam.[b]

COMMENTARY

Hsiang Lin says, "Sitting for a long time becomes toilsome." Understand? If you do understand, then you can put down your shield and spear on the hundred grasses. If you don't understand, then listen humbly to this treatment.

When the Ancients travelled on foot, forming associations with chosen friends to travel together as companions on the Path, they would pull out the weeds and look for the way. At the time Yun Men was causing the teaching to flourish throughout Kuang Nan. Hsiang Lin had made his way by stages out of Shu (Ssuchuan). He was contemporary with E Hu and Ching Ch'ing. He first went to Pao Tz'u Temple in Hunan; only later did he come to Yun Men's congregation, where he was an attendant for eighteen years.

At Yun Men's place he personally attained and personally heard; though the time of his enlightenment was late, nevertheless he was a man of great faculties. He stayed at Yun Men's side for eighteen years; time and again Yun Men would just call out to him, "Attendant Yuan!" As soon as he responded, Yun Men would say, "What is it?" At such times, no matter how much (Hsiang Lin) spoke to present his understanding and gave play to his spirit, he never reached mutual accord (with Yun Men). One day, though, he suddenly said, "I understand." Yun Men said, "Why don't you say something above and beyond this?" Hsiang Lin stayed on for another three years. Yun Men's eloquent elucidations of states uttered in his room were mostly so that Attendant Yuan could enter in actively wherever he was. Whenever Yun Men had some saying or remark, they were all gathered by Attendant Yuan.[c]

Later Hsiang Lin returned to Shu, where he stayed at the Crystal Palace Temple on Ch'ing Ch'eng Mountain.

Master Chih Men Tso was originally from Chekiang. Filled with what he had heard of Hsiang Lin teaching the Path, he came especially to Shu to meet him and pay homage. Tso was Hsueh Tou's master. Though Yun Men converted people without number, of all the wayfarers of that generation, Hsiang Lin's stream flourished most. After he came back to Shu, he lived in temples (teaching) for forty years; he didn't pass on until he was eighty. He once said, "Only when I was forty did I attain unity."

Ordinarily he would teach his assembly saying, "Whenever you go travelling on foot to search for men of knowledge, you must bring along the eye to distinguish initiate from uninitiate, to tell shallow from deep, then you'll be all right. First you must establish your resolve, just as old man Shakyamuni did when he was in the causal ground; wherever he thought or spoke, it was always to set his resolve."

Later a monk asked, "What is the saucer-lamp within the room?"[d] Lin said, "If three people testify that it's a turtle, then it's a turtle." Again he asked, "What is the affair underneath the patched robe?" Lin said, "The conflagration of the end of time burns up the mountain."

Since the old days, very many answers have been given for the meaning of the Patriarch's coming from the West. Only Hsiang Lin, right here in this case, has cut off the tongues of everyone on earth; there is no place for you to calculate or make up rationalizations. The monk asked, "What is the meaning of the Patriarch's coming from the West?" Lin said, "Sitting for a long time becomes toilsome." This could be called flavorless words, flavorless phrases; flavorless talk blocks off people's mouths and leaves you no place to show your energy. If you would see, then just see immediately. If you don't see, it's urgent you avoid entertaining intellectual understanding.

Hsiang Lin had encountered an adept; consequently he possessed Yun Men's technique and harmonious mastery of the 'three phrases' (of Yun Men). People often misunderstand and say, "The Patriarch came from the West and sat facing a wall for nine years; isn't this sitting for a long time and becoming weary?" What is there to hold on to? They don't see that the Ancient Hsiang Lin had attained the realm of great independence, that his feet tread upon the real earth; without so many views and theories of Buddha Dharma, he could meet the situation and function accordingly. As it is said, "The Teaching is carried on according to facts; the banner of the Teaching is set up according to the situation."

Hsueh Tou uses this wind to fan the fire, and from his position as a bystander points out one or a half:

VERSE

One, two, a thousand, ten thousand;
    **Why not practice accordingly?
    As plentiful as hemp and millet;
    why are they congregating into a crowd?*
Strip off the blinders, unload the saddle bags.
    **From today on, you must be purified, clean
    and at ease. Can you rest yet, or not?*

Turning to the left, turning to the right, following up behind;
  **You still can't let yourself go. Reflections upon reflec-
  tions, echoes upon echoes. I strike!*

Tzu Hu had to hit Iron Grindstone Liu.
  **I'd break the staff and no longer carry
  out this order. He draws his bow after
  the thief has gone, so I strike. Danger!*

COMMENTARY

Hsueh Tou strikes directly, like sparks struck from stone, like
the brilliance of a flash of lightening; he presses out and re-
leases to get you to see, which you can do only if you understand it immediately as soon as you hear it being brought up.

Undeniably Hsueh Tou is a descendant of Hsiang Lin's
house; thus he is able to talk this way. If you can directly and
immediately understand in this way, then nothing can stop
you from being extraordinary.

"One, two, a thousand, ten thousand; strip off the blinders,
unload the saddle bags." Purified, clean and at ease, they are
not stained by birth and death, they are not bound by emotional interpretations of sanctity and profanity. Above, there's
nothing to look to for support; below, they've cut off their
personal selves. They're just like Hsiang Lin and Hsueh Tou;
how could there be just a thousand or ten thousand? In fact all
the people in the world, each and every one, are all like this.
The past and future Buddhas are all like this too.

If you make up interpretative understandings on the words,
then this is like "Tzu Hu had to hit Iron Grindstone Liu." In
fact, as soon as (such interpretations) are raised, Hsueh Tou
strikes while you are still speaking. Tzu Hu studied under Nan
Ch'uan; he was a fellow student of Chao Chou and Tiger Ts'en
(Ch'ang Sha). At that time Iron Grindstone Liu had set up a hut
on Mt. Kuei. People from all over couldn't cope with her. One
day Tzu Hu came proudly to call on her; he asked, "You're Iron
Grindstone Liu, aren't you?" The Grindstone said, "I don't
presume (to say so)." Hu asked, "Do you turn to the left or turn
to the right?" The Grindstone said, "Don't tip over, Teacher."
Hu struck her while her words were still in the air.

Answering the monk who asked, "What is the meaning of
the Patriarch's coming from the West?" Hsiang Lin said, "Sit-

ting for a long time becomes toilsome." If you understand this way, you are "turning to the left, turning to the right, following up behind." But tell me, what is Hsueh Tou's meaning in versifying like this?

TRANSLATOR'S NOTES

a. Hsiang Lin's reply could also be glossed as "sitting for a long time becomes tiring," or "sitting for a long time becomes hard work." Tenkei said, "When you sit for a long time your legs hurt: it's nothing special—the eyes are horizontal, the nose vertical; though everyone knows, because they are not aware of it (Hsiang Lin) just lets everyone know that they breathe through their noses. Is there any patriarch's meaning in there? If you call it an answer as to the meaning of the coming from the West, it's a worthless bag, a worn-out loincloth." A popular legend has it that Bodhidharma's legs crumbled to dust as he sat still for nine years facing a wall at the Shao Lin monastery. Dogen said that the Way is actually realized by the body. This *kung an* should not be applied to person only, but also to things. The "ground of reality" which one must tread to see this case could also be glossed as "real earth" from a certain point of view.

b. According to commentators, this means that it is hard to penetrate.

c. It is said that Yun Men forbade the recording of his words; however, Hsiang Lin stealthily wrote them down on his paper robe. They were compiled by Shou Chien, another of Yun Men's successors.

d. The lamp symbolizes wisdom; the room symbolizes stability. Without the stability of meditation, the flame of wisdom is blown by the wind of passion.

National Teacher Chung's Seamless Monument

CASE

Emperor Su Tsung[1] asked National Teacher Hui Chung, "After you die, what will you need?"[2]

The National Teacher said, "Build a seamless monument for me."[3]

The Emperor said, "Please tell me, Master, what the monument would look like."[4]

The National Teacher was silent for a long time; then he asked, "Do you understand?"[5]

The Emperor said, "I don't understand."[6]

The National Teacher said, "I have a disciple to whom I have transmitted the Teaching, Tan Yuan, who is well versed in this matter. Please summon him and ask him about it."[7]

After the National Teacher passed on,[8] the Emperor summoned Tan Yuan and asked him what the meaning of this was.[9] Tan Yuan said,

> South of Hsiang, north of T'an;[10]
> Hsueh Tou added the comment, "A single hand does not make random sound."[11]
> In between there's gold sufficient to a nation.[12]
> Hsueh Tou added the comment, "A rough-hewn staff."[13]
> Beneath the shadowless tree, the community ferryboat;[14]
> Hsueh Tou added the comment, "The sea is calm, the rivers are clear."[15]
> Within the crystal palace, there's no one who knows.[16]
> Hsueh Tou added the comment, "He has raised it up."[17]

116   THE BLUE CLIFF RECORD

NOTES

1. This is a mistake; actually it was Tai Tsung.
2. He scratches before it itches. As it turns out, (Hui Chung) will create a model and draw a likeness; though great and venerable, he acts this way—he shouldn't point to the east as the west.[a]
3. It can't be grasped.
4. He gives (Chung) a good poke.
5. Confined in prison, he increases in wisdom. After all he points to the east as the west and takes the south as the north. All he can do is frown.
6. It's fortunate that he doesn't understand; if he had pressed (Chung) further at this time and made him gulp a mouthful of frost, then he would have gotten somewhere.
7. He's lucky that the Emperor did not overturn his meditation seat; why didn't (Chung) give him some of his own provisions? Don't confuse the man. (Chung) let the initiative go.
8. What a pity! After all (the Emperor) will mistakenly go by the zero point of the scale.
9. The son takes up the father's work. He too falls into the second level, into the third level.
10. This too can't be grasped. Two by two, three by three—what are you doing? Half open, half closed.
11. One blind man leading a crowd of blind men. After all (Hsueh Tou) is following his words to produce interpretations. Why follow falsehood and pursue evil?
12. Above is the sky, below is the earth. I've had no such news. Whose concern is this?
13. It's been broken. This too is creating a model and drawing a likeness.
14. The Patriarch has perished. What are you saying, Reverend?
15. When vast swells of expansive white waves flood the skies, this still only amounts to a little bit.
16. Bah!
17. He draws his bow after the thief has gone. The words are still in our ears.

COMMENTARY

Su Tsung and Tai Tsung were both descendants of Hsuan Tsung. When they were princes, they were always fond of studying meditation. Because there was a great upheaval in his realm,[b] Hsuan Tsung finally fled to Shu. The T'ang dynasty originally had its capital at Ch'ang An; but because it was occupied by An Lu Shan, later (the capital) was moved to Lo Yang.

When Su Tsung came to power, National Teacher Chung was dwelling in a hut on White Cliff Mountain in Teng Chou (in Hunan). Today this is the Fragrant Cliff (Hsiang Yen) monastery. Though he did not come down from the mountain for more than forty years, word of his practice of the Way reached the Imperial precincts. In 761 the Emperor Su Tsung sent his personal emissary to summon Chung to enter the Imperial palace (to teach). The Emperor treated Chung with the etiquette due a teacher, and greatly honored him. Chung once lectured on the Supreme Path for the Emperor. When the Master departed from court, the Emperor himself escorted his carriage and saw him off. The courtiers were all angry at this and wanted to make their displeasure known to the Emperor. But the National Teacher had the power to know the minds of others, so he saw the Emperor first and told him, "In the presence of Indra, I have seen Emperors scattered like grains, evanescent as a flash of lightening." The Emperor respected him even more after this.

When Tai Tsung succeeded to the throne (in 762) he again invited (Chung) to come to the Abode of Light Temple. Chung stayed in the capital for sixteen years, expounding the Dharma according to the occasion, until he passed on in 776.

Formerly the Master of Blue File Mountain in Shan Man Fu had been the National Teacher's travelling companion. The National Teacher once asked the Emperor to summon him to court, but he did not rise to three Imperial commands; he would always upbraid the National Teacher for being addicted to fame and fortune, and for liking the company of people.

Chung was National Teacher under two emperors, father and son. In that family father and son studied meditation at the same time. According to the *Record of the Transmission of the Lamp*, it was Tai Tsung who asked the questions in the present case. When the National Teacher was asked, "What is the Ten-Body Controller?" (case 99), this on the other hand was Su Tsung's question.

When the National Teacher's life was over and he was about to enter nirvana, he was taking leave of Tai Tsung. Tai Tsung asked, "After your death,ᶜ what will you need?" This is just an ordinary question. The old fellow (Chung) stirred up waves where there was no wind and said, "Build a seamless monument for me." Under the bright sun and blue sky, why answer like this? It should have been enough to build a monument; why then did he say to build a seamless monument? But Tai Tsung too was an adept: he pressed him and said, "Please tell me, Master, what the monument would look like?" The National Teacher remained silent for a long time, then said, "Do you understand?" How extraordinary this little bit is; it's most difficult to approach. When pressed by the Emperor, the National Teacher, supposedly so great, could only frown. Although this is so, anyone but this old fellow (Chung) would probably have been bowled over.

Quite a few people say that the National Teacher's not speaking is itself what the monument is like. If you understand in this fashion, Bodhidharma and all his family would be wiped off the face of the earth. If you say that keeping silent is it, then mutes too must understand Ch'an.

Haven't you heard how an outsider asked the Buddha, "I don't ask about the spoken, I don't ask about the unspoken." The World Honored One remained silent. The outsider bowed in homage and sighed in praise; he said, "The World Honored One's great mercy and great compassion has dispersed the clouds of my delusions and caused me to gain entry." After the outsider had left, Ananda asked the Buddha, "What did the outsider witness, that he said he had gained entry?" The World Honored One said, "In worldly terms he's like a good horse; he goes when he sees the shadow of the whip." People often go to the silence for their understanding. What is there to grasp?

My late teacher Wu Tsu brought up (the 'seamless monument') and said, "In front it is pearls and agate, in back it is agate and pearls; on the east are Avalokitesvara and Mahasthamaprapta, on the west are Manjusri and Samantabhadra;ᵈ in the middle there's a flag blown by the wind, saying 'Flap, flap.'"

The National Teacher asked, "Do you understand?" The Emperor said, "I don't understand," yet he had attained a little bit. But tell me, is this "I don't understand" the same as Emperor Wu's "I don't know" (case 1), or is it different? Although they seem the same, actually they're not.

The National Teacher said, "I have a disciple to whom I have transmitted the Teaching, Tan Yuan, who is well versed in this matter. Please summon him and ask him about it." Putting aside Tai Tsung's not understanding for the moment, did Tan Yuan understand? All that was needed was to say, "Please, Teacher, what would the monument look like?"—no one in the world can do anything about it. My late teacher Wu Tsu commented by saying, "You are the teacher of a whole nation; why is it that you don't speak, but instead defer to your disciple?"

After the National Teacher died, the Emperor summoned Tan Yuan, to ask about the meaning of this. Tan Yuan then came on behalf of the National Teacher and explained the principle with foreign words and native speech; naturally he understood what the National Teacher had said, and just needed a single verse (to explain):

> *South of Hsiang, north of T'an:*[e]
> *Within there's gold sufficient to a nation.*
> *Beneath the shadowless tree, the community ferryboat;*
> *Within the crystal palace, there's no one who knows.*

Tan Yuan, whose name was Ying Chen, served as an attendant at the National Teacher's place. Later he dwelt at Tan Yuan Temple in Chi Chou (in Kiangsi). At this time Yang Shan came to see Tan Yuan. Tan Yuan's words were severe, his nature harsh and unapproachable. It was impossible to stay there, so at first Yang Shan went and saw the Ch'an master Hsing K'ung. There was a monk who asked Hsing K'ung, "What is the meaning of the Patriarch's coming from the West?" Hsing K'ung said, "It's as if a man were down in a thousand foot deep well; if you could get this man out without using even an inch of rope, then I would tell you the meaning of the Patriarch's coming from the West." The monk said, "These days Master Ch'ang of Hunan is talking this way and that for people too." Hsing K'ung then called to Yang Shan, "Novice, drag this corpse out of here!"

Later Yang Shan took this up with Tan Yuan and asked, "How can you get the man out of the well?" Tan Yuan said, "Bah! Ignoramus! Who is in the well?" Yan Shan didn't under-

stand. Later he asked Kuei Shan. Kuei Shan immediately called
out (Yang Shan's name) "Hui Chi!" When Yang Shan responded, Kuei Shan said, "He's out." At this Yang Shan was
greatly enlightened. He said, "At Tan Yuan's I attained the
essence; at Kuei Shan's I attained the function."

As for this little verse of Tan Yuan's, it has led not a few
people into false interpretations. People often misunderstand
and say, "*Hsiang* is the *hsiang* of 'meet' (*hsiang-chien*); *T'an* is
the *t'an* of 'discuss' (*t'an-lun*). In between there's a seamless
memorial tower, hence the verse says, 'In between there's gold
sufficient to a nation.' 'Beneath the shadowless tree, the community ferryboat' is the interchange between the National
Teacher and the Emperor. The Emperor did not understand, so
the verse says, 'Inside the crystal palace there's no one who
knows.'"

Again, some say, "The first line means south of Hsiang
Chou and north of T'an Chou; 'In between there's gold sufficient to a nation' praises the Emperor." Then they blink their
eyes, look around, and say, "This is the seamless monument."
If you understand in such a way, you have not gone beyond
emotional views.

As for Hsueh Tou's four turning words, how will you understand them? People today are far from knowing the Ancient's
meaning. Tell me, how do you understand "South of Hsiang,
north of T'an"? How do you understand "Within there's gold
sufficient to a nation"? How do you understand "Beneath the
shadowless tree, the community ferryboat"? How do you understand "Within the crystal palace, there's no one who
knows"? If you can see this as Hsueh Tou and I do, nothing can
prevent a whole life of joy and happiness.

"South of Hsiang, north of T'an." Hsueh Tou says, "A single
hand does not make a random sound." He couldn't but explain
for you. "Within there's gold sufficient to a nation." Hsueh
Tou says, "A rough-hewn staff." An Ancient said, "If you know
the staff, the work of your whole life's study is complete."
"Beneath the shadowless tree, the community ferry." Hsueh
Tou says, "The sea is calm, the rivers are clear." Open the
windows and doors all at once—on all sides gleaming clarity.
"Inside the crystal palace, there's no one who knows." Hsueh
Tou says, "He's raised it." After all he's gotten somewhere.
Hsueh Tou has spoken clearly all at once; afterwards he simply
eulogizes the seamless monument.

VERSE

The seamless monument—
     ***How big is this one seam?*
     What are you saying?*
To see it is hard.
     ***It's not something eyes can see.*
     Blind!*
A clear pool does not admit the blue dragon's coils.
     ***Do you see? Great waves, vast, gigantic. Where*
     will the blue dragon go to coil up? Here it just
     cannot be found.*
Layers upon layers.
     ***No optical illusions! What are you doing,*
     seeing optical illusions?*
Shadows upon shadows—
     ***Your whole body is an eye. You*
     fall into sevens and eights. Two by
     two, three by three, walking the old
     road; turning to the left, turning
     to the right, following up behind.*
For ever and ever it is shown to people.
     ***Do you see? How will blind people see?*
     Can you catch a glimpse of it, Reverend?*

COMMENTARY

Right off Hsueh Tou says, "The seamless monument—To see it is hard." Though it stands alone revealed with nothing hidden, when you want to see it, it's still hard to do so. Hsueh Tou is exceedingly compassionate, and tells you more: "A clear pool does not admit the blue dragon's coils." My late master Wu Tsu said, "In Hsueh Tou's whole volume of eulogies on the ancients, I just like the line, 'A clear pool does not admit the blue dragon's coils.'" Still, this amounts to something.

Quite a few people go to the National Teacher's silence for their sustenance; if you understand in this way, you at once go wrong. Haven't you heard it said, "Reclining dragons aren't to be seen in stagnant water; where they are not, there's moonlight and the ripples settle, but where they are, waves arise without wind." Again, it was said, "Reclining dragons always fear the blue pool's clarity." As for this fellow Hsueh Tou, even if vast swelling billows of white waves flooded the sky, he still wouldn't coil up in there.

When Hsueh Tou gets to this, his verse is finished. Afterwards he applies a little bit of eye and carves a seamless monument. Following up behind he says, "Layers upon layers, Shadows upon shadows—For ever and ever it is shown to people." How will you look upon it? Where is it right now? Even if you see it clearly, don't mistakenly stick by the zero point of the scale.

TRANSLATOR'S NOTES

a. The three clauses of this sentence can be taken in reference to the Emperor or to Hui Chung. In the original these notes of Yuan Wu's are inserted right in the text; though they usually refer to the preceding passage, occasionally they apply to the succeeding sentence. The pronoun 'he'—absent in the original but added by the translator for grammatical English—normally refers to the same subject as the clause noted. Commentators frequently point out that it applies to you too.

b. In 755 the military man An Lushan, commander of powerful border armies on China's northern frontier, began a revolt aimed at supplanting the T'ang dynasty with his own regime. The fighting dragged on for more than five years, even after An Lushan himself had died, ravaging much of northern China, and dealing the ruling house of T'ang a blow from which it never fully recovered. Thereafter the sufferings of the people increased as rival military commanders struggled with each other and with the Imperial court for control of the revenues of the land. Hsuan Tsung fled from the capital Ch'ang An to the city of Ch'eng Tu in Szechuan (ancient Shu) in western China—a traditional route of flight before northern invaders.

c. The polite expression used is "after a hundred years."

d. Avalokitesvara represents compassion, Mahasthamaprapta represents empowerment, Manjusri represents wisdom and knowledge, and Samantabhadra represents goodness in all actions.

e. Hsiang-T'an was a district in Hunan, south of Ch'ang Sha. "South of Hsiang and north of T'an" can mean everywhere, or nowhere.

Chu Ti's One-Finger Ch'an

POINTER

When one speck of dust arises, the great earth is contained therein; when a single flower blooms, the world arises. But before the speck of dust is raised, before the flower opens, how will you set eyes on it? Therefore it is said, "It's like cutting a skein of thread: when one strand is cut, all are cut. It's like dyeing a skein of thread: when one strand is dyed, all are dyed."

This very moment you should take all complications and cut them off. Bring out your own family jewels and respond everywhere, high and low, before and after, without missing. Each and every one will be fully manifest. If you're not yet like this, look into the text below.

CASE

Whenever anything was asked,[1] Master Chu Ti would just raise one finger.[2]

NOTES

1. What news is there? Dull-witted teacher!
2. This old fellow too would cut off the tongues of everyone on earth. When it's warm, all heaven and earth are warm; when it's cold, all heaven and earth are cold. He snatches away the tongues of everyone on earth.

COMMENTARY

If you understand at the finger, then you turn your back on Chu Ti; if you don't go to the finger to understand, then it's like cast iron. Whether you understand or not, Chu Ti still goes on this way; whether you're high or low, he still goes on this way;

123

whether you're right or wrong, he still goes on this way. Thus it is said, "As soon as a speck of dust arises, the great earth is contained therein; when a single flower is about to open, the world immediately comes into being. The lion on the tip of a single hair appears on the tips of ten billion hairs."

Yuan Ming said, "When it's cold, all throughout heaven and earth are cold; when it's warm, all throughout heaven and earth are warm." The mountains and rivers and the great earth reach down through the Yellow Springs (Hades); the myriad images and multitude of forms penetrate upward through the heavens. But tell me, what is so extraordinary? For those who know, it's not worth taking hold of; for those who don't know, it blocks them off utterly.

Master Chu Ti was from Chin Hua in Wu Chou (in Chekiang). During the time he first dwelt in a hermitage, there was a nun named Shih Chi ('Reality') who came to his hut. When she got there she went straight in; without taking off her rain hat she walked around his meditation seat three times holding her staff. "If you can speak," she said, "I'll take off my rain hat." She questioned him like this three times; Chu Ti had no reply. Then as she was leaving Chu Ti said, "The hour is rather late: would you stay the night?" The nun said, "If you can speak, I'll stay over." Again Chu Ti had no reply. The nun then walked out. Chu Ti sighed sorrowfully and said, "Although I inhabit the body of a man, still I lack a man's spirit." After this he aroused his zeal to clarify this matter.

He meant to abandon his hermitage and travel to various places to call on teachers to ask for instruction, and had wrapped up his things for foot-travelling. But that night the spirit of the mountain told him, "You don't have to leave this place. Tomorrow a flesh and blood bodhisattva will come and expound the truth for you, Master. You don't have to go." As it turned out, the following day Master T'ien Lung actually came to the hermitage. Chu Ti welcomed him ceremoniously and gave a full account of the previous events. T'ien Lung just lifted up one finger to show him; suddenly Chu Ti was greatly enlightened. At the time Chu Ti was most earnest and single-minded, so the bottom of his bucket fell out easily. Later, whenever anything was asked, Chu Ti just raised one finger.

Ch'ang Ch'ing said, "Delicious food is not for a satisfied

man to eat." Hsuan Sha said, "If I had seen him then, I would have broken the finger off." Hsuan Chueh said, "When Hsuan Sha spoke this way, what was his meaning?" Hsi of Yun Chu said, "When Hsuan Sha spoke this way, was he agreeing with Chu Ti or not? If he agreed with him, why did he speak of breaking off the finger? If he didn't agree with him, where was Chu Ti's mistake?" The Former Ts'ao Shan said, "Chu Ti's realization was crude: he only recognized one device, one perspective. Like everyone else, he claps his hands and slaps his palms, but I look upon Hsi Yuan as exceptional."[a] Again, Hsuan Chueh said, "But say, was Chu Ti enlightened or not? Why was Chu Ti's realization crude?" If he wasn't enlightened, how could he say, "My whole life I've used one-finger Ch'an without ever exhausting it"? Tell me, where is Ts'ao Shan's meaning?

At that time, Chu Ti actually did not understand. After his enlightenment, whenever anything was asked, Chu Ti would just raise one finger; why couldn't a thousand people, even ten thousand people, entrap him or break him apart? If you understand it as a finger, you definitely won't see the Ancient's meaning. This kind of Ch'an is easy to approach but hard to understand. People these days who just hold up a finger or a fist as soon as they're questioned are just indulging their spirits. It is still necessary to pierce the bone, penetrate to the marrow, and see all the way through in order to get it.

At Chu Ti's hermitage there was a servant boy. While he was away from the hermitage, he was asked, "What method does your master usually use to teach people?" The servant boy held up a finger. When he returned, he mentioned this to the Master. Chu Ti took a knife and cut off the boy's finger; as he ran out screaming, Chu Ti called to him. The boy looked back, whereupon Chu Ti raised his finger; the boy opened up and attained understanding. Tell me, what truth did he see?

When he was nearing death, Chu Ti said to his assembly, "I attained T'ien Lung's one-finger Ch'an and have used it all my life without exhausting it. Do you want to understand?" He raised his finger, then died.

The One-Eyed Dragon of Ming Chao asked his 'uncle,' Shen of Kuo T'ai, "An Ancient said that Chu Ti just recited a three line spell and thereby became more famous than anyone else.

How can you quote the three line spell for someone else?" Shen also raised one finger. Chao said, "If not for Today, how could I know this borderlands traveller?" Tell me, what does this mean?

Mi Mo just used a forked branch all his life. The Earth-Beating Teacher would just hit the ground once whenever any-thing was asked. Once someone hid his staff and then asked, "What is Buddha?" The Teacher just opened his mouth wide. These (methods) too were used for a whole lifetime without ever being exhausted.

Wu Yeh said, "The Patriarch (Bodhidharma) observed that our country had people with the potential to be vessels of the Great Vehicle. He transmitted only the mind seal, in order to instruct those on the paths of illusion. Those who attain it do not choose between ignorance and wisdom, between worldly and holy. Much falsehood is not as good as a little truth. Any-one who is powerful will immediately rest right this moment and abruptly still the myriad entanglements, thus passing be-yond the stream of birth and death and going far beyond the usual patterns. Though you have family and estate, if you do not seek, it is attained of itself." Throughout his whole lifetime, whenever anything was asked, Wu Yeh would just say, "Don't think falsely!" Thus it is said, "Penetrate one place, and at once you penetrate a thousand places, ten thousand places. Clearly understand one device, and at once you clearly understand a thousand devices, ten thousand de-vices."

Generally people these days are not this way; they just in-dulge in conceptual and emotional interpretations, and don't understand what is most essential with these Ancients. How could Chu Ti have had no other devices to switch to? Why did he just employ one finger? You must realize that here is where Chu Ti helps people so profoundly and intimately.

Do you want to understand how to save strength? Go back to Yuan Ming's saying, "When it's cold, all throughout heaven and earth is cold; when it's warm, all throughout heaven and earth is warm." Mountains, rivers, and earth, extending up-ward to the solitary heights; myriad forms in profuse array penetrate down through dangerous precipices. Where will you find one finger Ch'an?

VERSE

For his appropriate teaching I deeply admire old Chu Ti;
    **A leper drags along his companions. Only those on*
    the same path know. Nevertheless it's (only) one
    *device, one perspective.**

Since space and time have been emptied, who else is there?
    **Two, three—there's still one more. He too should*
    *be struck dead.**

Having cast a piece of driftwood onto the ocean,
    **It's all this. So it is, but it's too*
    inaccessible. Worn out straw sandals; what
    *use does it have?**

Together in the night waves we take in blind turtles.
    **Dragging the sky, searching the earth; what end*
    will there be? When we take them in, what are they
    good for? We act according to what is imperative.
    I'd drive them towards a world where there is no
    *Buddha. I've taken you in, Reverend, one blind man.**

COMMENTARY

Hsueh Tou has mastered literary composition; he's consummately accomplished. He especially likes to make up verses for obscure and unusual public cases. For students of today he censures and praises the Ancients; as guest or host, with a question or an answer, he holds them up before you—this is how he helps people. Thus he says, "For his appropriate teaching I deeply admire old Chu Ti." Tell me, why does Hsueh Tou admire him? Since heaven and earth began, who else has there ever been? Just this one, old Chu Ti. If it had been anyone else, inevitably he would have been inconsistent; only Chu Ti just used one finger up until his old age and death.

People often interpret this wrongly and say, "Mountains, rivers, and the great earth are empty; man is empty; the Dharma is empty too. Even if time and space were emptied out all at once, it's just this one, old Chu Ti." But this has nothing to do with it.

"Having cast a piece of driftwood onto the ocean." Nowadays they call this the ocean of birth and death. Within the ocean of doing, sentient beings appear and disappear without understanding themselves clearly, without hope of getting out. Old Chu Ti extends his mercy to take people in; in the ocean of birth and death he uses one finger to rescue others. It's like letting down a piece of driftwood to rescue a blind turtle. He enables all sentient beings to reach the Other Shore.

"Together in the night waves we take in blind turtles." The Lotus Scripture says, "It's like a one-eyed turtle sticking his nose through a hole in a floating board."[b] When a great man of knowledge receives a fellow who is like a dragon or a tiger, he directs him towards a world where there is Buddha to act in turn as guest and host, and in worlds without Buddhas to cut off the essential way across. Having taken in a blind turtle, what use is it?

TRANSLATOR'S NOTES

a.   Once when Ch'an master T'an Tsang of Hsi Yuan, a successor of Ma Tsu, was making the fire to heat the bath, one of his disciples told him that such menial tasks should be done by one of the novices. The Master said nothing, but clapped his hands three times.

b.   The metaphor: a blind turtle surfacing at the precise moment a piece of driftwood with a hole in it is passing by; the turtle can climb through the hole up out of the sea. This symbolizes the rare opportunity of hearing the Buddhist Teaching while in human form, itself a rare opportunity.

Lung Ya's Meaning of the Coming from the West

Piled in mountains, heaped in ranges, up against walls, pressed against barriers; if you linger in thought, holding back your potential, you'll be bitterly cramped.

Or else, a man may appear and overturn the great ocean, kick over Mount Sumeru, scatter the white clouds with shouts, and break up empty space; straightaway, with one device, one object, he cuts off the tongues of everyone on earth, so that there is no way for you to approach. Tell me, since ancient times, who has ever been this way? To test, I cite this; look!

CASE

Lung Ya asked Ts'ui Wei, "What is the meaning of the Patriarch's coming from the West?"[1]

Wei said, "Pass me the meditation brace."[2]

Ya gave the meditation brace to Wei;[3] Wei took it and hit him.[4]

Ya said, "Since you hit me I let you hit me. In essence, though, there is no meaning of the Patriarch's coming from the West."[5]

Ya also asked Lin Chi, "What is the meaning of the Patriarch's coming from the West?"[6]

Chi said, "Pass me the cushion."[7]

Ya took the cushion and handed it to Lin Chi;[8] Chi took it and hit him.[9]

Ya said, "Since you hit me I let you hit me. In essence, though, there is no meaning of the Patriarch's coming from the West."[10]

NOTES

1. It's an old public case known everywhere; still he wants to put it to the test.
2. What will he use the meditation brace for? (Ts'ui Wei) almost let (Lung Ya) go. Danger!
3. He can't hold on to it; (Lung Ya) is given a fine steed, Green Dragon, but he doesn't know how to ride it. What a pity that he doesn't take charge right away.
4. Got him! What is accomplished by hitting a dead man? He too has fallen into the secondary.
5. This fellow's talk is in the secondary; he draws his bow after the thief has gone.
6. Again he inquires into the commonplace old public case; it's not worth half a cent.
7. If the waves of Ts'ao Ch'i resembled each other, endless numbers of ordinary people would get bogged down. One punishment for all crimes; they're buried in the same pit.
8. As before, he can't hold on to it; as before he's not very clever. What's like the land of Yueh is like Yang Chou.[a]
9. Got him! What a pity to be hitting this kind of dead man. Lin Chi comes out of the same pattern as Ts'ui Wei.
10. Obviously. He's making a living inside the demon cave. He thinks he's gained the advantage.

COMMENTARY

Master Chih of Ts'ui Yen said, "It was so at that time, but do patchrobed monks these days still have blood under their skin?"

Che of Mt. Kuei said, "Ts'ui Wei and Lin Chi can be called genuine masters of our sect."

Lung Ya was first rate at pulling out the weeds seeking the way; there's no reason why he shouldn't serve as a model for people of later times. After he had a fixed abode, a monk asked him, "Teacher, at that time did you agree with those two venerable adepts?" Ya said, "I agree, as far as agreement goes; it's just that there is no meaning of the Patriarch's coming from the West." Lung Ya looks carefully in front and behind, and dispenses medicine to suit the disease.

Ta Kuei, however, is not this way; when asked whether Lung Ya had agreed with the two venerable adepts, whether he understood or not, he would have brought his staff down across the back (of the questioner). This not only supports Ts'ui Wei and Lin Chi, but also doesn't turn away from the questioner.

Ts'ung of Shih Men said, "Lung Ya is still all right if there's no one to press him, but when he's pressed by a patchrobed one, he loses one eye."

Hsueh Tou said, "Lin Chi and Ts'ui Wei only knew how to hold still; they didn't know how to let go. If I had been Lung Ya at that time, when they asked for the cushion and meditation brace, I would have picked it up and immediately thrown it down right in front of them."

Wu Tsu Shih Chieh said, "The Teacher has such a long face!" He also said, "The patriarchal masters' star of ill-omen is over his head."

Hsin of Huang Lung Mountain said, "Lung Ya drove off the ploughman's ox, he snatched away the hungry man's food. Once he's clear, he's clear; why then is there no meaning of the Patriarch's coming from the West? Do you understand? On the staff there is an eye bright as the sun; to tell whether gold is real, see it through fire."

To extol the wonder of the essential, to advocate the fundamental vehicle, if you can understand it the very first instant, then you can cut off the tongues of everyone on earth. But if you vacillate, you fall into the secondary. These two old fellows Lin Chi and Ts'ui Wei, though they beat the wind and hit the rain, startle heaven and shake the earth, have never really hit a clear eyed fellow.

When the Ancients immersed themselves in meditation, they suffered some pains; having established powerful resolve, they would traverse mountains and rivers to call on venerable adepts. First Lung Ya met Ts'ui Wei and Lin Chi; later he called on Te Shan. There he asked, "How is it when a student holding a sharp sword tries to take the teacher's head?" Te Shan stretched out his neck and uttered a grunt. Ya said, "The teacher's head has fallen." Te Shan smiled slightly and let it go at that.

Next Lung Ya went to Tung Shan. Tung Shan asked, "Where did you come here from?" Ya said, "From Te Shan." Tung Shan said, "What did Te Shan have to say?" Ya then recounted the preceding story. Tung Shan asked, "What did he say?" Ya said, "He had no words." Tung Shan said, "Don't say that he had no words. Instead try to take Te Shan's fallen head and show it to me." At this Ya had insight; thereupon he burned incense and gazed far off towards Te Shan; he prostrated himself and repented.

When he heard of this, Te Shan said, "Old man Tung Shan can't tell good from bad; this fellow has been dead so long, what's the use of saving him? Let him wander over the earth carrying my head."

Lung Ya's basic nature was intelligent and acute. He went foot travelling carrying a bellyful of Ch'an. As soon as he got to Ts'ui Wei in Ch'ang An he immediately asked, "What is the meaning of the Patriarch's coming from the West?" Wei said, "Pass me the meditation brace," Ya took the meditation brace and gave it to Wei. Wei took it and hit him. Ya said, "Since you hit me I let you hit me; in essence, though, there is no meaning of the Patriarch's coming from the West." He also asked Lin Chi, "What is the meaning of the Patriarch's coming from the West?" Lin Chi said, "Pass me the cushion." Ya took the cushion and gave it to Lin Chi; Chi took it and hit him. Ya said, "Since you hit me I let you hit me; in essence, though, there is no meaning of the Patriarch's coming from the West."

When Lung Ya posed the question, he not only wanted to see the old fellows up on the carved wood seats, he also wanted to illumine the great concern of his own self. We can say that his words were not spoken in vain, that his effort was not expended haphazardly; they issued from his doing his work.

Haven't you heard? Wu Hsieh went to see Shih T'ou. He had made an agreement with himself beforehand saying, "If there's accord at the first word I'll stay; otherwise, I'll go." Shih T'ou just sat on his seat; Hsieh shook out his sleeves and went out. Shih T'ou knew that Wu Wsieh was a vessel of the truth, so he had extended his teaching to him. But Hsieh hadn't understood his meaning; he had announced his departure and gone out. When he got to the gate Shi T'ou called out to him, "Reverend!" When Hsieh looked back, Shih T'ou said, "From birth to death it's only this; don't seek anymore for anything else by turning your head and revolving your brain." At these words Hsieh was greatly enlightened.

Also, Ma Ku came to Chang Ching carrying his ring-staff; he

walked three times around the meditation seat, shook his staff once, and stood there upright. Ching said, "Right, right." He also went to Nan Ch'uan; as before he walked three times around the seat, shook his staff and stood there. Nan Ch'uan said, "Wrong, wrong. This is what the power of the wind can whirl around; in the end it decomposes." Ma Ku said, "Chang Ching said right; why do you say wrong?" Nan Ch'uan said, "Chang Ching was right; it is you who are wrong."[b]

Inevitably the Ancients had to take up and penetrate through this one matter. People today, as soon as they are questioned, have not made the slightest application of effort; they're this way today, and they'll be this way tomorrow too: if you just keep on like this, even into the endless future you will never have a day of completion. You must arouse and purify your spirit; only thus will you have some small share of realization.

Look at Lung Ya coming out with one question, saying, "What is the meaning of the Patriarch's coming from the West?" Ts'ui Wei said, "Pass me the meditation brace." When Ya gave it to him, he took it and immediately hit Ya. When Ya picked up the meditation brace, how could he have not known that Wei was going to hit him? And it won't do to say that Ya didn't understand, for why then did he pass the meditation brace to Wei? But tell me, at the moment he understood, how should Ya have acted? He didn't go to the living water to function, but took himself into the dead water for his sustenance. Acting as master throughout, he said, "Since you hit me I let you hit me; in essence, though, there is no meaning of the Patriarch's coming from the West."

Lung Ya also went to Hopeh to call on Lin Chi. He asked his question as before. Lin Chi said, "Pass me the cushion." When Ya gave it to him, he took it and immediately hit Ya. Ya said, "Since you hit me I let you hit me; in essence, though, there is no meaning of the Patriarch's coming from the West." Tell me, these two venerable adepts were not of the same lineage; why did their answers resemble each other, why was their functioning of one kind? You must realize that the one word, one phrase of the Ancients was not uttered at random.

Later when Lung Ya dwelt in a temple, a monk asked him, "Teacher, at that time, when you saw the two worthies, did you agree with them or not?" Ya said, "As far as agreement

goes, I agreed; but there is no meaning of the Patriarch's coming from the West." There are thorns in the soft mud. To let go
for people is already falling into the secondary; this old fellow
(Lung Ya) held steady—he only acted as an adept in the Tung
succession.[c] To be a disciple of Te Shan or Lin Chi, he would
have had to realize that there is a living side besides. As for me,
I am not this way; I would have told the monk, "As far as
agreement is concerned, I don't agree; in essence, though, there
is no meaning of the Patriarch's coming from the West."

Haven't you heard how a monk asked Ta Mei, "What is the
meaning of the Patriarch's coming from the West?" Mei said,
"The coming from the West has no meaning." Yen Kuan heard
of this and said, "One coffin, two dead men." Hsuan Sha heard
of this and said, "Yen Kuan is indeed an adept!" (To which)
Hsueh Tou said, "There are even three (dead men)." The monk
asked about the meaning of the Patriarch's coming from the
West; though Ta Mei told him that the coming from the West
has no meaning, if you understand in this way, you fall into the
realm of unconcern. Therefore Te Shan (Yuan Mi) said, "You
must study the living word; don't study the dead word. If you
can understand at the living word, you will never forget it; if
you understand at the dead word, you won't even be able to
save yourself."

When Lung Ya spoke this way, he had undeniably done his
best. The Ancient Tung Shan said, "Continuity is very difficult." The other Ancients, Ts'ui Wei and Lin Chi, were not
acting at random with their one word, one phrase; before and
after mutually illuminating, with both temporal and true, with
both illumination and function, guest and host obvious, inter-
changing vertically and horizontally.

If you want to discern the inside story, since Lung Ya was
not ignorant of the vehicle of our sect, how could he have fallen
into second place? At the time when the two venerable adepts
asked for the meditation brace and cushion, Ya could not have
but known their intention. It was just that he wanted to make
use of that which was within his own breast. Although he was
right, nevertheless his use of it was too extreme. Since Lung Ya
asked this way, and the two old ones answered this way, why
then is there no meaning of the Patriarch's coming from the
West? When you get here you must know that there's something else extraordinary. Hsueh Tou picks it up to show
people:

VERSE

In Dragon Tusk Mountain the dragon has no eyes;[d]
   **He's blind. He can fool other people all
   right, (but not me.) This is washing a clod
   of earth in the mud. Everyone on earth knows. *

When has dead water ever displayed the ancient way?
   **Should it suddenly come to life, nothing can
   be done. He drags in everyone on earth so that
   they can't get out. *

If you can't use the meditation brace and cushion,
   **Who would you have say this? What do you want
   to do with the meditation brace and cushion?
   Didn't he hand them over to you, Reverend?*

You should just give them over to Mr. Lu.
   **But they can't be given over. You
   lacquer bucket, don't entertain such
   views!*

COMMENTARY

Hsueh Tou settles the case according to the facts. Though he versifies this way, tell me, where is his meaning? Where does the dragon lack eyes? Where is he in dead water? At this point you must have the power to transform before you realize. That is why it is said, "In a clear pool there's no place for the blue dragon to coil up." Has there ever been a fierce dragon in stagnant water? Haven't you heard it said, "Stagnant water cannot conceal a dragon"? If it is a live dragon, it must go to where vast swelling billows of foamy waves flood the heavens. This is to say that Lung Ya went into the dead water and was hit by the others. Yet he did say, "Since you hit me I let you hit me; in essence, though, there is no meaning of the Patriarch's coming from the West." This prompted Hsueh Tou to say, "When has dead water ever displayed the ancient way?" Although this is so, tell me, was Hsueh Tou upholding (Lung Ya), or was he diminishing his dignity?

   People often misunderstand and ask, "Why did Hsueh Tou say, 'You should just give them over to Mr. Lu'?" They are far from knowing that Lung Ya did indeed give them to the others.

Whenever you visit masters to ask for instruction, you must discriminate in the midst of the action; only then will you see where those Ancients met.

"If you can't use the meditation brace and cushion." Ts'ui Wei said, "Pass me the meditation brace," and Lung Ya gave it to him; isn't this making a living within dead water? Clearly Lung Ya has been given a fine steed; it's just that he doesn't know how to ride it, that he is unable to make use of it.

"You should just give them over to Mr. Lu." People frequently say that Mr. Lu is the Sixth Patriarch; this is wrong. Hsueh Tou has called himself Mr. Lu previously in a verse called "Anonymous Bequest"—

> I saw its picture that year and loved Tung T'ing;[e]
> In the waves, seventy-two peaks of blue.
> Now, resting on high, I think back to what was before,
> To the picture, I've added Mr. Lu leaning against a wall.

Hsueh Tou wanted to walk on Lung Ya's head, but he still feared that people would misunderstand, so he made up another verse to cut away people's doubtful interpretations. Again he picks it up and says,

VERSE

Since this old fellow couldn't yet put an end to it, again he makes a verse:
**Obviously. How many people could there be who would know? He knew himself that he had attained only a half; luckily he has a final word.*

Once Mr. Lu has accepted them, why depend on them?
**Even if you search the whole world, such a man is still hard to find. Who would you have comprehend your words?*

Sitting, leaning—cease taking these to succeed to the lamp of the Patriarchs!

**A man in the weeds; he goes in to sit beneath the black mountain. He has fallen into the ghost cave.*

It's worth replying: the evening clouds, returning, have not yet come together;
**One, a half. Bring it up and already you're wrong. After all he can't get out.*

Distant mountains without end, layer upon layer of blue.
**They block off your eyes, they block off your ears. You sink into a deep pit. Study for thirty more years.*

COMMENTARY

"Once Mr. Lu has accepted them, why depend on them?" What is there to depend on? Here you must understand things directly this way; don't go on guarding a stump waiting for a rabbit. Smash what's before your skull all at once, so that there isn't the slightest bit of concern within your breast. Let go and become clean and at ease. Then what more need is there for something to rely on? Whether sitting (on the cushion) or leaning (on the brace), it's not worth considering it the principle of the Buddha Dharma. That is why Hsueh Tou said, "Sitting, leaning—cease to take these to succeed to the lamp of the Patriarchs." At once, Hsueh Tou has brought it up completely; he has a place to turn around in, and at the end reveals this scene where there's a bit of a nice place. He says, "It's worth replying: the evening clouds, returning, have not yet come together." Tell me, where is Hsueh Tou's meaning? When the evening clouds have returned and are about to join together but have not yet done so, tell me, how is it then? "Distant mountains without end, layer upon layer of blue." As before he's gone into the ghost cave. When you get here, when gain and loss, right and wrong, are cut off all at once, and you are clean and at ease, only then do you amount to something. "Distant mountains without end, layer upon layer of blue." Tell me, is this Manjusri's realm? Is this Samantabhadra's realm? Is this Avalokitesvara's realm? When you get here, tell me, whose affair is this?

TRANSLATOR'S NOTES

a. "What's like the land of Yueh is like Yang Chou" in that these two names refer to the same area of China: broadly speaking, the coastal plain river country north and south of the mouth of the Yangtse River, especially the modern provinces Chekiang and Kiangsu.

b. This story, quoted here in a somewhat different form, is the main example of the thirty-first case; Kato Totsudo thinks that it may have been inserted into this commentary by a later hand.

c. In Sung times some Lin Chi masters criticized the Ts'ao-Tung masters for being too fond of quiescence, abiding in extinction, absorbed by the vastness of the universe; the fifth rank of the Ts'ao-Tung's five ranks was symbolized by a solid black circle, which the Lin Chi masters often took to mean *nirvana* as extinction. Tenkei Denson sometimes remarked that Yuan Wu was not thoroughly familiar with the devices of the Tung lineage, and did not realize that there is a turning point, a pivot, in each rank. The Lin Chi masters emphasized the experience of *wu* (*satori*), enlightenment or awakening, and its active expression; they were foremost in the use of contemplation themes, upon which they would focus with a force known as 'doubt' or 'great doubt'. The tension of the doubt was used to rid the mind of wandering thought, unify the attention, and break mental habit patterns; the sudden dissolution of the 'mass of doubt' was sometimes brought about by blows or shouts, by a gesture, a word or phrase. After dying 'the great death' and entering the Path, one is supposed to return to life, awake and free; but it is said that many do not return, being absorbed by the peace of death, forsaking forever the clamor of life. Lung Ya is being 'criticized' for not showing his own initiative.

d. This refers to Lung Ya; the name Lung Ya means dragon's tusk, and is the name of the mountain on which the Ch'an master Chu Tun lived. As is customary, he is usually referred to by the name of the place where he lived.

e. This refers to Tung T'ing mountain in Su Chou (Soochow), Chekiang, eastern China, where Hsueh Tou lived at one time, on Ts'ui Feng (Green Peak). Hsueh Tou added a little picture of himself to a painting of Tung T'ing; this poem is just cited to show that 'Mr. Lu' refers to Hsueh Tou himself.

Chih Men's Lotus Flower, Lotus Leaves

INTRODUCTORY INSTRUCTION

Setting up the banner of the Teaching, establishing the essential meaning—this is adding flowers to brocade. Strip off the blinders, unload the saddle pack—this is the season of the great peace. If you can discern the phrase outside of patterns, then when one is raised you understand three. Otherwise, if you're not yet this way, as before humbly listen to this treatment.

MAIN CASE

A monk asked Chih Men, "How is it when the lotus flower has not yet emerged from the water?"[1] Chih Men said, "A Lotus flower."[2]

The monk said, "What about after it has emerged from the water?"[3] Men said, "Lotus leaves."[4]

NOTES

1. The hook is on the doubt-free ground. Washing a lump of dirt in the mud. How did he get this news?
2. One, two, three, four, five, six, seven. He stumps everyone on earth.
3. Don't go inside the ghost cave to make a living. Again the monk goes on this way.
4. Yu Chou (up north) is still alright: the worst suffering is south of the River. Two heads, three faces. He kills everyone on earth with laughter.

139

COMMENTARY

As for dealing with people in accordance with their potentials, Chih Men has attained a little. When it comes to cutting off the myriad streams, he's a million miles away. But say, is this flower before and after it emerges from the water the same or different? If you can see this way, I'll grant that you've had an entry. Nevertheless, if you say it's the same, you confuse your buddha-nature and becloud true thusness. If you say it's different, mind and environment are not yet forgotten, and you descend to travel the road of interpretation. When will you ever cease?

Tell me, what is the ancient's meaning? In reality there aren't so many concerns. That is why T'ou Tzu said, "Just don't attach names and words, classification and phrasing. If you have understood all things, naturally you won't be attached to them. Then there is no multiplicity of gradations of differences; you take in all things; but all things won't be able to take you in. Fundamentally there is no gain or loss, no illusions or dreams, no multiplicity of names. You should not insist on setting up names for them. Can I fool all of you people? Since all of you ask questions, therefore there are words. If you didn't ask, what could you have me say that would be right? All concerns are what you take up: none of it is any of my business." An ancient said, "If you want to know the meaning of the buddha nature, you must observe times and seasons, causes and conditions."

Haven't you seen Yun Men cite this story: A monk asked Ling Yun, "How was it before the Buddha appeared in the world?" Ling Yun raised his whisk. The monk asked, "What about after he appeared in the world?" Again Ling Yun raised his whisk. Yun Men said, "The first time he hit, the second time he missed." He also said, "Without speaking of appearing and not appearing, where would there be the time of his asking?"

With one answer for one question the ancients accorded with the time and season without a multitude of concerns. If you pursue words and follow after phrases, there will never be any connection. If in the midst of words you can penetrate through words, if in the midst of meanings you can pass through meanings, if within a device you can penetrate through the device, and if you let go and let yourself be at ease, only then will you see Chih Men's answer.ª

Yun Men said, "From ancient times till today, it's just been one thing. There is no right or wrong, no gain or loss, no born or not born." When they got here the ancients laid down one single path where there's an entrance and an exit. If it's a man who hasn't yet understood, then he's pressing against a fence, running his hands over a wall,ᵇ (like a ghost) haunting the weeds and trees. If you make him let go, he still goes into the wild vast desolation. If it is a man who has attained, then twenty-four hours a day he won't depend on a single thing. While he doesn't depend on a single thing, when he reveals one device, one object, how will you search him out?

This monk asked, "How is it when the lotus flowers have not yet emerged from the water?" Chih Men said, "A Lotus flower." This then is just an answer that blocks the question, nevertheless it's exceptional. All over it's called "upside-down words." How so? Haven't you heard: Yen T'ou said, "I always hope you would attain a little before you open your mouths."

Where the ancient one Chih Men revealed his mind, he was already leaking and tarrying. Students these days don't wake up to the ancient's meaning: they just go on talking theoretically of "emerged from the water" and "not yet emerged from the water." What connection is there?

Haven't you heard: A monk asked Chih Men, "What is the body of Wisdom?" Men said, "An oyster enclosing the bright moon." The monk asked, "What is the functioning of Wisdom?" Men said, "A rabbit becomes pregnant." Look at him responding like this: no one on earth can search out the stream of his words.

If someone asked me, "How is it when the lotus flowers have not yet emerged from the water?" I would just answer him by saying, "The pillar and the lamp."ᶜ Tell me, is this the same as the lotus flowers or different? If I were asked, "What about after they've emerged from the water?" I would answer, "The staff upholds the sun and moon, underfoot how muddy and deep!" You tell me, is this right or wrong? And don't mistakenly stick by the zero point of a scale.

Hsueh Tou is extremely compassionate, breaking up people's emotional interpretations, so he comes out with his verse:

VERSE

Lotus flower, lotus leaves—he reports for you to know
   **Grandmotherly kindness. A manifest public case. Its
      pattern is already revealed.*

*How can emerging from the water compare to when it has not
      yet emerged?*
   **Washing a lump of dirt in the mud. Dividing them is
      alright, but you can't lump them together.*

North of the river, south of the river, ask Old Wang
   **Where is the master? Why ask Old Master Wang?
      You're just wearing out your straw sandals.*

Fox-doubt after fox-doubt
   **I bury them in one hole. It's you who doubt. You won't
      avoid feelings of doubt without respite. Having struck
      I say, "Do you understand?"*

COMMENTARY

Originally Chih Men was from Chekiang. He made his way by
stages to Szechuan to call on Hsiang Lin. After he had penetrated (this affair under Hsiang Lin's guidance), he returned to
dwell at Chih Men in Sui Chou.

Hsueh Tou was Chih Men's true successor: he saw well
Chih Men's most hidden, most subtle point and says directly,
"Lotus flower, lotus leaves—he reports for you to know/How
can emerging from the water compare to when it has not yet
emerged?" Here he wants people to understand directly and
immediately.

I say, "How is it when they've not yet emerged from the
water? The pillar and lamp. What about after they've emerged?
The staff upholds the sun and moon, underfoot how muddy
and deep!" But don't mistakenly abide by this as the zero point
of a scale. What limit is there to people these days chewing
over the words and phrases of others?

But tell me, when they emerge from the water, what time
and season is this? When they've not yet emerged from the
water, what time and season is this? If you can see to this
point, I'll allow that you've seen Chih Men personally.

Hsueh Tou says, if you don't see, "North of the river, south of the river, ask Old Wang." Hsueh Tou means that you should just go north of the river and south of the river to ask the venerable adepts about "emerged from the water" and "not emerged from the water." If you add two phrases south of the river, add two phrases north of the river, add one load upon another load, creating doubts over and over, just tell me, when will you get so that you don't doubt? You're like wild foxes, full of doubt, walking on river ice: they listen for the sound of the water (below); if it doesn't make a sound, then they can cross the river. If students have "fox-doubt after fox-doubt," when will they attain peace and tranquility?

TRANSLATOR'S NOTES

a.   Following this, the Chang book inserts, "'How is it before the Buddha appeared in the world?' 'How was it before Niu T'ou saw the fourth patriarch?' 'How is it when a conglomerate stone is still undifferentiated inside?' 'How was it before your parents bore you?'" These are supposed to be in the same category as 'How is it before the lotus emerges from the water?' The lotus is a traditional symbol for enlightenment.

b.   Pressing against a fence, running his hands over a wall, as a blind man would.

c.   "The pillar and the lamp": Physical reality, the world of objects, such as the pillar and the lamp that would have been present in the Dharma Halls right in front of the eyes of Yuan Wu's listeners.

Hsueh Feng's Turtle-Nosed Snake

POINTER

There's nothing outside the great vastness; it's as fine as atomic dust. Holding on and letting go are not another's (do-ing): rolling up and rolling out^a rest with oneself. If you want to free what is stuck and loosen what is bound, you simply must cut away the traces (of thought) and swallow the sounds (of words). All people occupy the essential crossing place; each and every one towers up like a thousand fathom wall. But tell me, whose realm is this? To test, I'm citing this old case: look!

CASE

Hsueh Feng taught the assembly saying, "On South Mountain there's a turtle-nosed snake.[1] All of you people must take a good look."[2]

Ch'ang Ch'ing said, "In the hall today there certainly are people who are losing their bodies and their lives."[3]

A monk related this to Hsuan Sha.[4] Hsuan Sha said, "It takes Elder Brother Leng (Ch'ang Ch'ing) to be like this. Nevertheless, I am not this way."[5] The monk asked, "What about you, Teacher?"[6] Hsuan Sha said, "Why make use of 'South Mountain'?"[7]

Yun Men took his staff and threw it down in front of Hsueh Feng, making a gesture of fright.[8]

NOTES

1. If you see something strange as not strange, it's strangeness dis-appears by itself. What a strange thing! Unavoidably it causes people to doubt.
2. Aha! A case of over-indulgence.

3. The man from P'u Chou (Ch'ang Ch'ing) escorts the thief. He judges others on the basis of himself.
4. There's no different dirt from the same hole. When the manservant sees the maidservant he takes care. Those with the same disease sympathize with each other.
5. He doesn't avoid forming a wild fox spirit view. What news is this? His poison breath afflicts others.
6. He too presses the old fellow well.
7. On a boat fishing, the third son of the Hsiehs (Hsuan Sha). Only this wild fox spirit has attained a little. He's lost his body and his life and doesn't even realize it.
8. Why be afraid of it? One son has intimately attained. All of them are giving play to their spirits. All of you try to discern this.

COMMENTARY

If you spread it out evenly, I let you spread it out evenly; if you break it up, I let you break it up.

Hsueh Feng travelled with Yen T'ou and Ch'in Shan. In all, he went to Mt. T'ou Tzu three times, and climbed Mt. Tung nine times. Later he called on Te Shan, and only then did he smash the lacquer bucket.

One day he went along with Yen T'ou to visit Ch'in Shan. They got as far as an inn on Tortoise Mountain (in Hunan) when they were snowed in. Day after day Yen T'ou just slept, while Hsueh Feng constantly sat in meditation. Yen T'ou yelled at him and said, "Get some sleep! Every day you're on the meditation seat, exactly like a clay image. Another time, another day, you'll fool the sons and daughters of other people's families." Feng pointed to his breast and said, "I am not yet at peace here; I don't dare deceive myself." T'ou said, "I had thought that later on you would go to the summit of a solitary peak, build a hut of straw, and propagate the great teaching: but you're still making such a statement as this." Feng said, "I am really not yet at peace." T'ou said, "If you're really like this, bring forth your views one by one; where they're correct I'll approve them for you, and where they're wrong I'll prune them away for you."

Then Hsueh Feng related, "When I saw Yen Kuan up in the

hall bringing up the meaning of form and void, I gained an entry." Yen T'ou said, "Henceforth for thirty years avoid mentioning this." Again Feng said, "When I saw Tung Shan's verse on crossing the river,[b] I had an insight." T'ou said, "This way, you won't be able to save yourself." Feng went on, "Later when I got to Te Shan I asked, 'Do I have a part in the affair of the vehicle of the most ancient sect, or not?' Shan struck me a blow of his staff and said, 'What are you saying?' At that time it was like the bottom of the bucket dropping out for me." Thereupon Yen T'ou shouted and said, "Haven't you heard it said that what comes in through the gate is not the family jewels?" Feng said, "Then what should I do?" T'ou said, "In the future, if you want to propagate the great teaching, let each point flow out from your own breast, to come out and cover heaven and earth for me." At these words Hsueh Feng was greatly enlightened. Then he bowed, crying out again and again, "Today on Tortoise Mountain I've finally achieved the Way! Today on Tortoise Mountain I've finally achieved the Way!"

Later Hsueh Feng returned to Min (Fukien) and lived on Elephant Bone Mountain. He left behind this verse about himself:

> Human life so hectic and hurried is but a brief instant;
> How can you dwell for long in the fleeting world?
> As I reached thirty-two I emerged from the mountains;
> Already over forty, I return to Min.
> No use bringing up the faults of others again and again;
> One's own mistakes must be cleared away continually.
> I humbly report to the purple-clad nobles who fill the court:
> The King of Death has no awe of the golden emblems of rank you wear.

Usually Hsueh Feng would go up into the hall and teach the assembly by saying, "In every respect cover heaven and cover earth." He talked no more of mystery or marvel, nor did he speak of mind or nature. He appeared strikingly, alone, like a

great fiery mass; approach and he burns off your face. Like the
T'ai Ya sword, fool around with him and you lose your body
and your life. If you linger in thought, holding back your activity, then you lose contact.

Pai Ching asked Huang Po, "Where are you coming from?"
Po said, "I've been at the foot of Mt. Ta Hsiung picking mush-
rooms." Chang said, "See any tigers?" Po then made a tiger's
roar. Then Chang picked up an axe and made a chopping motion; Po then slapped him. Chang chuckled and went back and
ascended his seat and told the assembly, "There's a tiger on Mt.
Ta Hsiung; all of you should watch out for him. Today I myself
was bitten by him."

Whenever Chao Chou saw a monk, right away he would say,
"Have you ever been here?" Whether the monk said he had or
he hadn't, Chou would always say, "Go drink some tea." The
temple overseer asked, "The teacher always asks monks if
they've been here or not, then always says, 'Go drink some tea.'
What is the meaning?" Chou said, "Overseer!" When the overseer responded, Chou said, "Go drink some tea."

Beneath the gate at Tzu Hu stood a signboard; the writing on
the plaque said, "At Tzu Hu there's a dog: on top he takes
people's heads, in the middle he takes people's midsections,
and below he takes people's legs; hesitate and you're lost." As
soon as he saw any newcomer, the Master of Tzu Hu would
immediately give a shout and say, "Look at the dog!" The
moment the monk turned his head, the master would return to
his abbot's room.

(These examples) are just like Hsueh Feng's saying, "On
South Mountain there is a turtle-nosed snake; all of you people
should watch it carefully." At just such a time, how would you
reply? Without following in your former tracks, try to say
something for me to see. When you get here, you must understand the phrase outside of patterns; then, when all the public
cases are brought up, you will immediately know where they
come down. See how Hsueh Feng teaches the assembly this
way, without speaking to you of practice or understanding.
Can you figure him out by means of intellectual discrimination?

Since Ch'ang Ch'ing, Hsuan Sha, and Yun Men are sons of
his house, what they say is exactly appropriate. This is why the
Ancient said, "On hearing words, you must understand the

source; don't set up standards on your own." Words must have that which is beyond patterns; phrases must penetrate the barrier. If your words don't leave their nest of cliché, you fall into the poison sea.

Hsueh Feng's teaching the assembly this way can be called flavorless talk that blocks off people's mouths. Ch'ang Ch'ing and Hsuan Sha are both men of his family, thus they understand when he speaks this way.

What about "On South Mountain there's a turtle-nosed snake"? Do all of you know what this really means? Here you must be possessed of the all-pervasive eye in order to understand. Haven't you seen Chen Ching's verse which says,

> Beating the drum, strumming the lute,
> Two men of understanding meet.
> Yun Men is able to harmonize—
> Ch'ang Ch'ing knows how to follow his vagaries;
> The ancient song has no rhyme.
> South Mountain's turtle-nosed snake;
> Who knows this meaning?
> Truly it's Hsuan Sha.

When Ch'ang Ch'ing replied as he did, tell me, what was his meaning? To get here you must be like a stone-struck spark, like a lightning flash; only then will you be able to reach. If there's as much as a fine hair that you can't get rid of, then you won't be able to reach his depths. It's a pity that people mostly make intellectual interpretations of Ch'ang Ch'ing's words. They say, "As soon as anything is heard in the hall, then this is 'losing body and life.'" Some say, "Fundamentally there's not the slightest speck of anything; to say this kind of thing on even blank ground makes people doubt. People hear him say, 'On South Mountain there's a turtle-nosed snake,' and immediately they have doubts." If you understand in such ways, you have no contact; you just go on making a living on the words. If you don't understand this way, then how will you understand?

Later a monk related this to Hsuan Sha. Hsuan Sha said, "It takes Elder Brother Leng (Ch'ang Ch'ing) to be like this; nevertheless, I am not thus." The monk asked, "What about you, teacher?" Hsuan Sha said, "Why make use of 'South Mountain'?" Just observe how within Hsuan Sha's words there is a place where he shows himself. Immediately he said, "Why make use of 'South Mountain'?" If it hadn't been Hsuan Sha, it would have been very difficult to reply. When Hsueh Feng speaks this way, "On South Mountain there's a turtle-nosed snake," tell me, where is it? To get here you must be a transcendent person; only then will you be able to understand such talk. The man of old Hsueh Tou said, "Up on the boat fishing, the third son of the Hsieh doesn't like South Mountain; he prefers the turtle-nosed snake."

Then again we get to Yun Men; he took his staff and threw it down in front of Hsueh Feng, making a gesture of fright. Yun Men has the ability to handle snakes, and doesn't run afoul of the sharp point. He strikes home in light, and he strikes home in darkness too. As he helps people it's always like doing a sword dance; sometimes he flies onto people's eyebrows and eyelashes, sometimes he flies three thousand miles away and snatches people's heads. His throwing down his staff and making a gesture of fright—isn't this giving play to his spirit? Doesn't he lose his body and life too? Expert teaching masters never go to a word or phrase to make a living. Just because he likes the way Yun Men accorded perfectly with Hsueh Feng's meaning, therefore Hsueh Tou makes his verse on it:

VERSE

Elephant Bone Cliff is so high no one goes there;
     ***A thousand, ten thousand, search but cannot
     find. It's not your realm, sir.**

Those who get there must be master snake handlers.
     ***This is a spirit recognizing a spirit, a thief
     recognizing a thief. Why gather in crowds?
     Still, you must be of the same group to make it.**

Master Leng and Master Pei can't do anything—
     ***Their crimes are listed on the same indictment.
     They passed up the first move.**

How many lose their bodies and their lives?
     ***A crime is not judged twice. He drags
     in common people.**

Shao Yang knows:
>   **He's just attained a little.
>   This old fellow has just one single
>   eye. The old fellow is just
>   being clever.*

Again he searches the weeds—
>   **He's a fellow fallen in the weeds;
>   what is the use? After all, where
>   is (the 'snake')? I strike!*

South, north, east, west; no place to search.
>   **Is there? Is there? Your eyes are
>   blind, Reverend.*

Suddenly he thrusts out his staff,
>   **Look! Set your eyes high. I strike!*

And throws it down before Hsueh Feng; it opens wide its
>   mouth.
>   **Self-contrived, self-experienced. It swallows a
>   thousand, ten thousand, but what is accomplished?
>   No one on earth can find it.*

The gaping mouth is like a lightning flash;
>   **A double case. After all. Fortunately
>   there is a final word.*

Raise your eyebrows (to look) and you won't see.
>   **It's already gone by. Search all over for
>   such a man, and still it's hard to find one.
>   Right now where is (the snake)?*

Right now it's hidden here on Ju Peak;
>   **Where has it gone? Even the
>   great Hsueh Tou acts this way
>   too. Today I too have been bitten.*

Those who come, one by one observe expedient methods.
>   **Blind! Don't look under his feet; look under
>   your own feet. He's shot an arrow.*

The Master (Hsueh Tou) shouted loudly and said, "Look right
>   under your feet!"
>   **He draws his bow after the thief has gone. Secondary,
>   tertiary. Repeated words are not worth enduring.*

COMMENTARY

"Elephant Bone Cliff is so high that no one goes there; those who get there must be master snake handlers." On Hsueh Feng Mountain there is an Elephant Bone Cliff. Hsueh Feng's active edge is lofty and steep; rarely is there anyone who reaches his place. Hsueh Tou is a man of his house; they're birds of a feather. Answering each other with the same voice, seeking each other with the same spirit; it takes all-competent adepts to join in the mutual witness of enlightenment.

Still, this turtle-nosed snake is unavoidably hard to handle; you must know how to handle it before you can do so. Conversely, if you don't know how to handle it, you'll be bitten by the snake. My late teacher Wu Tsu said, "With this turtle-nosed snake, you must have the ability not to get your hands or legs bitten. Hold him tight by the back of the neck with one quick grab. Then you can join hands and walk along with me."

Ch'ang Ch'ing and Hsuan Sha had this kind of ability. When Hsueh Tou says that Master Leng and Master Pei couldn't handle it, people often say that Ch'ang Ch'ing and Hsuan Sha couldn't do anything about it, and thus Hsueh Tou only praises Yun Men. But this has nothing to do with it. How far they are from knowing that among the three men there is no gain or loss in ability; it's just that there is close and far away. Now I ask all of you people, where is it that Master Leng and Master Pei couldn't manage?

"How many lose their bodies and their lives?" This praises Ch'ang Ch'ing's saying, "In the hall today there certainly are people who lose their bodies and lives." To get here, first you must be thoroughly versed in snake handling.

Hsueh Tou is descended from Yun Men, so he brushes the others away all at once and just keeps one, Yun Men: Hsueh Tou says, "Shao Yang knows; again he searches the weeds." Since Yun Men knew the meaning of Hsueh Feng's saying, "On South Mountain there's a turtle-nosed snake," therefore "Again he searches through the weeds."

After Hsueh Tou has taken his verse this far, he still has more marvels. He says, "South, north, east, west; no place to search." You tell me where the snake is. "Suddenly he thrusts out his staff." From the beginning the snake has been right here. But you must not then go to the staff for sustenance. Yun Men took his staff and threw it down in front of Hsueh Feng, making a gesture of fright. Thus Yun Men used his staff as the turtle-nosed snake. Once, though, he said, "The staff changed into a dragon and has swallowed the universe; where are mountains, rivers and the great earth to be found?" Just this one staff—sometimes it's a dragon, sometimes it's a snake. Why is it like this? Only when you get here will you know (the meaning of the) ancient saying, "Mind revolves along with myriad phenomena; the turning point is truly mysterious."

The verse says, "He throws it down before Hsueh Feng; it opens wide its mouth. The gaping mouth is like a lightning flash." Hsueh Tou has extra talent; he picks up Yun Men's poisonous snake and says, "Just this gaping mouth is like a flash of lightning." If you hesitate, then you lose your body and life. "Raise your eyebrows (to look), and you won't see." Where has it gone?

His verse finished, Hsueh Tou must go to a living place to help others; he takes Hsueh Feng's snake and picks it up and plays with it himself. Nothing can stop him from killing or bringing to life in accordance with the occasion. Do you want to see? He says, "Right now it's hidden here on Ju Peak." Ju Peak is a name for Hsueh Tou Mountain.

Though Ch'ang Ch'ing, Hsuan Sha, and Yun Men can handle the snake, they don't see. After all Hsueh Tou says, "Right now it's hidden here on Ju Peak; those who come, one by one observe expedient methods." Hsueh Tou is still too subtle; he doesn't say, "Use it right away," but instead shouted loudly and said, "Look right under your feet!" Since ancient times how many people have picked up the snake and played with it? Tell me, has the snake ever wounded anyone or not?

Then the Master Yuan Wu struck.

TRANSLATOR'S NOTES

a.   In the *Chueh Kuan Lun* by Master Fa Jung of Ox Head Mountain it says: Q: What is 'rolling out'? A: Illumination and action is 'rolling out.' Q: What is 'rolling up'? A: Mind quiescent and extinct (nirvana) is 'rolling up.' When rolling out he travels everywhere throughout the universe; when rolling up even the traces of his concentration are impossible to look for.

b.   See the biography of Tung Shan Liang Chieh. After leaving his teacher Yun Yen, he happened to see a reflection of himself as he crossed a river, and thereupon was greatly enlightened and composed the verse.

Pao Fu's Summit of the Mystic Peak

POINTER

Jewels are tested with fire, gold is tested with a stone; a sword is tested with a hair, water is tested with a pole. In the school of the patchrobed monks, in one word, one phrase, one act, one state, one exit, one entry, one encounter, one response, you must see whether someone is deep or shallow, you must see whether he is facing forwards or backwards. But tell me, what will you use to test him with? I bring this up: look!

CASE

Once when Pao Fu and Ch'ang Ch'ing were wandering in the mountains,[1] Pao Fu pointed with his hand and said, "Right here is the summit of the mystic peak."[2]

Ch'ang Ch'ing said, "Indeed it is. What a pity!"[3]

Hsueh Tou added a word, saying, "Today what is the purpose of travelling the mountains together with these fellows?"[4] He also said, "Hundreds of thousands of years hence, I don't say there are none, just that they will be few."[5]

Later this (dialogue between Pao Fu and Ch'ang Ch'ing) was quoted to Ching Ch'ing.[6] Ching Ch'ing said, "If it hadn't been Mr. Sun (Pao Fu), then you would have seen skulls covering the fields."[7]

NOTES

1. These two fellows have fallen into the weeds.
2. He raises a pile of bones on level ground. Just avoid speaking of it. Dig a hole and bury it deep.
3. If you don't have iron eyes or brass eyes, you'll probably be confused. Those with the same disease sympathize with each other. The two men are buried in the same hole.

4. Inevitably Hsueh Tou diminishes people's worth. Still it amounts to something. The bystander wields the double-edged sword.
5. A petty boast; here's another cloud-dwelling saint.
6. There's good, there's bad.
7. Only those on the same path know. The great earth is so vast and desolate it kills people with sadness. When the manservant sees the maidservant, he takes care. Even if Lin Chi and Te Shan appeared, they too would have to take a beating.

COMMENTARY

Pao Fu, Ch'ang Ch'ing, and Ching Ch'ing were all successors of Hsueh Feng; these three men attained alike and realized alike, saw alike and heard alike, picked up alike and used alike. With one exit and one entrance, they pressed back and forth one after the other. Since they were men born of the same lineage, as soon as one raised something the others knew where it came down. In Hsueh Feng's congregation it was just these three who always engaged in questioning and answering. Whether walking, standing, sitting, or lying down, the ancients were mindful of this path; that is why as soon as it is brought up, they know where it comes down.

One day when he was wandering in the mountains Pao Fu pointed with his hand and said, "Right here is the summit of the mystic peak." When Ch'an men these days are questioned this way, then they only frown; fortunately it was Ch'ang Ch'ing who was asked. Tell me, when Pao Fu spoke this way, what was his purpose? When the ancient Pao Fu acted like this, he wanted to test whether Ch'ang Ch'ing had eyes or not.

Ch'ang Ch'ing was a man of his house, so naturally he knew what Pao Fu was getting at; thus he replied to him by saying, "Indeed it is. What a pity!" But tell me, when Ch'ang Ch'ing spoke this way, what was his meaning? You can't always go on this way. Though there are those who seem so, (actually) there is rarely anyone at ease without the slightest concern. Fortunately Ch'ang Ch'ing understood Pao Fu completely.

Hsueh Tou added a word saying, "Today, travelling the mountains with these fellows, what is the purpose?" Tell me, where does this come down? Again he said, "Hundreds of thousands of years hence, I don't say there are none, just that

they will be few." Hsueh Tou knows how to point to himself.
This is just like Huang Po's saying, "I don't say that there is no
Ch'an, just that there are no teachers." Hsueh Tou speaking
this way is also undeniably dangerous and steep. If Hsueh Tou
hadn't answered back with the same voice, how could it have
been this unique and marvelous? This is called an added comment; it comes down on both sides, but though it comes down
on both sides, it doesn't remain on either side.

Later this was quoted to Ching Ch'ing. He said, "If it hadn't
been Mr. Sun, then you would have seen skulls covering the
fields." Sun is Ch'ang Ch'ing's lay surname. Haven't you heard
how a monk asked Chao Chou, "What is the lone summit of
the mystic peak?" Chou said, "I won't answer this question of
yours." The monk asked, "Why won't you answer this question?" Chou said, "I fear that if I answered you, you would fall
onto the level ground."

In the teachings it says that the mendicant Meghasri always
stayed on the lone summit of the peak of wonder; he never
came down from the mountain. Sudhana went to call on him
and searched for seven days without encountering him. But
then one day they met on a separate peak. When he had seen
him, Meghasri explained for Sudhana that the three worlds are
a moment of thought and the wisdom and illumination of all
the Buddhas, the gate of Dharma that appears everywhere.
Given that Meghasri never came down from the mountain,
why then did they meet on a separate peak? If you say Meghasri
must have come down from the mountain, yet in the teachings
it says that he never did come down from the mountain, that
he was always on the solitary summit of the peak of wonder.
At this point, where are Meghasri and Sudhana really?

Later, Elder Li created some complications, and made up a
verse quite well:

> *The lone summit of the mystic peak*
> *Is the teaching of one-flavor equanimity.*
> *Each and every one—they're all real;*
> *Each and every one—they're all complete.*
> *Where there's no gain and no loss,*
> *No affirmation and no negation,*
> *There it stands alone revealed;*
> *Therefore Sudhana couldn't see him.*

When you get to the point of merging with nature, it's like "the eye does not see itself, the ear does not hear itself, the finger does not feel itself; it's like a sword doesn't cut itself, fire does not burn itself." At this point there are many instances of compassionate assistance in the teachings; this is why they let down a single path, and in methods of the secondary truth set up host and guest, devices and objects, questions and answers. Thus it is said, "The Buddhas have not appeared in the world, nor is there any nirvana. They manifest such things as expedient means to rescue sentient beings."

But tell me, in the end, how will you avoid Ching Ch'ing and Hsueh Tou talking as they did? If they hadn't been able to clap along in unison at that time, that would have been why "human skulls cover the fields all over the world." Ch'ang Ch'ing comes up with this testimony, and both Pao Fu and Ch'ang Ch'ing use it this way. Afterwards, Hsueh Tou comes out with a verse even more brilliant. The verse says,

VERSE

On the lone summit of the mystic peak, weeds grow in profusion;
　　**You lose your body too. (The weeds) are already several fathoms deep beneath your feet.*

Clearly it is brought up—to be given to whom?
　　**And used for what? There's no one on earth who knows. A dry piece of shit; what is it good for? You've got your nostrils, but lost your mouth.ᵃ*

If it hadn't been Mr. Sun discerning the real point,
　　**Wrong! Watch the arrow! He's caught the thief Without even realizing it.*

Skulls would cover the ground, but how many people would know?
　　**They won't live again. They're numerous as hemp or millet seeds. You've got the nostrils but lost the mouth, Reverend.*

COMMENTARY

"On the lone summit of the mystic peak, weeds grow in profusion." If you roll around in the weeds, when will you ever have done? "Clearly it is brought up—to be given to whom?" Where is the clarity? This praises Pao Fu saying, "Right here is the summit of the mystic peak."

"If it hadn't been Mr. Sun discerning the real point." What truth did Mr. Sun see that he could say, "So it is. What a pity!"? As for "Skulls would cover the ground, but how many people would know?" Do all you people know? Blind!

TRANSLATOR'S NOTES

a. "Getting the nostrils, but losing the mouth" connotes getting something vital but at the same time losing something else equally necessary by focussing exclusively on the first objective.

Kuei Shan and Iron Grindstone Liu

POINTER

Stand on the summit of the highest peak, and demons and outsiders cannot know you; walk on the bottom of the deepest sea, and even the Buddha's eye cannot catch sight of you. Even if your eyes are like shooting stars and your intellect is like flashing lightning, still you won't avoid (being like) the spirit tortoise dragging his tail (leaving traces.) At this point, what is proper? To test, I'm citing this: Look!

CASE

Iron Grindstone Liu arrived at Kuei Shan.[1] Kuei Shan said, "Old cow, so you've come!"[2]

The Grindstone said, "Tomorrow there's a great communal feast on T'ai Shan; are you going to go, Teacher?"[3]

Kuei Shan relaxed his body and lay down;[4] the Grindstone immediately left.[5]

NOTES

1. Unavoidably it'll be hard to stay there. This old lady is out of her depth.
2. Check! A probing pole, a reed shade. Where should you look to see the obscurity?
3. The arrow is not shot to no purpose. In China they beat the drum, in Korea they dance. The letting go was too fast, the gathering in is too slow.
4. The arrow got him. Where will you see Kuei Shan? Who realizes that in the far-off misty waves there is another more excellent realm of thought?
5. She's gone. She saw the opportunity and acted.

COMMENTARY

The nun 'Iron Grindstone' Liu was like a stone-struck spark, like a lightening flash; hesitate and you lose your body and your life. In the path of meditation, if you get to the most essential place, where are there so many things? This meeting of adepts is like seeing horns on the other side of a wall and immediately knowing there's an ox, like seeing smoke on the other side of a mountain and immediately knowing there's a fire. When pushed they move, when pressed they turn about.

Kuei Shan said, "After I die, I'll go down the mountain to an alms-giver's house and be a water buffalo. On my left flank five words will be written, saying, 'A Kuei Shan monk, me.' At that time, would it be right to call it a Kuei Shan monk, or would it be right to call it a water buffalo?" When people these days are questioned about this, they are stymied and can't explain.

Iron Grindstone Liu had studied for a long time; her active edge was sharp and dangerous. People called her "Iron Grindstone Liu." She built a hut a few miles from Kuei Mountain. One day she went to call on Kuei Shan. When he saw her coming, he said, "Old cow, so you've come." The Grindstone said, "Tomorrow there's a great communal feast on Mt. T'ai; are you going to go, Teacher?" Kuei Shan relaxed his body and lay down, whereupon the Grindstone left. All of you look—throughout they seemed to be conversing, but this is not Ch'an, neither is it Tao. Can it be understood by calling it unconcern?

Kuei Shan is over six hundred miles from Mt. T'ai; how then did Iron Grindstone Liu want to have Kuei Shan go to the feast? Tell me, what was her meaning? This old lady understands Kuei Shan's conversation: fiber coming, thread going, one letting go, one gathering in; they answer back to each other like two mirrors reflecting each other, without any reflection image to be seen. Action to action, they complement each other; phrase to phrase, they accord.

People these days can be poked three times and not turn their heads, but this old lady couldn't be fooled one little bit. By no means is this an emotional view based on mundane truth; like a bright mirror on its stand, like a bright jewel in the palm of the hand, when a foreigner comes, a foreigner is reflected, and when a native comes a native is reflected. It's that she knows there is something transcendent; that's why she acts like this.

Right now you are content to understand this as unconcern. Master Yen of Wu Tsu said, "Don't take having concerns as not having concerns; time and time again concern is born of unconcern." If you can immerse yourself in this and penetrate through, you will see that Kuei Shan and Iron Grindstone Liu acting in this way is the same sort as ordinary people's conversation. People are often hindered by the words, that's why they don't understand. Only an intimate acquaintance can understand them thoroughly.

It's like Ch'ien Feng teaching his assembly saying, "If you raise one, you shouldn't raise two; let the first move go and you fall into the secondary." Yun Men came forward and said, "Yesterday there was a monk who came from T'ien T'ai and returned to Nan Yueh." Ch'ien Feng said, "Chief cook, don't participate in the general labor today."

Observe these two, Liu and Kuei Shan; when letting go, both let go, and when gathering in, both gather in. In the Kuei-Yang tradition, this is called "merging of perspectives."

In the wind-blown dust the grasses move; thoroughly comprehend the whole from the surface. This is also called "a phrase which hinders one"—the meaning is conveyed but the words obstruct. When you get here, you must be able to sweep to the left and turn to the right; then you are an adept.

VERSE

Once riding an iron horse she entered the fortress;
> **An adept accustomed to battle. Beyond the borders
> is the general's place. She's equipped with the
> seven items.* [a]*

*The edict comes down reporting that the six nations are
    cleared.*
> **A dog carries the amnesty in its mouth. In the heart of
> the realm is the emperor's place. What about (the fact
> that) the sea is calm, the rivers clear?**

*Still holding the golden whip, she questions the returning
    traveller;*

What's the news? Two people are supported by a single staff. They call to each other, going together and coming together.

In the depths of the night, who will go along to walk the royal
    road?
    **You're headed southeast, I'm headed northwest. But tell me, why go?*

COMMENTARY

Hsueh Tou's verses are universally considered the best of their kind. Among the hundred verses this one verse is the most logical, among them it is the most wondrously arrayed and clearly set out.

"Once, riding an iron horse, she entered the fortress." This praises Iron Grindstone Liu coming as she did to Kuei Shan. "The edict comes down, reporting that the six nations are cleared." This praises the way Kuei Shan questioned her. "Still holding the golden whip, she questions the returning traveller." This praises the Grindstone saying, "Tomorrow there's a great communal feast on T'ai Shan; are you going to go, Teacher?" "In the depths of the night, who will go along to walk the royal road?" This praises Kuei Shan relaxing his body and the Iron Grindstone immediately leaving.

Hsueh Tou has this kind of ability: where they hurry he praises their hurrying, and where they are easygoing he praises their being easygoing. Feng Hsueh too once commented on this case, and his meaning was the same as Hsueh Tou's; people all over praise this verse:

> Standing on the summit of the highest peak,
> Unknown to demons and outsiders;
> Walking on the bottom of the deepest sea,
> Unseen even by Buddhas' eyes.

Look at Kuei Shan and Liu: one relaxed his body and lay down, one immediately left. If you go on wandering around, you won't ever be able to find the road. The meaning of Hsueh Tou's verse is most excellent. If he didn't have the same attainment and the same realization, how could he be capable of this? But say, what meaning was attained?

Haven't you heard how a monk asked Feng Hsueh, "When Kuei Shan said, 'Old cow, so you've come!' what was his inner meaning?" Feng Hsueh said, "In the depths of the white clouds the golden dragon leaps." The monk asked, "When Iron Grindstone Liu said, 'Tomorrow there's a great communal feast on T'ai Shan; are you going to go, Teacher?' what was her inner meaning?" Hsueh said, "In the heart of the blue waves the Jade Rabbit bolts." The monk asked, "When Kuei Shan immediately lay down, what was his inner meaning?" Hsueh said, "Old and worn-out, decrepit and lazy, days without concern; lying idly deep in sleep, facing the blue mountains." This meaning too is the same as Hsueh Tou's.

TRANSLATOR'S NOTES

a.   The seven items of a teacher are: 1) great capacity and great function; 2) swiftness of wit and eloquence; 3) wondrous spirituality of speech; 4) the active edge to kill or bring life; 5) wide learning and broad experience; 6) clarity of mirroring awareness; and 7) freedom to appear or disappear. In light of the military metaphor of the verse, it should also be noted that "the seven items" can also refer to a warrior's equipment.

TWENTY-FIFTH CASE

The Hermit of Lotus Flower Peak Holds up His Staff

POINTER

If your potential does not leave (its fixed) position, you tumble down into the poison sea. If your words don't startle the crowd, you fall into the streams of the commonplace.

Suddenly, if you can distinguish initiate from lay in the light of sparks struck from stone, if you can decide between killing and giving life in the light of a flash of lightning, then you can cut off the ten directions and tower up like a thousand fathom wall.

But do you know that such a time exists? To test I'm citing this old case: look!

CASE

The hermit of Lotus Flower Peak held up his staff and showed it to the assembly saying,[1] "When the ancients got here, why didn't they consent to stay here?"[2]

There was no answer from the assembly,[3] so he himself answered for them, "Because they did not gain strength on the road."[4]

Again he said, "In the end, how is it?"[5] And again he himself answered in their place, "With my staff across my shoulder, I pay no heed to people—I go straight into the myriad peaks."[6]

NOTES

1. Look! He has the one eye on his forehead. Still, this is a nest for people these days.
2. You can't drive stakes into empty space. Provisionally the hermit sets up an illusionary city (to teach).

3. A thousand, ten thousand, (numerous as) hemp and millet. They've attained a little, though. What a pity! Swift falcons on a roost.

4. If you go to the road to discern this, you'll still be struggling for half a month's journey. Even if you gain strength, what's it good for? How could there be none at all?

5. A thousand people, ten thousand people, are sitting right here. Among a thousand or ten thousand people, one or two will understand.

6. Still, he deserves thirty blows, because he's carrying a board on his shoulder. If you see cheeks on the back of his head, don't go along with him.

COMMENTARY

Can all of you judge the hermit of Lotus Flower Peak? His feet still aren't touching the ground. Early in Sung times he built a hut on T'ien T'ai's Lotus Flower Peak. After they had attained the Path, the ancients would dwell in thatched huts or stone grottos, boiling the roots of wild greens in broken legged pots, passing the days. They didn't seek fame and fortune: unconcerned, they accorded to conditions. They would impart a turning word, wanting to repay the benevolence of the buddhas and patriarchs and transmit the Buddha Mind Seal.

As soon as he saw a monk coming, the hermit would hold up his staff and say, "When the ancients got here, why didn't they consent to stay here?" For more than twenty years, there was never even one person who could answer. This one question has both provisional and true, both illumination and function. If you know his snare, it isn't worth taking hold of.

But tell me, why did he ask this question for twenty years? Since this is the action of a master of the school, why did he just keep to one peg? If you can see here, naturally you won't be running in the dusts of the senses.

During the course of twenty years, there were quite a few people who laid out their remarks to the hermit to present their views, trying all their clever devices. Even if someone could speak of it, still he did not reach the place of the hermit's ultimate point. Moreover, although this matter is not in words and phrases, if not for words and phrases, it could not be distinguished. Haven't you heard it said: "The Path is fundamentally without words. We use words to reveal the Path"? Therefore the essential point in testing others is to know them intimately the minute they open their mouths.

The ancient man let down a word or half a phrase for no other purpose than to see whether or not you know that 'this matter exists.' He saw that the people did not understand; that is why he himself answered for them, "Because they did not gain strength on the road." See how what he says spontaneously accords with principles and meshes with the circumstances. When did he ever lose the essential meaning? The ancient Shih T'ou said, "When you receive words you must understand the source: don't set up standards on your own."

When people these days bump into it, they think that's enough. Though they get to it, what can be done about their fat headedness and confusion? When they come before an adept, he uses the three essential seals[a]—sealing space, sealing water, sealing mud—to test them. Then the adept sees whether the square peg is stuck in the round hole with no way to come down.

When the time comes where, will you search to look for one here with the same attainment and realization? If it's a person who knows that 'this matter exists,' then open your heart and convey the message. What is there that can be wrong? If you don't meet with such a person, then keep it to yourself for the time being.

Now I ask all of you: the staff is something patchrobed monks ordinarily use; why then does the hermit say that they didn't gain strength on the road? Why does he say that when the ancients got here, they didn't consent to stay here? In truth, though gold dust is precious, when it falls into your eyes it becomes a blinding obstruction.

Master Shan Tao of the Stone Grotto, when he was subject to the persecution (of 845) would always take his staff and show it to the assembly saying, "All the buddhas of the past are thus, all the buddhas of the future are thus, all the buddhas of the present are thus."

One day in front of the monk's hall Hsueh Feng held up his staff and showed it to the crowd saying, "This one is just for people of medium and low faculties." At the time there was a monk who came forward and asked, "When you unexpectedly encounter someone of the highest potential, then what?" Feng picked up his staff and left. Yun Men said, "I'm not like Hsueh Feng when it comes to breaking up confusion." A monk asked, "How would you do it, Teacher?" Yun Men immediately hit him.

Whenever you study and ask questions, there aren't so many things to be concerned with. (Concerns arise) because outside you perceive that mountains and rivers and the great earth exist; within you perceive that seeing, hearing, feeling, and knowing exist; above you see that there are various buddhas that can be sought; and below you see that there are sentient beings who can be saved. You must simply spit them all out at once: afterwards, whether walking, standing, sitting, or lying down, twenty-four hours a day, you fuse everything into one. Then, though you're on the tip of a hair, it's as broad as the universe; though you dwell in a boiling cauldron or in furnace embers, it's like being in the land of peace and happiness; though you dwell amidst gems and jewels in profusion, it's like being in a thatched hut. For this kind of thing, if you are a competent adept, you get to the one reality naturally, without wasting any effort.

The hermit saw that no one could reach his depths, so again he pressed them saying, "In the end, how is it?" Again they couldn't deal with him. He himself said, "With my staff across my shoulder, I pay no heed to people—I go straight into the myriad peaks." Again, what is the meaning of this? Tell me, what place is he pointing to as his whereabouts? Undeniably, there are eyes in his words, but his meaning is outside the words. He gets up by himself, he falls down by himself; he lets go by himself, he gathers up by himself.

Haven't you heard: The venerable Yen Yang met a monk on the road. He raised his staff and said, "What's this?" The monk said, "I don't know." Yen Yang said, "You don't even recognize a staff?" Again he took his staff and poked the ground saying, "Do you recognize this?" The monk said, "No, I don't." Yen Yang said, "You don't even recognize a hole in the ground?" Again, he put his staff across his shoulder and said, "Do you understand?" The monk said, "I don't understand." Yen Yang said, "With my staff across my shoulder, I pay no heed to people—I go straight into the myriad peaks." When the ancients got here, why didn't they agree to stay here?

Hsueh Tou has a verse which says:

Who,
Confronting the situation,
Brings it up without deception;
Such a person is rare:
He destroys the steep lofty peaks,
He melts down the mysterious subtlety.
The double barrier has been wide open:
Adepts do not return together.
The Jade Rabbit—now round, now partial
The Golden Raven seems to fly without flying. [b]
Old Lu doesn't know where he's going—
To go along together as before with white clouds
*   and flowing streams.*

Why did I say, "If you see cheeks on the back of his head, don't go along with him"? As soon as you make a comparative judgment, you're in the demon cave of the mountain of darkness making your living. If you can see all the way through and your faith is thoroughgoing, then naturally a thousand or ten thousand people won't be able to trap you or do anything about you. When pushed or pressed, you will kill or give life spontaneously.

Hsueh Tou understood the hermit's meaning when he said, "I go straight into the myriad peaks." At that point he begins to make his verse. If you want to know where this is at, look at Hsueh Tou's verse.

VERSE

Dust and sand in his eyes, dirt in his ears,
   **Blocked up with tons of dirt. What limit is there to the*
      confusion? There are other such people. *
He doesn't consent to stay in the myriad peaks.
   **Where will you go? But say, what scene is this?* *
Falling flowers, flowing streams, very vast.
   **A good scene. With the lightning flash intellect, if you*
      vainly toil tarrying in thought, look to the left—a

thousand lives; look to the right—ten thousand eons. *
Suddenly raising my eyebrows (to look)—where has he gone?
  ***Right beneath your feet another pair of eyes is given to
  you. From the beginning he's just been right here.
  Have you cut off the hermit's footsteps? Although it's
  like this, it's still necessary to get to this realm to
  begin to attain. I'll hit, saying, "Why is he just right
  here?"*

COMMENTARY

Hsueh Tou versifies very well: he has a place to turn around in
and doesn't stick to one corner. Immediately he says, "Dust
and sand in his eyes, dirt in his ears." This one line praises the
hermit of Lotus Flower Peak. When patchrobed monks get
here, they have nothing above to cling to or venerate, and
below they have no personal selves: at all times they are like
fools and dunces. Haven't you read of Nan Ch'uan saying,
"Among men of the Path, those that are like fools and dullards
are hard to come by." Ch'an Yueh's poem says, "I often recall
Nan Ch'uan's fine words/Such fools and dullards are indeed
rare." Fa Teng said, "What man knows the meaning of this? He
makes me think back to Nan Ch'uan." Nan Ch'uan also said,
"The seven hundred eminent monks (at the Fifth Patriarch's
place) were all men who understood the Buddhist Teachings.
There was only Workman Lu who didn't understand the Buddhist Teachings. He just understood the Path: that's why he
obtained the Patriarch's robe and bowl." Tell me, how far apart
are the Buddhist Teachings and the Path?
  Hsueh Tou brought up this saying of Nan Ch'uan's and said,
"Sand can't get in his eyes, and water can't get in his ears. If
there is a fellow whose faith is thoroughgoing and who can
hold fast, he isn't deceived by others. (For such a man) what a
bunch of meaningless noises are the verbal teachings of the
buddhas and patriarchs! So I invite you to hang up your bowl
and bag, break your travelling staff, and just become an unconcerned man of the Path."
  Hsueh Tou also said, "Mount Sumeru can be put in his eyes,
the waters of the great ocean can be put in his ears. There is a
kind of fellow who accepts people's haggling discussions and

the verbal teachings of the buddhas and patriarchs like a dragon reaching the water, like a tiger taking to the mountains. He must pick up his bowl and bag and put his staff across his shoulder. He too is an unconcerned man of the Path."

Hsueh Tou also said, "Neither way will do; after all, there is no connection."

Among the three unconcerned men of the Path (that Hsueh Tou has described), if you would choose one man to be your teacher, the correct choice is this kind of cast iron fellow. Why? Whether he encounters environments of evil or of wonders, to him what he faces is all like a dream. He doesn't know there are six senses, nor does he know there is sunrise and sunset. Even if you get to this realm, you must not cling to the cold ashes of a dead fire, you must not plunge into the flood of darkness. You still must have a way to turn around before you attain. Haven't you read of an ancient saying, "Don't cling to the greenness of the strange plants on the cold cliff. If you cut off the white clouds, the source is not marvellous."

Thus the hermit of Lotus Flower Peak said, "It's because they didn't gain strength on the road." To get it you simply must go into the myriad peaks. But say, what is being called "the myriad peaks"?

Hsueh Tou just likes him saying, "With my staff across my shoulder, I pay no heed to people—I go straight into the myriad peaks." Therefore he comes out with the verse. But tell me, where does he go? Is there anyone who knows where he goes?

"Falling flowers, flowing streams, very vast." Falling flowers in profusion, flowing streams vast, endless. For the lightning flash mind, what is before the eyes?

"Suddenly raising my eyebrows to look—where has he gone?" Why doesn't Hsueh Tou know where he's gone either? It's just like me raising my whisk just now: tell me, where is it now? If all of you people can see, you're studying with the hermit of Lotus Flower Peak. If not, go back to your places and try to investigate and observe carefully.

TRANSLATOR'S NOTES

a.   The three seals: Sealing mud, for the lower sort, who considers that something has been attained and leaves traces. Sealing water, for the middling sort, for whom there is something attained and the understanding mind still remains, but who leaves no traces. Sealing space, for the superior ones, who attain without attainment and leave no traces.

b.   The Jade Rabbit is the moon; the Golden Raven is the sun.

Pai Chang's Sitting Alone on Ta Hsiung Mountain

CASE

A monk asked Pai Chang, "What's the extraordinary affair?"[1]
Chang said, "Sitting alone on Ta Hsiung Mountain."[2]
The monk bowed;[3] Chang thereupon hit him.[4]

NOTES

1. There's an echo in the words. He demonstrates his ability in a phrase. He flabbergasts people. Though this monk has eyes, he's never seen.
2. His awesome majestic air extends over the whole country. The one standing and the one sitting both are defeated.
3. A clever patchrobed monk! There still is such a man who wants to see such things.
4. Chang is a competent teacher of our school: why does he not speak much? The imperative is not carried out vainly.

COMMENTARY

He has the eye to face situations and not heed danger or death. Thus it is said, "How can you catch tiger cubs without entering the tiger's lair?" Pai Chang was ordinarily like a tiger with wings. Nor does this monk shun birth and death: he dares to grab the tiger's whiskers and asks, "What's the extraordinary affair?" This monk too has eyes. Pai Chang immediately took up the burden with him saying, "Sitting alone on Ta Hsiung Mountain." The monk then bowed. Patchrobed monks must be able to discern the meaning before the question.

This monk's bowing was not the same as ordinary bowing: he had to have eyes before he could do this. He didn't spill all his guts to others. Though they knew each other, they acted like they didn't.

As for "A monk asked Pai Chang, 'What's the extraordinary affair?' Chang said, 'Sitting alone on Ta Hsiung Mountain.' The monk bowed; then Chang hit him": observe how when they let go, they both do so at once, and when they gather back, they wipe away the tracks and obliterate the traces. But say, when the monk bowed right then, what was his meaning? If you say it was good, then why and for what did Pai Chang then hit him? If you say it was no good, what was wrong about his bowing? When you get here, you must be able to tell right from wrong, distinguish initiate from outsider, and stand on the summits of a thousand peaks, to begin to understand.

This monk's bowing was like grabbing the tiger's whiskers: he was just contending for a pivotal position. Fortunately there's an eye on Pai Chang's forehead and a talisman behind his elbow, shining through the four quarters and profoundly discerning oncoming winds. Therefore he immediately hit the monk. If it had been someone else, he wouldn't have been able to handle the monk. The monk met mind with mind, conveyed intention with intention: that is why he bowed.

Nan Ch'uan said, "Last night at midnight, Manjusri and Samantabhadra came up with views of Buddha and Dharma. I gave them each twenty blows and sentenced them to be hemmed in by twin iron mountains." At the time Chao Chou came forward and said, "Who should take your beating, Teacher?" Nan Ch'uan said, "Where was my fault?" Chou bowed.

Masters of our school do not idly observe how the other takes action. The moment they are in charge of the situation and bring it into play, they are naturally leaping with life.

My late teacher Wu Tsu would often say, "It's like coming to grips in the front lines." I'm always telling you simply to cut off seeing and hearing, form and sound, all at once—then you'll be able to hold fast and act with mastery. Only then will you see Pai Chang. But tell me, how about when letting go? Look at Hsueh Tou's verse:

VERSE

In the realm of the patriarchs gallops the heavenly colt.
> ** (Such a man) is born once in five hundred years.
> Among a thousand or ten thousand people there's one
> or a half. The son (Pai Chang) takes up the father's (Ma
> Tsu's) work. *

*Among expedients rolling out and rolling up are not the same
path—*
> **Already so before the words. Pai Chang gains inde-
> pendence: it's a matter of his adepts' methods. *

*In a flash of lightning or sparks struck from stone he retains
the ability to change with circumstances.*
> **He came head-on, turning to the left, turning to the
> right. Do you see where Pai Chang helps people or
> not? *

How laughable—a man comes to grab the tiger's whiskers!
> **He deserves thirty blows. Where there's a great re-
> ward, there must be a valiant man. He doesn't avoid
> losing his body and his life. I leave this move to
> you . . . *

COMMENTARY

Hsueh Tou can see all the way through: thus he can come out
with the verse. The heavenly colt runs a thousand miles in a
day, runs back and forth and up and down, gallops as though
flying: thus he is called the heavenly colt. Hsueh Tou is prais-
ing Pai Chang—in the territory of the patriarchs he runs from
east to west and from west to east, a single coming, a single
going, free in all directions, totally without the slightest hindrance, just like the heavenly colt. He was well able to gallop:
only thus can we see how free he is. This is because he attained
Ma Tsu's great ability and great function.

Haven't you heard? A monk asked Ma Tsu, "What is the
great meaning of the Buddhist Teachings?" Tsu then hit him
and said, "If I didn't hit you, all the people in the world would
be laughing at me." Again, the monk asked, "What is the

meaning of the Patriarch's coming from the West?" Tsu said, "Come here and I'll tell you." The monk approached and Tsu boxed his ears saying, "Six listeners don't draw the same conclusions (as to what was said.)" Observe how Ma Tsu attained the great independence in such fashion: within the gate of expedients, sometimes he rolls out, sometimes he rolls up. Sometimes the rolling out isn't in the rolling up, sometimes the rolling up isn't in the rolling out. Sometimes rolling out and rolling up both aren't there. Hence the saying, "On the same path but not in the same groove."

Hsueh Tou says, "In a flash of lightning or sparks struck from stone he retains the ability to change with circumstances." This praises the monk for being like sparks struck from stone, like the brilliance of a flash of lightning— it's just a matter of a bit of changing with the situation. Yen T'ou said, "Turning away from things is superior; pursuing things is inferior. In battle each man occupies a pivotal position." Hsueh Tou said, "The wheel of potential has never turned. If it turns, it surely must go both ways." And if it can't be turned, what's the use? Even powerful men must know a little of changing with circumstances. People these days just offer (their teacher) their true feelings and get their nostrils pierced by him. What end will there be?

This monk was able in the midst of lightning flashes and sparks to retain the ability to change with the situation, so he bowed. Hsueh Tou says, "How laughable—a man comes to grab the tiger's whiskers!" Pai Chang was like a tiger—how laughable that this monk went to grab the tiger's whiskers.

Yun Men's The Body Exposed, The Golden Wind

POINTER

Ask one, answer ten. Raise one, understand three. Seeing the rabbit he looses the falcon—he uses the wind to fan the flame—he doesn't spare his eyebrows.

This I leave aside for the moment. How is it when entering the tiger's lair? To test I'm citing this old case: look!

CASE

A monk asked Yun Men, "How is it when the tree withers and the leaves fall?"[1]

Yun Men said, "Body exposed in the golden wind."[2]

NOTES

1. What season is this? When the family breaks up, the people perish; when the people perish, the family breaks up.
2. He holds up the sky and supports the earth. He cuts nails and shears through iron. Clean and naked, bare and purified. Walking with even steps through the blue sky.

COMMENTARY

If you can comprehend here, then you begin to see where Yun Men helped people. Otherwise, if you still can't, as before you'll be pointing to a deer and calling it a horse: your eyes are blind, your ears are deaf. Who arrives at this realm?

Tell me, do you think Yun Men answered the monk's question, or do you think he was harmonizing with him? If you say he answered his question, you are wrongly sticking to the zero point of a scale. If you say he harmonized with him, this has nothing to do with it. Since it's not this way, ultimately, how is it? If you can see all the way through, patchrobed monks' nostrils are not worth a pinch. Otherwise, if you still can't, as before you'll plunge into the ghost cave.

In general, to uphold and establish the vehicle of our sect, you must take up the burden with your entire being and not fear for your eyebrows, you must stretch out in the tiger's mouth and allow others to pull you back and forth and drag you down. If you're not like this, how will you be able to help people?

This monk posed a question that was indeed dangerous and lofty. If you look at him in ordinary terms, he just seems to be a monk involved in idle concerns. If you go by the traditions of patchrobed monks, when you go into his life line and look, then he undeniably has something marvellous about him. But say, when the tree withers and the leaves fall off, whose realm is this? In Fen Yang's scheme of eighteen kinds of questions, this is called "a question to test the host." It is also called "a question that uses things."

Yun Men did not stir a hairsbreadth, but just said to him, "Body exposed in the golden wind." He answered most wondrously, and without presuming to turn his back on the monk's question either. Since his question had eyes, Yun Men's answer too was straight to the point. An ancient said, "If you want to attain Intimacy, don't ask with a question." If you really know someone, you know what he's getting at as soon as he mentions it. If you go to the vein of Yun Men's words to look, you've immediately gone wrong. It's just that in his phrases Yun Men was often wont to provoke people's emotional interpretations. If I made up emotional interpretations to understand him, I wouldn't avoid being bereft of my successors.

Yun Men liked to ride the thief's horse to pursue the thief in this way. Haven't you heard: a monk asked him, "What is that which is not within reach of thought?" Men said, "Impossible for cognition to fathom." This monk asked, "How is it when the tree withers and the leaves fall?" Men said, "Body exposed in the golden wind." In his words he unstoppably seizes and cuts off the essential bridge and doesn't let ordinary or saintly through. You must understand how Yun Men raises one and illuminates three, raises three and illuminates one. If you go to his three phrases to seek, then you're pulling an arrow out of the back of your head. In a single phrase of Yun Men's, three phrases are inevitably present: the phrase that contains heaven and earth, the phrase that follows the waves and pursues the currents, and the phrase that cuts off the myriad streams. (What he says) is naturally exactly appropriate. But tell me, of the three phrases, which one does Yun Men use to receive people? Try to discern this.

The verse says:

VERSE

Since the question has the source,
> **Hsueh Tou profoundly discerns the oncoming wind. The arrow is not shot in vain.**

The answer too is in the same place.
> **How could there be two? Yun Men is like a bell waiting to be struck. His efforts are not expended excessively.**

Three phrases should be distinguished:
> **Above, between, below. Which phrase is his answer here? First you must comprehend outside of the three phrases.**

An arrowpoint flies far into the void.
> **On target! It's gone by. Hitting, striking. The arrow flies past Korea.**

Over the great plains—chilling windblasts howling, wailing,
> **Throughout the heavens, all over the earth. Do you feel your hairs standing on end? He's let go.**

In the eternal sky—intermittent misty rains.
> **The winds are great, the waters vast. Above your heads, boundless vastness; below your feet, boundless vastness.**

Haven't you seen the traveller sitting so long at Shao Lin, who hasn't returned?
> **Here's another dunce. He's gotten others involved. The Yellow River flows turbid from its source.**

Tranquil up on Bear Ears Mountain, a single gathering.
　**Open your eyes and you see, shut your eyes and you*
　see too. Making a living in the ghost cave. Your eyes
　are blind, your ears are deaf. Who arrives at this
　*realm? You don't avoid smashing your gap-teeth.**

COMMENTARY

The ancient man Shih T'ou said, "When you receive words, you must understand the source. Don't set up standards on your own." The ancient man's words were not empty talk. Hence it is said, "In general to ask about this affair you must have some knowledge of right and wrong. If you don't know noble from base behavior, if you can't recognize pure and defiled, if you let your mouth speak at random, what will be the gain?"

Whenever one utters words and spews out breath, it must be like clamps, like tongs, it must have hooks and chains, it must have unbroken continuity. This monk's question had the source meaning; Yun Men's answer was also this way. Yun Men always taught people with three phrases (in one): this is his ultimate pattern.

Hsueh Tou's verse on this case is similar in kind to his verse on the (eighty-second) case, about Ta Lung. "Three phrases should be distinguished." Three phrases are inevitably present in each phrase of Yun Men's. If you can distinguish them, then you penetrate beyond the three phrases. "An arrowpoint flies far into the void." He shot it so far that you must set your eyes on it quickly to catch sight of it. And if you can see it clearly, you can open out the universe in a single phrase.

At this point the verse is completed, but Hsueh Tou has extra talent so he opens out and says, "Over the great plains—chilling windblasts howling, wailing/In the eternal sky—intermittent misty rains." Tell me, is this mind or is this object? Is this mysterious or is this wondrous? An ancient said, "The truth of things is not hidden—from ancient times till now it's always been obvious."

The monk asked, "What's it like when the tree withers and the leaves fall?" Yun Men said, "Body exposed in the golden wind." Hsueh Tou's intent was just to create a single environment. What's in front of your eyes right now, the whistling wind, is either the southeast wind or the northwest wind. It will be all right only if you understand Hsueh Tou's meaning this way. If you go further and understand it as Ch'an or Tao, this has nothing to do with it.

"Haven't you seen the traveller sitting so long at Shao Lin, who hasn't returned?" Before he returned to the West Bodhidharma sat facing a wall for nine years, utterly silent. But say, is this "the tree withers, the leaves fall"? Is this "body exposed in the golden wind"? If here all past and present fools and sages, sky, earth, and the great world are all fused into one, then you will see how Yun Men and Hsueh Tou really helped people.

"Tranquil up on Bear Ears Mountain, a single gathering." Bear Ears Mountain is Shao Lin on Sung Shan near the Western Capital. In front and behind, the mountains are clustered thickly by the thousands. Where will all of you people see? Do you see where Hsueh Tou helps people? Even if you do, this is still the spirit tortoise dragging his tail (leaving traces).

Nan Ch'uan's Truth That's Never Been Spoken

CASE

Nan Ch'uan went to see Master Nirvana of Pai Chang (Mountain.)

Chang asked, "Have all the sages since antiquity had a truth that they haven't spoken for people?"[1]

Ch'uan said, "They have."[2]

Chang said, "What is the truth that hasn't been spoken for people?"[3]

Ch'uan said, "It's not mind, it's not buddha, it's not any thing."[4]

Chang said, "You said it."[5]

Ch'uan said, "I am just thus. What about you, Teacher?"[6]

Chang said, "I am not a great man of knowledge either: how would I know whether it has been spoken or not?"[7]

Ch'uan said, "I don't understand."[8]

Chang said, "I've already spoken too much for you."[9]

NOTES

1. A master should know. It stands like a wall ten thousand fathoms high. Does Chang feel his teeth falling out?

2. He's fallen into the weeds. Why so brash? Then there is such a thing!

3. Look how his hands are flustered, his feet frantic. He adds error to error. Just try and ask!

4. As it turns out he suffers defeat. After all he indulges quite a bit.

5. Don't explain it all for him: Let him go wrong his whole life. Chang shouldn't speak this way to him.

6. Fortunately he has a place to turn around. With the long, he's long; with the short, he's short. When the reasoning is superior, he goes to it.

7. Look how his hands are flustered, his feet frantic. He hides his body but reveals his shadow. He acts totally dead. There are thorns in the soft mud. Though he acts like this, how could he swindle me?

8. He can only act this way. Luckily he doesn't understand. If you understand I'll immediately break your head open! Fortunately this fellow is just this way.

9. Adding frost on top of snow. Why the dragon's head and snake's tail?

COMMENTARY

At this point he doesn't use "it's mind" or "it's not mind," nor does he use "not mind" or "not not mind." Even though from head to foot he doesn't have one hair of his eyebrows, still, he's gotten somewhere. Meditation Master Shou calls "it's mind" a revealing-explanation and "it's not mind" a concealing-explanation.

This Master Nirvana is Meditation Master Fa Cheng. Formerly he dwelled as retired abbot in the western hall at Pai Chang: (he had the monks) clear fields for him and (in return) he preached the great meaning for them.

At this time Nan Ch'uan had already seen Ma Tsu, but he was going around to various places to settle (what's right) and pick out (what's wrong.)

When Pai Chang posed this question it was indeed very difficult to respond to. He said, "Have all the sages since antiquity had a truth that they haven't spoken for people?" If it had been me, I would have covered my ears and left. Look at this old fellow's scene of embarrassment. If an adept had seen him asking this way, he would have been able to see through him immediately. But Nan Ch'uan just went by what he had seen, so he said, "They have." This was indeed brash.

Pai Chang then added error to error and followed up behind saying, "What is the truth that hasn't been spoken for people?" Ch'uan said, "It's not mind, it's not buddha, it's not any thing." Greedily gazing at the moon in the sky, this fellow has lost the pearl in the palm of his hand. Chang said, "You said it." Too bad—he explained in full for Nan Ch'uan. At the time I would have simply brought my staff down across his back to get him to know real pain.

Although it was like this, you tell me, where did he say it? According to Nan Ch'uan's view, it's not mind, it's not buddha, it's not any thing, it's never been spoken. So I ask all of you, why did Pai Chang nevertheless say, "You said it"? And there aren't any tracks or traces in Nan Ch'uan's words. If you say he didn't say it, then why did Pai Chang talk like this?

Nan Ch'uan was a man who could shift and get through, so after this he pressed Pai Chang and said, "I am just thus. What about you, Teacher?" If it had been anyone else, he wouldn't have been able to explain. But Pai Chang was an adept: his answer is undeniably extraordinary. Immediately he said, "I am not a great man of knowledge either: how would I know whether it has been spoken or not?" Nan Ch'uan then said his "I don't understand." He said "I don't understand" while actually he did understand: this is not genuine not understanding. Pai Chang said, "I've already spoken too much for you." But tell me, where did he speak?

If they had been two fellows playing with mud balls, both would have been covered with slime. If both were adepts, they were like bright mirrors in their stands. In fact in the beginning both were adepts; in the end they both let go. If you're a fellow with eyes, you'll judge them clearly. But say, how will you judge them?

Look at Hsueh Tou's verse:

VERSE

Patriarchs and Buddhas never helped people.
> ***Each guards his own territory. If you have standards, hang onto standards. If you keep even a single word in your mind, you go to hell fast as an arrow.* *

Patchrobed monks present and past running neck and neck.
> ***Having worn out your straw sandals, break your staff and hang up your bowl and bag.* *

When the bright mirrors are on their stands, the range of images differs.

> ****They've fallen, they've broken. Come smash the mirror and I'll meet with you.***

One by one they all face south and see the northern dipper.
> ****Do you see me astride the buddha hall going out through the mountain gate? In Korea they've gone up to the hall; in China they haven't yet beaten the drum.***

The dipper handle is hanging down.
> ****You still don't know where it comes down. Where is it?***

There's no place to seek.
> ****Blind men! Too bad! The cup falls to the ground, the plate shatters to pieces.***

When you pick up your nostrils, you lose your mouth.
> ****Where did you get news of this? After all, it's so, so I strike!***

COMMENTARY

Old Shakyamuni appeared in the world and in forty-nine years never said a single word. Beginning from the Land of Brilliance, ending at the river Hiranyavati, and for all the time in between, he never spoke a single word. Tell me, was such talk speaking or not? Right now it fills the Dragon Palace and fills the Oceanic Treasurehouse—how can this not be speaking? Haven't you heard Lord of the Mountain Hsiu say:

> The buddhas have not appeared in the world:
> Forty-nine years of talk.
> Bodhidharma didn't come from the West:
> Shao Lin has a wondrous secret.

Again it's said:

> The buddhas have not appeared in the world,
> Nor is there any truth to be given to people.
> They just were able to observe the hearts of living beings,
> Responding to their ills according to circumstances,
> Giving medicines and dispensing prescriptions.

Thus we have the twelve part teaching of the Triple Vehicle.

In fact from ancient times till now, the patriarchs and buddhas have never spoken for people. This very not helping people deserves thoroughgoing investigation. I always say, though I were to add a phrase as sweet as honey, when properly viewed it's just poison. If you bring down your staff across their backs and strike as soon as they blurt something out and push them away, only then are you helping people on an intimate level.

"Patchrobed monks present and past running neck and neck." Everywhere they go they ask questions about is and is not, about buddhas and patriarchs, about facing upwards and facing down. Though they act like this, if they haven't arrived at this realm, they can't do without this questioning.

"When the bright mirrors are on their stands, the range of images differs." With just this one line you can distinguish clearly. An ancient said, "The myriad forms are all the impression of the single truth." Again it's said, "The myriad forms are all perfect within this." The great teacher Shen Hsiu said:

The body is the tree of enlightenment,
The mind is like a bright mirror.
Constantly take care to wipe it clean:
Don't let it be defiled with dirt and dust.

(The Fifth Patriarch) said that Shen Hsiu was still outside the gate.[a] When Hsueh Tou talks this way, tell me, is he inside or outside the gate?

You people, each of you has an ancient mirror. All the myriad forms—long, short, square, round—each and every one appears in it. If you go to the longness or shortness to understand, in the end you'll never be able to find it. This is why Hsueh Tou said, "When the bright mirrors are on their stands, the range of images differs."

Instead you must "All face south and see the northern dipper." When you're facing south why are you nevertheless to look at the northern dipper? You'll see where Pai Chang and Nan Ch'uan met only if you can understand this way. These two lines (the third and fourth of the verse) praise Pai Chang pressing and pressing again. Chang said, "I am not a great man of knowledge either: how would I know whether it has been spoken or not?"

At this point Hsueh Tou's verse has come down into dead water. Fearing people would misunderstand he turned around and picked it up himself, saying, "The dipper handle is hanging down right now before your eyes: where else will you go to look for it? As soon as you pick up your nostrils you lose your mouth." Hsueh Tou has picked up the nostrils and lost the mouth.[b]

TRANSLATOR'S NOTES

a. The Fifth Patriarch Hung Jen asked the members of his congregation to submit verses demonstrating their attainment, so that he could choose his successor and pass on the robe and bowl. Of the more than seven hundred disciples, none felt he could outdo Shen Hsiu, who was considered the foremost among them: thus only Shen Hsiu offered a verse. The Fifth Patriarch praised his verse and had it written on a wall for the congregation to learn and recite. Hui Neng, an illiterate workman in the congregation, happened to hear Shen Hsiu's verse being recited: knowing that Shen's verse reflected a lack of true understanding, he had a boy write another verse on the wall:

Fundamentally enlightenment is not a tree,
Nor is the mind-mirror a mirror.
From the beginning there hasn't been a single thing—
What's the use of wiping away dust?

When the Fifth Patriarch saw this, he made as if to disapprove, so that the monks of his congregation would not become jealous of Hui Neng, a layman and a barbarian. He came secretly to Hui Neng and handed on the robe and bowl to him, sealing him as the Sixth Patriarch.

b. This means to gain one thing, but at the same time to lose something else equally vital.

Ta Sui's It Goes Along with It

POINTER

When fish swim through, the water is muddied; when birds fly by, feathers drop down. He clearly discriminates host and guest, he penetratingly distinguishes initiate and outsider, just like a bright mirror in its stand, like bright pearl in the palm of the hand. When a native comes, a native is reflected; when a foreigner comes, a foreigner is reflected. The sound is obvious, the form is evident. But say, why is it like this? As a test I'm citing this old case: look!

CASE

A monk asked Ta Sui, "The conflagration at the end of the eon sweeps through and the universe is totally destroyed. I wonder, is this one destroyed or not?"[1]
Sui said, "It is destroyed."[2]
The monk said, "If so, then this goes along with it."[3]
Sui said, "It goes along with it."[4]

NOTES

1. What thing is "this one"? No one on earth can get ahold of this phrase. He scratches in advance, anticipating the itch.
2. An iron hammer head with no handle-hole is thrown down in front of him. He's lost his nostrils. Before he opens his mouth, he's already thoroughly exposed.
3. Immeasurably great men whirl around in the stream of words. After all he misunderstands.
4. The first arrow was still light but the second arrow was deep. Just this is what so many people cannot find. When the water rises, the boats ride high; with a lot of mud, the buddha image is big. If you say "It goes along with that," where is it? If you say that it doesn't go along with that, then what? I'll hit!

187

COMMENTARY

Master Fa Chen of Ta Sui was a successor of Meditation Master Ta An. He was from Yen T'ing county in Tung Ch'uan (in Szechuan). He called on more than sixty men of knowledge.

Formerly he was the keeper of the fire in Kuei Shan's congregation. One day Kuei Shan asked him, "You have been here several years, yet you still don't know how to pose a question, so I can see what's what with you." Sui said, "What questions would you have me ask to be right?" Kuei Shan said, "Since you don't understand, ask, 'What is buddha?'" Sui covered Kuei Shan's mouth with his hand. Shan said, "Later you will not even find anyone to sweep the ground."

Later Ta Sui returned to Tung Ch'uan. At first he stayed by the road on P'eng K'ou Mountain, making tea and waiting on travellers for about three years in all. Only later did he finally appear in the world and open a mountain monastery, dwelling at Ta Sui.

There was a monk who asked him, "The conflagration at the end of the eon sweeps through and the universe is totally destroyed. I wonder, is this one destroyed or not?" This monk just came up with a question based on an idea in the Teachings. In the Teachings it says, "Formation, abiding, destruction, emptiness.ᵃ When the age of the triple cataclysm occurs, the destruction reaches to the third meditation heaven." Basically this monk did not know the meaning of this statement.

Tell me, what is "this one"? People often make emotional interpretations and say, "'This one' is the fundamental nature of sentient beings." Sui said, "It is destroyed." The monk said, "If so, then this goes along with it." Sui said, "It goes along with it." As for "this one," so many people make emotional interpretations and are unable to find it. If you say that it goes along with it, where is it? If you say it doesn't go along with it, then what? Haven't you heard it said: "If you want to attain Intimacy, don't ask with questions"?

Later there was a monk who asked Master of the Mountain Hsiu, "The conflagration at the end of the eon sweeps through and the universe is totally destroyed. I wonder, is this one destroyed or not?" The Master of the Mountain said, "It's not destroyed." The monk said, "Why isn't it destroyed?" The Master said, "Because it's the same as the universe." Both "it's destroyed" and "it's not destroyed" obstruct people fatally.

Since the monk didn't understand what Ta Sui said, he inevitably had this matter on his mind. He took this question straight to Mt. T'ou Tzu in Shu Chou. T'ou Tzu asked him, "Where did you come here from?" The monk said, "From Ta Sui in western Szechuan." T'ou Tzu said, "What did Ta Sui have to say?" The monk then recounted the former conversation. T'ou Tzu burned incense and bowed and said, "In western Szechuan there's an ancient buddha who has appeared in the world. As for you, hurry back to him!" The monk returned to Ta Sui but Sui had already passed on. What an embarrassment for this monk!

Later there was a monk at the T'ang court named Ching Tsun who said of Ta Sui:

> *Clearly there is no other truth—*
> *Who says (the Fifth Patriarch) approved the southerner Neng?*
> *The one phrase "it goes along with it"*
> *Makes a patchrobed monk run over a thousand mountains.*
> *A cricket who's cold cries in the piled up leaves;*
> *By night a ghost bows to the lamp before a crypt.*
> *The humming stops outside the lonely window,*
> *He wanders back and forth, unable to overcome his regret.*

Hence Hsueh Tou draws on two of these lines afterwards to make his verse.

Right now, you shouldn't make the understanding that it is destroyed, and you shouldn't make the understanding that it is not destroyed. In the end, how will you understand? Quick, set your eyes on it and look!

VERSE

In the light of the conflagration ending the age he poses his question—
> **What is he saying? He's already gone wrong.*
The patchrobed monk is still lingering within the double barrier.
> **If you squash this man how can he be saved? A hundred layers, a thousand levels.*

How touching—for a single phrase, "going along with that,"
  **The world's patchrobed monks all make this sort of
    judgment. It's not even worth it for a thousand
    phrases, for ten thousand phrases. What's hard about
    cutting off his footsteps?*
*Intently he travelled out and back alone for ten thousand
  miles.*
  **His active consciousness is very chaotic. He stumbled
    by without knowing it. He's just wearing out his
    straw sandals.*

COMMENTARY

Hsueh Tou takes charge of the situation and comes out with
his verse: in his words there's a place where he shows himself.

"In the light of the conflagration ending the age he poses his
question/The patchrobed monk is still lingering within the
double barrier." From the first this monk's question was concerned with "it is destroyed" and "it is not destroyed"—this is
the double barrier. A person who has attained has a place to
show himself whether he is told "it is destroyed" or he is told
"it is not destroyed."

"How touching—for a single phrase, 'going along with
that,'/Intently he travelled out and back alone for ten thousand
miles." This versifies this monk taking the question to T'ou
Tzu, then returning again to Ta Sui—this can indeed be called
being intent for ten thousand miles.

TRANSLATOR'S NOTES

a.   According to traditional Buddhist cosmology, these are the four
     phases an eon goes through.

Chao Chou's Big Turnips

CASE

A monk asked Chao Chou, "Teacher, I have heard that you have personally seen Nan Ch'uan. Is this true or not?"[1]

Chou said, "Chen Chou produces big turnips."[2]

NOTES

1. A thousand hearings are not as good as one seeing. He's pressing him. Everyone has a pair of eyebrows.
2. He holds up the sky and supports the earth. He cuts nails and shears through iron. The arrow flies past Korea.

COMMENTARY

This monk too is one who has studied for a long time: inevitably, there's an eye in his question. Nevertheless, Chao Chou is an adept: he immediately says to him, "Chen Chou produces big turnips." This can be called flavorless talk that blocks off people's mouths. This old fellow Chao Chou greatly resembles a thief who steals in broad daylight. As soon as you open your mouth he immediately plucks your eyes out.

If you are an exceptional brave-spirited fellow, then amidst sparks struck from stone and the brilliance of a lightning flash, as soon as you hear it raised, you immediately get up and go. Otherwise, if you linger in thought and hold back your potential, you won't avoid losing your body and your life.

In judging this case the wild sage Ch'eng of Kiangsi called it "asking about the east, answering about the west." He said that Chao Chou didn't answer and didn't climb into his trap. If you understand this way, how will you get it?

Jurist Yuan said, "These are words (affording) a glimpse from the side." This is contained in the *Nine Belts*. If you understand this way, you haven't even seen it in dreams, and, moreover, you're dragging Chao Chou down.

Some say, "Chen Chou has always produced big turnips, as everyone in the country knows. Chao Chou had called on Nan Ch'uan: everyone in the country knows this. That's why, when this monk nevertheless still asked whether or not Chao Chou had personally seen Nan Ch'uan, Chao Chou said to him, 'Chen Chou produces big turnips.'" But this has nothing to do with it.

If you don't understand in any of these ways, in the end, how will you understand? Chao Chou has his own road through the skies.

Haven't you heard: A monk asked Chiu Feng, "Teacher, I have heard that you personally saw Yen Shou. Is this true or not?" Feng said, "Is the wheat in front of the mountain ripe yet or not?" This matches exactly what Chao Chou said to the monk: both are like iron hammer heads with no handle holes.

Old man Chao Chou is an unconcerned man. If you question him carelessly he immediately snatches your eyes out. If you're a man who knows what is, you'll chew it carefully and swallow it. If you're a man who doesn't know what is, it will be like swallowing a date whole.

VERSE

Chen Chou produces big turnips—
> **Everyone knows. Just avoid saying so. Each time it's brought up it's brand new.*

All the patchrobed monks in the country seize upon this as a principle;
> **Nevertheless, it isn't so. Who has a use for these idle words, this long-winded speech?*

They only know it as extending from past to present:
> **Half open, half closed. (They're as numerous) as hemp or millet. In ancient times it wasn't so; right now it isn't so either.*

How can they discern that the swan is white and the crow is black?
> **The whole capacity comes through. What's long is long

*of itself; what's short is short of itself. Those who can
recognize this are precious. Still, it's not worth discerning.**

Thief! Thief!
   ***Bah! It's none other: Hsueh Tou himself is wearing
   stocks, giving evidence of his crime.**

He has snatched patchrobed monks' nostrils.
   ***He's pierced them, snapped them around.**

COMMENTARY

"Chen Chou produces big turnips." If you seize upon this as
the ultimate principle, you've already gone wrong. When the
ancients joined hands and ascended high mountains, they
couldn't avoid the laughter of onlookers. People all know that
this answer of Chao Chou's is a statement of the ultimate
principle, though in the end they don't know where the ultimate principle is. That's why Hsueh Tou says, "All the patchrobed monks in the country seize upon this as a principle/They
only know it as extending from past to present/How can they
discern that the swan is white and the crow is black?"

Though they know that both ancient people and modern
people have answered this way, when have they ever been able
to distinguish expert from naive? Hsueh Tou says, "To really
understand you must discern the swan's whiteness and the
crow's blackness within the sparks Chao Chou strikes from
stone, within the brilliance of Chao Chou's lightning flash."

At this point the verse on this case is completed, but Hsueh
Tou brings out his own opinion and goes to the place leaping
with life to tell you more: "Thief! Thief!/He has snatched
patchrobed monks' nostrils." All the buddhas of past, present,
and future are thieves too; the successive generations of patriarchs are thieves too. They were well able to snatch away
people's eyes. As for the skill not to blunder, I only approve
Chao Chou. But tell me, how does he make a good thief?
"Chen Chou produces big turnips."

Ma Ku Carrying his Ring-Staff

POINTER

Move, and a shadow appears; become aware, and ice forms. Yet if you don't move and are not aware, you will not avoid entering into the wild fox cave.

If you can penetrate thoroughly, trust completely, without a hair of blinding obstruction, you'll be like a dragon finding water, like a tiger taking to the mountains. Let go, and even tiles and pebbles emit light; hold still, and even real gold loses its color.

The ancients' public cases could not avoid being roundabout, but tell me, what were they discussing? To test, I cite this. Look!

CASE

Ma Ku, carrying his ring-staff,[a] went to Chang Ching. He circled the meditation seat three times, then shook his staff once and stood there upright.[1] Chang Ching said, "Correct. Correct."[2] (Hsueh Tou added a word, saying "Wrong!")[3]

Ma Ku also went to Nan Ch'uan: he circled the meditation seat three times, shook his staff once and stood there upright.[4] Nan Ch'uan said, "Incorrect. Incorrect."[5] (Hsueh Tou added a word, saying, "Wrong!")[6]

Ma Ku then said, "Chang Ching said 'Correct'; why do you say 'Incorrect,' Master?"[7]

Nan Ch'uan said, "Chang Ching is correct; it's you who are incorrect.[8] This is what is turned about by the power of the wind; in the end it breaks down and disintegrates."[9]

NOTES

1. He bursts forth in the same fashion as (Yung Chia did at) Ts'ao Ch'i; he startles the heavens and stirs the earth.

194

2. He's washing a clod of earth in the mud. He completely fools everyone. What talk is this? A donkey-tethering stake.
3. It won't do to let him go. There's still a move to go.
4. As before, he's washing a clod of earth in the mud: again he bursts forth; but though the frog leaps, he can't get out of the basket.
5. Why not accept it? He kills the man without blinking an eye. What is this talk?
6. It won't do to let the error go.
7. Where is the master? This fellow from the beginning grasps people's words; he has broken down considerably.
8. Good! When one kills someone, one must see blood; when one helps someone, he should do his utmost for them. How many people has he deceived?
9. After all, Ma Ku is trapped by Nan Ch'uan.

COMMENTARY

When the ancients travelled on foot to visit the monasteries everywhere, they only had this matter on their minds: they wanted to discern whether the old teacher on the carved wood seat possessed eyes or did not possess eyes. The people of old would stay if there was mutual agreement in a single word, and would leave if they did not agree in one word.

Observe how that Ma Ku went to Chang Ching, circled the meditation seat thrice, shook his staff once, and stood there upright. Chang Ching said, "Correct. Correct." (To use) the sword that kills people, the sword that brings people to life, one must be a master in his own right.

Hsueh Tou says "Wrong!" This falls on both sides, but if you go to either side to understand, you will not see Hsueh Tou's meaning. Ma Ku stood there upright, but tell me, what did he do it for? Why does Hsueh Tou then say "Wrong"? Where is it that he is wrong? Chang Ching said "Correct. Correct." Where is it that he is wrong? Hsueh Tou seems to be sitting there reading the judgment.

Ma Ku, carrying this word "correct," then went to see Nan Ch'uan. As before, he circled the meditation seat thrice, shook his staff once, and stood there upright. Ch'uan said, "Incorrect. Incorrect." For the sword that kills people, the sword that gives people life, one must be a master of the school in his own right. Hsueh Tou says "Wrong!" Chang Ching said, "Correct. Correct." Nan Ch'uan said "Incorrect. Incorrect." Are these the same or different? The first says "Correct": why is he also wrong? The latter says "Incorrect": why is he too wrong? If you attain understanding at Chang Ching's saying, you will not even be able to save yourself: if you attain understanding at Nan Ch'uan's saying, you can be the teacher of Buddhas and Patriarchs. Even so, patchrobed monks must prove it themselves before they will understand; do not just accept other people's verbal explanations.

Since Ma Ku's question was the same, why did one say "correct" and one say "incorrect"? If one is a thoroughly competent master, a man who has attained great liberation, he must have a life apart (from "correct" and "incorrect"). One who has not forgotten mind and objects will certainly be stuck over these two sides. If you want to clearly understand past and present, and cut off the tongues of everyone in the world, first you must clearly apprehend these two "wrongs." This is so because Hsueh Tou wants to bring up the livingness. If you are a fellow with blood under your skin, you will naturally not go to the words and phrases to create interpretations; you will not go to a donkey-tethering stake to make up theories. Some people say that Hsueh Tou utters these two "wrongs" on behalf of Ma Ku, but what has that got to do with it? They are far from knowing that the ancient's added comments lock off the essential gate; this side is correct, and that side is also correct, but ultimately they do not remain on either of the two sides. The librarian Ch'ing said, "Holding his staff, circling the meditation seat, 'correct' and 'incorrect' are both wrong. The reality of it does not lie herein."

Have you not read how Yung Chia came to Ts'ao Ch'i and saw the Sixth Patriarch? He circled the meditation seat three times, shook his staff once, and stood erect. The Patriarch said, "A monk is to have three thousand modes of dignity, and eighty-four thousand refinements of conduct; where have you come from, O Worthy, that you bear such great self-conceit?" Why did the Sixth Patriarch say that he bore great self-conceit? This one did not say "correct" or "incorrect"; "correct" and "incorrect" are both donkey-tethering stakes. There is only Hsueh Tou who, pronouncing two "wrongs," has thus attained something.

Ma Ku said, "Chang Ching said 'correct'; why do you say

'incorrect,' Master?" This old fellow didn't spare his eyebrows; he indulged considerably—Nan Ch'uan said, "Chang Ching is correct; it's you who are incorrect." One might say that Nan Ch'uan, seeing a rabbit, released a falcon. Librarian Ch'ing said, "Nan Ch'uan was excessively doting; whereas he might have let the matter rest with 'incorrect,' still he went on to bring out the other's fault for him, saying, 'This is what is turned around by the power of the wind; eventually it breaks down and disintegrates.'" The *Sutra of Complete Enlightenment* says, "This here body of mine is a combination of four major elements. The so-called defiled form of hair, nails, teeth, skin, flesh, sinews, bone, marrow, and brains, all return to earth. Saliva, tears, pus, and blood, all return to water. Warm breath returns to fire, and movement returns to wind. When the four major elements each separate, where could this illusory body be?"[b] When that Ma Ku circled the meditation seat holding his staff, already this was what is turned around by the power of the wind; eventually it breaks down and disintegrates. Then tell me, ultimately where does the matter of discovering the source of mind lie? When you get here, you must be a man made of cast iron in order to realize it.

Have you not read how the scholar Chang Ch'o called on the Ch'an Master Tsang of Hsi T'ang? He asked, "Do the mountains, rivers, and earth exist or not? Do the Buddhas of the three times exist or not?" Tsang said, "They exist." Chang Ch'o the scholar said, "Wrong!" Tsang said, "Who have you seen?" Ch'o said, "I have seen the Master of Ching Shan: whatever I asked about, Ching Shan said it doesn't exist." Tsang said, "What family do you have?" Ch'o said, "I have a wife and two children." Tsang then asked, "What family does Ching Shan have?" Ch'o said, "Ching Shan is an Ancient Buddha; you should not slander him, Master." Tsang said, "Wait till you are like Ching Shan; then I'll tell you everything doesn't exist." Chang Ch'o just bowed his head. A competent teacher of the sect always wants to melt the sticking points, remove the bonds, pull out the nails and draw out the pegs for people; he should not just hold to one side, but sweep to the left and turn to the right, sweep to the right and turn to the left.

Just observe how Yang Shan went to Chung Yi's place to thank him for ordination. When Yi saw him coming, he beat his hand on the meditation seat and said, "Wa wa." Yang Shan thereupon stood to the east; then he stood to the west, and then stood in the middle. After that, once he had finished giving thanks for ordination, he then retreated and stood there. Chung Yi said, "Where did you get this concentration?" Yang Shan said, I took it off the Seal of Ts'ao Ch'i." Chung Yi said, "You tell me, whom did Ts'ao Ch'i use this concentration to receive?" Yang Shan said, "To receive the Overnight Enlightened Guest (Yung Chia)." Yang Shan too asked Chung Yi, "Master, where did you get this concentration?" Chung Yi said, "I got this concentration at Ma Tsu's place." Isn't such conversation by fellows who raise one and understand three, see the root and pursue the branches?

Lung Ya said to his community, "Those people who penetrate the study must pass beyond buddhas and patriarchs. (Tung Shan) the Master of Hsin Feng said, 'If you see the verbal teachings of the buddhas and patriarchs as if they were your mortal enemies, only then will you have the qualifications for penetrating the study.' If you can't pass beyond them, then you will be deceived by the patriarchs and buddhas." At the time there was a monk who asked, "Do the patriarchs and buddhas have any intention to deceive people or not?" Lung Ya said, "Tell me, do rivers and lakes have any intention to obstruct people or not?" He went on to say, "Although rivers and lakes have no intention to obstruct people, it's just that people now can't cross them. Therefore, rivers and lakes after all become barriers to people. You cannot say that rivers and lakes do not obstruct people. Although the patriarchs and buddhas have no intention to deceive people, it's just that people now cannot pass beyond them. So patriarchs and buddhas after all deceive people. Again, you cannot say that patriarchs and buddhas do not deceive people. If one can pass beyond the patriarchs and buddhas, this person surpasses the patriarchs and buddhas. Still, one must completely realize the intent of the patriarchs and buddhas: only then can one be equal to those transcendent people of old. If you have not yet been able to pass through, if you study the Buddhas and study the Patriarchs, then you'll have no hope of attaining even in ten thousand aeons." The monk also asked, "How can I be able to avoid being deceived by the Patriarchs and Buddhas?" Lung Ya said, "You must be enlightened yourself." When you get here, you must be like this.

Why? When you help someone, you should do your utmost for them; when you kill someone, you must see their blood. Hsueh Tou is such a man, so he dares to pick up and play.

VERSE

This "wrong" and that "wrong"—
  **Be careful of your eyebrows! Still, this is acting according to the imperative. 'In heaven and on earth, I alone am the sole honored one.'*
It is important not to take them away.
  **A pair of hammerheads without holes; even the great Compassionate One with a thousand hands cannot lift them up. If you take them away, Reverend, you'll receive thirty blows.*
Then the waves are calm in the four seas,
  **No one in the world dares to move. East, West, South, North, all have the same family style. Recently there has been much rain and water.*
The hundred rivers return to the ocean tide.
  **Clean and naked, peace and tranquility in one's own house is realized; the sea being at rest, the rivers are clear.*
The standard of the ancient rod is lofty, with twelve gates;
  **How does it compare with this one! There is no eye on the staff. It is important to avoid going to the staff to make a living.*
In each gate there is a road, empty and desolate.
  **There's not a single thing. It belies your everyday life. If you look, you'll go blind.*
Not desolate—
  **After all. Luckily there's a place to turn around in. Already blind—so I strike!*
The adept should seek medicine without disease.
  **Once having died, you won't come back to life again. Why are you fast asleep all day long? Why search through the heavens and grope over the earth?*

COMMENTARY

This verse resembles the case of Te Shan seeing Kuei Shan: first (Hsueh Tou) adds two turning words, piercing it through on one string; then he produces his verse. "This 'wrong' and that 'wrong'—it is important not to take them away." Hsueh Tou's meaning is that the "wrong" here and the "wrong" there should absolutely not be taken away; if you take them away, you're mistaken. It is necessary to add this double "wrong" like this, and thus you realize right away: "The waves are calm in the four seas, the hundred rivers return to the ocean tide." How pure the wind, how bright the moon! If you gain understanding at these two "wrongs," you will no longer have the slightest concern: mountains are mountains, rivers are rivers, what is long is of itself long, and what is short is of itself short; one breeze every five days, one rainfall every ten days. That is why he said, "The waves are calm in the four seas; the hundred rivers return to the ocean tide."

The latter part eulogizes Ma Ku carrying his staff; "The standard of the ancient rod is lofty, with twelve gates." The people of old used a whip for a rod; patchrobed monks use the staff as a rod. The "ancient rod" is the staff; the pure wind is higher than the twelve vermillion gates. If you can understand this two-fold "wrong," then your staff will emit light; even the ancient rod can't be put to use. An Ancient said, "If you know the staff, your life's study is finished." It is also said, "This is not displaying form and vainly holding to things; the Tathagata's precious staff has personally left its traces." This is in the same category. When you get here, through all upsets and downfalls, throughout all times, you attain great freedom.

"In each gate there is a road, empty and desolate." Although there is a road, it is just that it's empty and desolate. At this point Hsueh Tou feels that he has indulged, so he goes on to strike a smashing blow for you; although it is so, still there is a place which is not desolate. Even if you are an adept, when you have no illness, still you must seek a bit of medicine to take.

TRANSLATOR'S NOTES

a.   Monks' travelling staffs were often adorned with six or twelve rings at the top; these symbolize the causal chain: ignorance—

volition—consciousness—name and form—the six senses—contact — sensation — love — grasping — existence — birth — old age and death. The jingling of the rings is supposed to constantly remind the travelling monk of his condition. The "twelve gates" mentioned in the verse also may be taken to refer to these.

b. Fugai regards this passage from the *Sutra of Complete Enlightenment* as a later addition; in the Chinese style, it was customary to insert "footnotes" right into a text.

Elder Ting Stands Motionless

POINTER

The ten directions cut off, a thousand eyes abruptly open; when one phrase cuts off all streams, myriad impulses cease. Are there after all any who will die together and be born together? The public case is completely manifest, but if you cannot get it together, please look at the Ancients' trailing vines:

CASE

Elder Ting asked Lin Chi, "What is the great meaning of the Buddhist Teaching?"[1]
    Chi came down off his meditation seat, grabbed and held (Ting), gave him a slap, and then pushed him away.[2] Ting stood there motionless.[3] A monk standing by said, "Elder Ting, why do you not bow?"[4] Just as Ting bowed,[5] he suddenly was greatly enlightened.[6]

NOTES

1. So many people are at a loss when they get here. There is still this here. Oh, why is he so feeble-minded?
2. Today he caught him. He's kind as an old woman. No patchrobed monk in the world can leap clear.
3. He's already fallen into the ghost's cave. He's already stumbled past. He can't avoid losing his nostrils.
4. On neutral ground there is a man who can see through it all. He has completely attained the other's power. When someone dies in the eastern house, the people of the western house help them mourn.
5. He uses diligence to make up for his incompetence.

6. Like finding a lamp in the darkness; like a poor man finding a jewel. (Still, this is) adding error upon error. But tell me, what did Elder Ting see, that he bowed?

COMMENTARY

See how he was; directly leaving, directly entering, directly going, directly coming—this indeed is the True School of Lin Chi, to have such dynamic function. If you can go all the way through, then you can overturn the sky and make it into earth, attaining the use of the endowment yourself.

Elder Ting was such a fellow; slapped once by Lin Chi, as he bowed and rose he immediately understood the ultimate. He was a man of the North, extremely simple and direct. Once he had attained this, he did not appear in the world thereafter. He thenceforth made complete use of the ability of Lin Chi; unavoidably his sharpness came through. One day on the road he met Yen T'ou, Hsueh Feng, and Ch'in Shan. Yen T'ou asked, "Where do you come from?" Ting said, "Lin Chi." T'ou said, "Is the teacher in good health?" Ting said, "He has already passed on." T'ou said, "We three were going especially to pay him our respects; our good fortune is shallow and thin, that we find he has 'returned to silence.' When the teacher was living, what did he have to say? Elder, please cite one or two examples for us." Ting then cited one day when Lin Chi instructed the assembly by saying, "In the lump of red flesh there is a true man with no station: he is always going in and out through the gates of your senses; those who have not witnessed proof of this, look! Look!" At the time there was a monk who came forth and asked, "What is the true man with no station?" Lin Chi immediately grabbed him and said, "Speak! Speak!" The monk hesitated, whereupon Lin Chi pushed him away and said, "The true man of no station: what a piece of crap he is!" Then Lin Chi returned to the abbot's room.

(Hearing this,) Yen T'ou unconsciously stuck out his tongue (in awe). Ch'in Shan said, "Why did he not say, 'Not a true man of no station'?" Ting grabbed him and said, "How far apart are 'a true man of no station' and 'not a true man of no station'? Speak quickly! Speak quickly!" Ch'in Shan did not speak; his face turned yellow and green. Yen T'ou and Hsueh Feng approached and bowed and said, "This novice does not know good from bad; he has offended you, Elder: we hope you will be merciful and forgive his error." Ting said, "If not for you two old fellows, I would have choked this bed-wetting sprite to death."

Again, once in Chen Chou, as he was returning from a vegetarian feast, he rested on a bridge. There he met three lecturing monks. One of them asked, "What is the meaning of 'Where the river of Ch'an is deep, you must plumb the very bottom'?" Ting grabbed him and was about to throw him off the bridge, when the other two lecturers frantically tried to rescue him, saying, "Stop! Stop! He has offended you, Elder, but we hope you will be merciful." Ting said, "If not for you two, I would have let him plumb the very bottom."

Observe such methods of his. This is wholly the dynamic function of Lin Chi. Also take a look at Hsueh Tou's verse:

VERSE

Tuan Chi's entire ability continues in his footsteps;
   **The Yellow River is muddy from the very source. The son inherits the father's work.*

Brought forth, why should it remain at ease?
   **Where is it? What can be done about the fact that there is such a man? Can a man without feet or hands attain that, or not?*

The great spirit lifted his hand without much ado
   **He scares people to death. A little boasting. Striking once with a whisk, I will not test any further.*

And split apart Flower Mountain's ten million layers.
   **The whole world appears at once. It's fallen.*

COMMENTARY

Hsueh Tou eulogizes, "Tuan Chi's entire ability continues in his footsteps; brought forth, why should it remain at ease?" Only Lin Chi alone continued in the footsteps of Huang Po's[a] great ability and great function. Once it is brought forth, it does not admit of any attempt to discuss it; if you hesitate, you'll immediately fall into the realm of ignorance.[b]

The *Surangama Sutra* says, "Just as when I put my finger on it, the Ocean Seal emits light, if you arouse your minds even momentarily, anxiety over the material world will come up first."

"The great spirit lifted his hand without much ado, and split apart Flower Mountain's ten million layers." The great spirit (of the Yellow River) had great supernatural powers; with his hand he broke open Mt. T'ai Hua and let the water of the Yellow River run through. Elder Ting's feeling of doubt was like a massive mountainous heap; struck once by Lin Chi, immediately he found the tiles had scattered, the ice had melted.

TRANSLATOR'S NOTES

a.   Tuan Chi was a posthumous title of Huang Po Hsi Yun, Lin Chi's teacher.

b.   "Realm of ignorance" is used here to translate "the heaps and the elements"; that is, form, feeling, perception, volition, and consciousness (the five heaps), and the six sense organs, their objects, and their associated consciousnesses (the eighteen elements). These are considered identical to fundamental ignorance.

Ministry President Ch'en Sees Tzu Fu

POINTER

He does not discriminate east from west, nor distinguish south from north, from morning till evening, evening till morning; but can you say he is fast asleep? Sometimes his eyes are like comets, but can you say he is wide awake? Sometimes he calls south north; but tell me, is he mindful or mindless? Is he a man of the Way or an ordinary man? If you can pass through here, for the first time you will know the ultimate, and then you will know how the ancients were so or not so. But tell me, what time is this? To test, I cite this. Look!

CASE

Ch'en Ts'ao, ministry president, went to see Tzu Fu. When Fu saw him coming, he immediately drew a circle.[1] Ts'ao said, "My coming here like this has already missed the point; how much more so, to go on and draw a circle!"[2] Fu thereupon closed the door of his room.[3]

Hsueh Tou said, "Ch'en Ts'ao has just one eye."[4]

NOTES

1. This is a spirit recognizing a spirit, a thief recognizing a thief. If he were not relaxed and at ease, how could he discern this fellow? But do you see the adamantine cage?[a]
2. Today he has encountered a man who's fast asleep. This old thief!
3. A thief does not break into a poor man's house. He has already entered the other's cage.
4. Hsueh Tou has an eye on his forehead. But tell me, where does his meaning lie? He should give him another circle. Clearly. Ch'en

206

Ts'ao has a dragon's head, but a snake's tail; at that time he should have given Tzu Fu such a thrust that he would have had no gate to advance through, and no road to retreat upon. But tell me, what further pressure could he bring to bear on him?

COMMENTARY

Ministry president Ch'en Ts'ao was a contemporary of P'ei Hsiu and Li Ao.[b] Whenever he saw a monk come, he would first invite him to a meal, and would give him three hundred cash, wishing thereby to test the monk. One day Yun Men came; seeing him, Ch'en Ts'ao immediately asked, "I do not ask about what is in the Confucian books, and the twelve part teachings of the three vehicles have their own professors: what is the purpose of a patchrobed monk's journey on foot?" Yun Men said, "How many people have you asked?" Ts'ao said, "I am asking you right now." Yun Men said, "Leaving aside 'right now' for the moment, what is the meaning of the teachings?" Ts'ao said, "Yellow scrolls on red rollers." Yun Men said, "These are written words and letters: what is the meaning of the teachings?" Ts'ao said, "When the mouth wishes to speak of it, words flee; when the mind seeks affinity with it, thought vanishes." Yun Men said, "'When the mouth wishes to speak of it, words flee' is to refer to maintaining verbalization; 'when the mind seeks affinity with it, thought vanishes' is to refer to false conceptualization. What is the meaning of the teachings?" Ts'ao was speechless. Yun Men said, "I have heard it said that you read the *Lotus of Truth* scripture; is this true or not?" Ts'ao said, "True." Yun Men said, "In that scripture it says that all livelihood and productive labor are not contrary to the characteristics of reality. But tell me, in the heaven that is beyond thought and thoughtlessness,[c] right now how many people fall back from that position?"[d] Ts'ao again was speechless. Yun Men said, "Do not be so careless. A real monk abandons the three scriptures and five discourses[e] to enter a monastery; after ten or twenty years, he still can do nothing himself. So how could you, ministry president, be able to understand?" Ts'ao bowed and said, "I am at fault."

Also one day as (Ch'en Ts'ao) had climbed up in a tower with a group of officials, they looked out and saw several monks coming. One of the officials said, "Those people approaching are all Ch'an monks." Ts'ao said, "No, they're not." The official said, "How do you know they're not?" Ts'ao said, "Wait till they come near, and I will put them to a test for you." When the monks reached the foot of the tower, Ts'ao suddenly called out, "O Elders!" The monks raised their heads. Ts'ao said to the group of officials, "Didn't you believe what I said?" There was only one man, Yun Men, whom Ch'en Ts'ao could not expose.

Ch'en Ts'ao had seen Mu Chou. One day he went to call upon Tzu Fu. When Fu saw him coming, he immediately drew a circle. Tzu Fu was an honorable adept in the Kuei-Yang lineage; he always liked to use the meeting of perspectives[f] to deal with people. When he saw the ministry president Ch'en Ts'ao coming, he thereupon drew a circular figure. But what could he do? Ts'ao was after all an adept, and didn't submit to the deceit of others; he knew himself how to make a test—he said, "My coming here like this has already missed the point; how is it worth going on to draw a circle?" Fu closed the door. This kind of public case is called "discerning the target within the words, concealing ability within a phrase." Hsueh Tou says, "Ch'en Ts'ao has just one eye." Hsueh Tou may be said to have an eye on his forehead. But tell me, where does his meaning lie? (Tzu Fu) should have produced another circular figure; but if he always acted like this, how could a patchrobed monk benefit others? Now I ask you, if you were Ch'en Ts'ao at that moment, what could you have said in order to avoid Hsueh Tou's saying that he has just one eye? Thus Hsueh Tou kicks over everything and versifies:

VERSE

Round and round the jewel turns, ringing like jade—
     **With a three foot pole he tries to stir the Yellow River.*
     *Only the Blue-eyed Barbarian (Bodhidharma) could do
     it. Made of cast iron.**

Horses carry it, asses bear it; load it on an iron ship;
     **Why do you need so many for? What limit is there?*
     *I give it to you.**

Share it with an unconcerned traveller of sea and mountain.
   ***There is someone who has no need of it. If one is a real
   unconcerned traveller, he has no use for it. But you must
   be a traveller without concern before you will get it.**

When fishing for a tortoise, he lets down a cage-trap.
   ***Coming this way, going this way; none can escape.
   If it is a frog, what is the use of it? What's to
   be done about prawns, mussels, snails, and oysters?
   It is necessary to hook a tortoise.**

Hsueh Tou also said, "No patchrobed monk in the world can
   jump out."
   ***You too are inside it. All are buried in the same hole;
   but can you manage to jump out, your reverence?**

COMMENTARY

"Round and round the jewel turns, tinkling like jade: horses
carry it, asses bear it; load it on an iron ship." The beginning of
Hsueh Tou's poem just eulogizes the circle. If you can merge
with it, you'll be like a tiger with horns. This bit requires you
to have the bottom fall out of your bucket, your mental machi-
nations to come to an end; throw away gain and loss, right and
wrong all at once, do not make your understanding in terms of
principle anymore, and do not understand it as a mysterious
wonder. Ultimately, how to understand? This must be carried
by horses, borne by asses, loaded on an iron ship. You will only
get it if you see it here. Anyplace else, it cannot be imparted: it
must be taken and shared with an unconcerned traveller of sea
and mountain. If you have the slightest bit of concern in your
belly, you will not be able to take it up properly. Here you must
be a person who is not affected by concerns or absence of concerns, by unpleasant feelings or pleasing situations, or by Buddhas or Patriarchs: only then can you take it up properly. If
there is any Ch'an to seek, any measure of profane or holy
feelings, you will certainly not be able to fully attain mastery.
But once you have attained mastery, how will you understand
his saying, "When fishing for a tortoise, he lowers a cage-trap"?
In fishing for tortoises, only a cage will do. That is why Feng
Hsueh said, "Used to fishing for whales, I scour the great

ocean; instead I'm disappointed by a frog crawling in the muddy sand." He also said, "O great tortoise, do not carry away the three mountains! I want to walk on the summit of P'eng Lai." Hsueh Tou also said, "No patchrobed monk in the world can leap out." If one is a great tortoise, he will not entertain the view of a patchrobed monk; if one is a patchrobed monk, he will not entertain the view of a great tortoise.

TRANSLATOR'S NOTES

a. The word for cage also means circle.

b. Like Ch'en Ts'ao, P'ei Hsiu and Li Ao were laymen who were adept at Ch'an. P'ei Hsiu was a student of Huang Po; Li Ao was a student of Yao Shan.

c. Or: "neither perception nor non-perception," *naivasamjnana-samjnanayatana*, the highest of the "four trances" which were cultivated by Buddhist mendicants since ancient times.

d. According to the Lotus Scripture, five thousand monks and nuns who thought they had attained nirvana got up and left when the Buddha began to preach the Lotus. They represent the lesser vehicle, whose devotees abide in detachment, without being able to detach from detachment itself.

e. According to the *Hekigan-Sho*, the three scriptures are the Hua Yen ("Flower Garland"), the Fa Hua ("Flower of Dharma," the Lotus), and the Nieh Pan (Nirvana) Scriptures; its list of the five discourses is redundant and thus incomplete, but it included the Wei Shih ("Consciousness Only"), Chi Hsin ("Arousal of Faith"), and the Ta Chih Tu Lun ("On the Great Perfection of Wisdom") Discourses.

f. Or: "meeting at objects," "concentration on objects." This refers specifically to circular figures, with or without characters added. Yan Shan especially is known for his use of these figures. The perspective of teacher and student meet in the object, and there's a special series of circular figures to represent this. Also, various phases and processes of Buddhist Teaching were represented symbolically in circles, figures, and words; no doubt at times these were used as meditation objects.

Yang Shan Asks "Where Have You Come From?"

CASE

Yang Shan asked a monk, "Where have you just come from?"[1]
  The monk said, "Mount Lu."[2]
  Yang Shan said, "Did you visit Five Elders Peak?"[3]
  The monk said, "I didn't get there."[4]
  Yang Shan said, "You never visited the mountain at all."[5]
  (Later,) Yun Men said, "These words were all for the sake of compassion; thus they had a conversation in the weeds."[6]

NOTES

1. Everyone in the world is the same. Still it is necessary to ask. (The monk) will inevitably construe it in the ordinary way.
2. A truthful man is hard to find.
3. He uses the wind to fan the fire. How could he have ever passed it by?
4. Take a step. A red face is not as good as honest speech. He seems to be at a loss.
5. Too much ado! He should be careful of his eyebrows. What is this old fellow's hurry?
6. The sword that kills people, the sword that gives people life. Two, three. If you want to know the mountain road, you must be the man who travels on it.

COMMENTARY

The point of testing someone is to know him intimately as soon as he opens his mouth. An Ancient said, "Immeasurably great people are turned about in the stream of speech." If you are one who has the eye on your forehead, as soon as it is being brought up, you immediately know where it comes down. See their one question, one answer; each is distinctly clear. Why did Yun Men then say that these words were all for the sake of compassion, so they had a conversation in the weeds? When that man of old gets here, he is like a clear mirror on its stand, like a bright jewel in the palm of the hand: when a foreigner comes, a foreigner is reflected, and when a native comes, a native is reflected. Not even a single fly could get past his scrutiny. But tell me, how is it that there was a conversation in the weeds for the sake of compassion? It was nevertheless dangerously steep; getting to this realm, only this fellow could hold up. This monk had personally come from Mount Lu; why did (Yang Shan) then say, "You have never visited the mountain"?

Kuei Shan one day asked Yang Shan, "When there are monks coming from various places, what do you use to test them?" Yang Shan said, "I have a way of testing." Kuei Shan said, "Try to show me." Yang Shan said, "Whenever I see a monk coming, I just lift up my whisk and say to him, 'Do they have this in other places?' When he has something to say, I just say to him, 'Leaving this aside for the moment, what about That?'" Kuei Shan said, "This has been the tooth and nail of our sect since time immemorial."

Haven't you read how Ma Tsu asked Pai Chang, "Where do you come from?" Chang said, "From down the mountain." Tsu said, "Did you meet anyone on the road?" Chang said, "Not at all." Tsu said, "Why did you not meet anyone at all?" Chang said, "If I had met anyone, I would mention it to you, teacher." Tsu said, "How could this have been happening?" Chang said, "I am at fault." Tsu said, "On the contrary, I am at fault."

Yang Shan's questioning the monk was just like these examples. At that time, when he said, "Did you ever get to Five Elders Peak?" if that monk had been a man, he would simply have said, "A disaster." Instead, he said, "I never got there." Since this monk was not an adept, why did Yang Shan not act according to the rule, so as to avoid the many complications that subsequently appeared? Instead he said, "You never visited the mountain." That is why Yun Men said, "These words were all for the sake of compassion, thus they had a conversation in the weeds." If it were a talk outside the weeds, then it would not be like this.

VERSE

Leaving the weeds, entering the weeds;
  **Above the head, vast expanse; below the feet,
  vast expanse. Half open, half closed. He is
  so, and I too am so.**

Who knows how to seek them out?
  **He has a single eye on his forehead. You do not
  know how to seek them out?**

White clouds, layer upon layer;
  **A thousand levels, a hundred layers. He puts
  another head on top of his head.**

Red sun, clear and bright.
  **It has broken through. Blind! If you lift up
  your eyes, you'll miss it.**

Looking to the left, there are no flaws;
  **Blind fellow! As before, there's nothing to
  be concerned about. Why are you displaying so
  much cleverness?**

Looking to the right, already old.
  One thought, ten thousand years. Gone past.

Have you not seen the man of Cold Mountain?
  A leper drags his companion along.

He travelled so swiftly;
  Still he's not fast.

Ten years he couldn't return,
  Where is he right now? It's obvious.

And forgot the road by which he came.
  **He has attained freedom. (Hsueh Tou) passes up
  the initiative, so (I'll) strike. Better not to
  act so lost.**

COMMENTARY

"Leaving the weeds, entering the weeds; who knows how to
seek them out?" Hsueh Tou after all knows where they are at;
when he gets there, with one hand he upholds, and with the

other hand he pushes down. "White clouds, layer upon layer; red sun, clear and bright." This is much like "Grasses in profusion, mist overhanging." At this point there is not even so much as a single hair that belongs to the ordinary, nor so much as a single hair that belongs to the holy. The whole world has never concealed it; each particular cannot cover it. This is what is called the realm of no-mind; when cold, it doesn't feel cold, and when hot it doesn't feel hot—the whole thing is one great gate of liberation. "Looking to the left, there are no flaws; looking to the right, already old."

Master "Lazy" Ts'an dwelt in seclusion in a stone grotto on Mount Heng. Emperor Su Tsung of T'ang heard of his name and sent an emissary to summon him. The emissary went to his grotto and made the announcement, "The Emperor has a command; you should rise and give thanks for his favor, Reverend." Just then Ts'an poked into his ox-dung fire, took out a baked yam and ate it; cold nose-water dripped from his chin. He did not answer at all. The emissary laughed and said, "I suggest that you wipe off that snot, Reverend." Ts'an said, "What leisure time do I have to wipe snot for a worldly man?" After all he never arose. The emissary returned and reported this to the Emperor. Su Tsung praised him highly. Someone so pure and calm, so clear and direct as this, is not at the disposal of others; he just holds still, as though made of cast iron. It is just like the case of Master Shan Tao, who after the purge never again became a monk; people called him "the stone-grotto worker." Whenever he tread the pestle, he forgot the movement of his footsteps. A monk asked Lin Chi, "What is the essential meaning of the stone grotto worker's forgetfulness of the movement of his footsteps?" Chi said, "Sunken in a deep pit."

Fa Yen's verse on Completely Perfect True Nature reads,

> When reason is exhausted, feelings and considerations are forgotten:
> How could there be any adequate comparison?
> Wherever I go there's the frosty night's moon;
> It falls as it may into the valley ahead.
> When the fruits are ripe, they are heavy with monkeys;
> The mountains go on so long, it seems I have lost my way;

*When I raise my head, there is some light remain-
   ing—*
Actually this is west of my dwelling place.

Hsueh Tou said, "Have you not seen the man of Cold Mountain? He travelled so swiftly: for ten years he couldn't return,
and forgot the road by which he came." In one of the Cold
Mountain Man's poems it says, "If you want a place to rest
your body, you can preserve it long on Cold Mountain. The
gentle wind blows in the dense pines; heard from nearby, the
sound is even better. Underneath there is a man with half-grey
hair furiously reading Huang-Lao.ᵃ For ten years he couldn't
return, and forgot the road he took when he came." Yung Chia
also said, "Mind is the organ, phenomena are the objects: both
are like flaws in a mirror. When the defilement of the flaws is
gone, only then does the light appear; when mind and
phenomena are both forgotten, nature is identical to reality."
When you get here, be like a fool, like a blockhead, and then
you will perceive this public case. If you do not reach this
realm, you will just be running around in the words; what end
will there ever be?

TRANSLATOR'S NOTES

a.   That is, the Taoist teachings: a book on internal medicine by the
     Yellow Emperor (Huang Ti) and the Tao Te Ching of Laotzu,
     explaining the way to long life.

The Dialogue of Manjusri and Wu Cho

POINTER

Determining dragons and snakes, distinguishing jewels and stones, separating the profound and the naive, to settle all uncertainty: if you haven't an eye on your forehead and a talisman under your elbow, time and again you will miss the point immediately. Right at this very moment seeing and hearing are not obscured; sound and form are purely real. Tell me, is it black? Is it white? Is it crooked? Is it straight? At this point, how will you discriminate?

CASE

Manjusri asked Wu Cho, "Where have you just come from?"[1]
Wu Cho said, "The South."[2]
Manjusri said, "How is the Buddhist Teaching being carried on in the South?"[3]
Wu Cho said, "Monks of the Last Age have little regard for the rules of discipline."[4]
Manjusri said, "How numerous are the congregations?"[5]
Wu Cho said, "Some three hundred, some five hundred."[6]
Wu Cho asked Manjusri, "How is it being carried on hereabouts?"[7]
Manjusri said, "Ordinary people and sages dwell together; dragons and snakes intermingle."[8]
Wu Cho said, "How numerous are the congregations?"[9]
Manjusri said, "In front, three by three; in back, three by three."[10]

NOTES

1. It is necessary to pose the question. There is still this news.
2. He sticks his head up from his nest in the weeds. Why should he hoist it on to his eyebrows? There is nothing outside the great vastness; why is there nevertheless a South?
3. If he asked someone else, a disaster would happen. It still lingers on his teeth and lips.
4. A truthful man is hard to find.
5. At that moment I would immediately give him a shout. With one nudge he pushes him over.
6. They are all wild fox spirits. After all he's let slip.
7. He's pushed! Immediately he turns the spear around and comes back with it.
8. He's suffered quite a loss. In fact his feet are frantic, his hands in confusion.
9. Give me back the words. Still he can't be let go.
10. Crazy words, insane talk. But tell me, how many are they? Even the Great Compassionate One with a thousand hands could not count them all.

COMMENTARY

When Wu Cho was visiting Mt. Wu T'ai, when he came to a place on the way where it was wild and rough, Manjusri produced a temple to take him in for the night. So he asked, "Where have you just come from?" Cho said, "The South." Manjusri asked, "How is the Buddhist Teaching being carried on in the South?" Cho said, "Monks of this Last Age have little regard for the rules of discipline." Manjusri asked, "How numerous are the congregations?" Cho said, "Some three hundred, some five hundred." Wu Cho then asked Manjusri, "How is it being carried on hereabouts?" Manjusri said, "Ordinary people and sages dwell together; dragons and snakes intermingle." Cho asked, "How numerous are the congregations?" Manjusri said, "In front, three by three; in back, three by three."

Then they drank tea; Manjusri held up a crystal bowl and

asked, "Do they also have this in the South?" Cho said, "No." Manjusri said, "What do they usually use to drink tea?" Cho was speechless. After all he took his leave and departed. Manjusri ordered Ch'un T'i the servant boy to see him to the gate. When they got to the portals of the gate, Wu Cho asked the boy, "Before, he said, 'In front three by three; in back, three by three'; how many is this?" The boy said, "O Worthy!" Cho responded "Yes?" The boy said, "How many is this?" Cho also asked, "What temple is this?" The boy pointed beyond the Vajrasattva; when Cho turned his head, the illusory temple and the boy had vanished completely out of sight: it was just an empty valley. Later that place was called the Vajra (Adamantine) Cave.

Later on a monk asked Feng Hsueh, "What is the Master of Ch'ing Liang Mountain?"[a] Hsueh said, "One phrase did not settle Wu Cho's question; to this very day he is still a monk who sleeps in the fields."

If you want to penetrate the peaceful equanimity of actual truth, so that your feet tread upon the real earth, go to Wu Cho's words to get attainment; then naturally though you stay in a cauldron of hot water or the embers of a stove, still you would not feel hot, and though you stay on cold ice, neither would you feel cold.

If you want to go through to use the solitary peril, the steep and sharp, like the Jewel Sword of the Diamond King, go to Manjusri's words to get attainment; then naturally water poured will not wet, and wind blowing cannot enter.

Have you not seen how Ti Tsang of Cheng Chou asked a monk, "Where have you just come from?" The monk said, "The South." Tsang said, "How is Buddhism there?" The monk said, "There is much deliberation." Tsang said, "How can that compare with us here sowing fields and having a lot of rice to eat?" Now tell me, is this the same as Manjusri's answer, or is it different? Some say that Wu Cho's answers were wrong, while in Manjusri's answers there is both snake and dragon, there is both the ordinary and the sage. What bearing does this have on it? Can you clearly discern three by three in front, three by three in back? The first arrow will still light; the second arrow went deep. Now tell me, how many is this? If you can pass through here, then a thousand phrases, ten thousand phrases, are only one phrase. If at this one phrase you can cut off and hold still, in the next moment you will reach this realm.

The thousand peaks twist and turn, the color of indigo.
But do you see Manjusri?

Who says Manjusri was conversing with him?
Even if it were Samantabhadra, I wouldn't pay any attention. He's already stumbled past.

It is laughable, "How many the people?" on Ch'ing Liang:
Tell me, what is he laughing at? It's already there before speaking of it.

In front three by three, and in back three by three.
Please observe it under your feet. There are thorns in the soft mud. The tea bowl falls to the ground, the dish breaks in seven pieces.

COMMENTARY

"The thousand peaks twist and turn, blue as indigo; who says Manjusri was conversing with him?" Some say that Hsueh Tou is just reciting it a second time, without ever eulogizing it. It is just like a monk asked Fa Yen, "What is a drop of water from the source of the Ts'ao stream?" Yen said, "A drop of water from the source of the Ts'ao stream." Also a monk asked Master Hui Chueh of Lung Ya, "How does fundamental purity and clarity suddenly give rise to mountains, rivers, and earth?" Chueh said, "How does fundamental purity and clarity suddenly give rise to mountains, rivers, and earth?" You cannot say either that these were just repetitions.

The One-Eyed Dragon of Min Ch'ao also versified the meaning of this, with the ability to cover heaven and earth; he said,

> Extending throughout the world is the beautiful monastery:
> The Manjusri that fills the eyes is the one conversing.
> Not knowing to open the Buddha-eye at his words,

(Wu Cho) turned his head and saw only the blue mountain crags.

"Extending throughout the world is the beautiful monastery." This refers to the illusory temple nestled in the weeds. This is what is called having the ability to carry out both the provisional and the real together. The Manjusri which fills the eyes is talking; if you don't know how to open the Buddha-eye at his words, when you turn your head you'll only see the blue mountain crags. At such a time, could you call it the realm of Manjusri, Samantabhadra,[b] or Avalokitesvara?[c] In essence it is not this principle. Hsueh Tou just changes Ming Ch'ao's usage; instead he has a needle and thread—"Ten thousand peaks twist and turn, blue as indigo." He does not run afoul of the point and hurt his hand. Within the phrase there is the provisional, there is the real; there is principle, there are phenomena. Who says Manjusri was conversing with him? They talked all night, but he didn't know it was Manjusri.

Later Wu Cho stayed on Mt. Wu T'ai and worked as a cook. Every time Manjusri appeared on the rice pot, Wu Cho lifted the rice stirrer and hit him. Still, this is drawing the bow after the thief has left.

This time, as soon as he said, "How is the Buddhist Teaching being carried on in the South?" he should have hit him right on the spine; then he would have gotten somewhere.

"It's laughable, 'How many are the people?' on Ch'ing Liang." There is a sword in Hsueh Tou's laughter. If you can understand what he's laughing about, you will see the other's saying, "In front three by three; in back three by three."

TRANSLATOR'S NOTES

a.   Ch'ing Liang ("Pure and Cool") was another name for Mt. Wu T'ai. One of the five holy mountains of China, it was traditionally thought to be the abode of Manjusri, who symbolizes wisdom and knowledge. The Vajra, or Diamond, is also a symbol of wisdom, because it can cut through everything, while itself being firm and indestructible.

b.   Samantabhadra, universal goodness, is the bodhisattva representing the ultimate principle.

c.   Avalokitesvara is the bodhisattva representing compassion.

Biographical Supplement

The following excerpts from the lives and sayings of the eminent Ch'an masters appearing in the main cases of *The Blue Cliff Record* are taken mostly from the classic Ch'an history *Ching Te Ch'uan Teng Lu* (briefly, *Ch'uan Teng Lu*, hereafter referred to as CTL), the "Record of the Transmission of the Lamp (compiled in) the Ching Te era (of the Sung dynasty, 1004)." Containing information on over six hundred Ch'an masters, the CTL usually gives only a few bare biographical facts such as birth, death, and enlightenment stories; most "biography" consists of dialogues, sayings and doings of the teachers. The CTL also includes three chapters of sermons, poems, and short writings. It is a standard Ch'an book and a primary source of many *kung an.*

Some material is also taken from the *Tsu T'ang Chi*, "Collection from the Halls of the Ancestors"; *Wu Teng Hui Yuan*, "Five Lamps Merged in the Source"; and *Ku Tsun Su Yu Lu*, "Records of Sayings of Ancient Venerable Adepts." (These will hereafter be referred to as TTC, WT, and KTS, respectively.)

The TTC antedates the CTL by about fifty years; though a much smaller collection, it contains a number of stories not found in CTL or later collections. The WT, a later and more extensive compilation, draws on five so-called "Lamp" records, including the CTL and its continuation, plus the *Kuang Teng Lu, Lien Teng Hui Yao,* and *P'u Teng Lu.* The title "Five Lamps" refers to these five source collections, but is also sometimes taken to refer to the five houses of classical Ch'an. The WT covers a longer period of time than CTL, and often contains more material on individual masters than does the former. Tenkei Denson, one of the main commentators consulted on *The Blue Cliff Record,* usually cites the WT as most detailed and authoritative.

The KTS contains extensive records of sermons and sayings of numerous Ch'an masters, and includes whole volumes which have been published as individual books, such as the *Lin*

221

Chi Lu, "Record of Lin Chi"; and the *Yun Men Kuang Lu,* "Extensive Record of Yun Men."

The order of the biographies is as follows:

Bodhidharma (case 1)
Pao Chih (cases 1, 67)
Chao Chou Ts'ung Shen (cases 2, 9, 30)
Ma Tsu Tao I (case 3)
Te Shan Hsuan Ch'ien (case 4)
Kuei Shan Ling Yu (cases 4, 24, 70)
Hsueh Feng I Ts'un (cases 5, 22, 49, 51)
Yun Men Wen Yen (cases 6, 8, 14, 15, 22, 27, 34)
Fa Yen Wen I (case 7)
Ts'ui Yen Ling Ts'an (case 8)
Pao Fu Ts'ung Chan (cases 8, 22, 23, 95)
Ch'ang Ch'ing Hui Leng (cases 8, 22, 23, 95)
Mu Chou Tao Tsung (case 10)
Huang Po Hsi Yun (case 11)
Tung Shan Shou Ch'u (case 12)
Pa Ling Hao Chien (cases 13, 100)
Ching Ch'ing (cases 16, 23, 46)
Hsiang Lin Teng Yuan (case 17)
Nan Yang Hui Chung (cases 18, 99)
Lung Ya Chu Tun (case 20)
Ts'ui Wei Wu Hsueh (case 20)
Lin Chi I Hsuan (cases 20, 32)
Chih Men Kuang Tso (cases 21, 90)
Hsuan Sha Tsung I (cases 22, 88)
Lotus Flower Peak Hermit (case 25)
Pai Chang Huai Hai (cases 26, 53, 70, 71, 72, 73)
Nan Ch'uan P'u Yuan (cases 28, 31)
Ta Sui Fa Chen (case 29)
Ma Ku Pao Che (case 31)
Chang Ching Huai Hui (case 31)
Tzu Fu Ju Pao (case 33)
Yang Shan Hui Chi (cases 34, 68)

LINEAGE OF MASTERS

Those appearing in the main examples of volume one of *The Blue Cliff Record* are marked by asterisks.

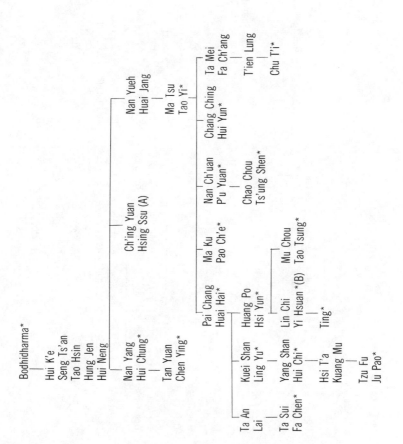

Bodhidharma*
Hui K'e
Seng Ts'an
Tao Hsin
Hung Jen
Hui Neng

Nan Yang Hui Chung*
Ch'ing Yuan Hsing Ssu (A)
Nan Yueh Huai Jang

Tan Yuan Chen Ying*

Ma Tsu Tao Yi*

Pai Chang Huai Hai*
Ma Ku Pao Ch'e*
Nan Ch'uan P'u Yuan*
Chang Ching Hui Yun*
Ta Mei Fa Ch'ang

Huang Po Hsi Yun*
Chao Chou Ts'ung Shen*
T'ien Lung

Mu Chou Tao Tsung*
Lin Chi Yi Hsuan*(B)
Chu T'i*

Ting*

Ta An Lai
Kuei Shan Ling Yu*

Ta Sui Fa Chen*
Yang Shan Hui Chi*

Hsi T'a Kuang Mu

Tzu Fu Ju Pao*

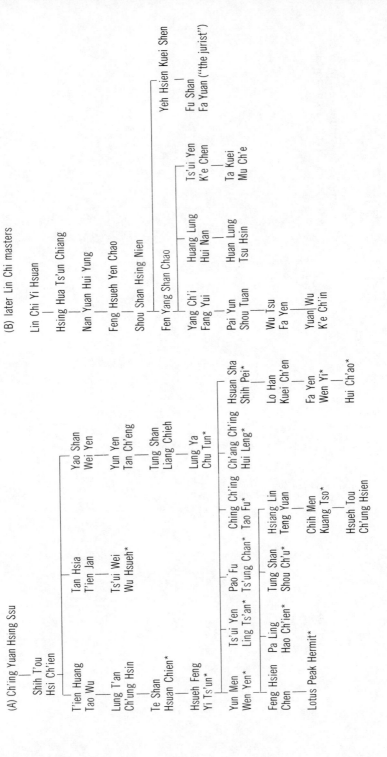

BODHIDHARMA (4–6 cent. A.D.)
CASE 1

Bodhidharma was a meditation master from southern India; by the time of *The Blue Cliff Record* his life was veiled in legend. Regarded as the first patriarch of Ch'an in China, most stories of Bodhidharma popular in Ch'an circles are what may be called illustrative history, and are used as teaching materials or guides to contemplation.

Bodhidharma did not associate with kings, did not translate any scriptures or found any temples, and transmitted his bequest to only a few successors. Though his immediate impact on the Buddhist world in China was not very great, he was influential enough locally to be opposed and assassinated. Although there were many meditation teachers in China in Bodhidharma's time, the Buddhist historian Tao Hsuan (7th century A.D.) wrote that Bodhidharma was one of only two teachers who founded continuous transmission lines.

Bodhidharma claimed to be over one hundred and fifty years old when he died. Many stories are told of him: popular legend has it, for example, that his legs fell off after sitting still for nine years; that tea plants first grew from his eyelids, which he cut off in anger after falling asleep during his nine year vigil; and that he introduced *kung-fu* combat techniques to the monks in Shao Lin monastery, to bridle aggressive tendencies and tone otherwise inactive bodies.

Bodhidharma's meeting with Emperor Wu of Liang (r. 502–549) may be part of the legend which grew up around the great teacher. In his youth Wu had mastered many branches of learning, and in 498 was appointed Inspector of Ying Chou (in Hunan); he later took advantage of internal disputes over the authority of the Ch'i dynasty, his employer, to rebel and set up his own kingdom in southern China, called Liang. Turning from warfare to culture, Wu lavishly patronized Confucianism, Taoism, and especially Buddhism, hiding from the responsibilities of sovereignty under the cloak of personal piety. Bodhidharma's blunt deflation of Emperor Wu's pretensions to sanctity and merit is emblematic of the independence of the Ch'an school; because Wu was deceived by outward forms and the concept of holiness, it is said that he did not understand Bodhidharma.

PAO CHIH (417/421–514)
CASES 1, 67

Pao Chih is recognized as a master of Ch'an; thus he is said to have "seen" Bodhidharma even though the two never met.* The *Chuan Teng Lu* (27) says,

"Meditation master Pao Chih was a man from Chin Ling (the area of Nanking, the southern capital). His surname was Shu. As a youth he left home and stayed in Tao Lin monastery and cultivated meditative concentration.

"In the beginning of the T'ai Shih era of Sung (465–472), suddenly he no longer dwelt in any fixed abode. He ate and drank without consideration of the hour of the day. His hair was several inches long. He walked barefoot, holding a staff; the staff was armed with dagger, scissors, and a mirror."

Scissors are a conventional Chinese metaphor for appointment and dismissal, promotion and demotion; a mirror is a Buddhist metaphor for clear awareness without biased views—like a mirror that reflects anything that comes before it. The record continues:

"Sometimes he wore one or two feet of silk. Even when not eating for several days, he had no appearance of hunger. Sometimes he might sing songs; his words seemed to be prophecies. The gentry and peasants alike did things for him.

"During the Yung Ming era of Ch'i, the Martial Emperor (r. 483–493) declared that the master was deluding the masses; so he had him captured and bound over to the prison at Chien K'ang.

"When it was morning, the people saw him going into the market place; but when an investigation was made, they found him in prison as before. The prefect of Chien K'ang reported the matter to the Emperor, who invited the master to dwell in the rear hall within the palace.

"The master stayed at the Flower Forest Manor. Suddenly one day he put on three cloth caps: it was not known where he had gotten them. All of a sudden the Prince of Yu Ch'ang, Wen Hui, and the Crown Prince died in succession. The Ch'i dynasty too was now at its last. Due to this, they imprisoned the master.

"When the Exalted Ancestor of Liang (the Emperor Wu of ex. I) assumed that rank, he sent down an imperial rescript stating,

'Master Chih's tracks are within the province of the defilements of the Dusts, but his spirit wanders in hidden tranquility. Water or fire could not burn or wet him; snakes or tigers
could not bother him or cause him fear. To speak of his enlightenment into the Principle, he is higher than a disciple of
Buddha; to talk about his mysterious obscurity, he is a lofty
one among the Escaped Immortals. How could we regulate him
according to the empty forms of the ordinary feelings of uninitiated people? Henceforth do not censor him again.' "

A few cryptic answers to imperial questions are attributed to
Pao Chih; they are recorded along with the interpretations of
"those who knew" among the court. In this case, his recognition of Bodhidharma as the bodhisattva of compassion is symbolic of the eye of the source.

"In the winter of 514, when his life was about to end, he
suddenly ordered the community to move the temple's statue
of the Adamantine Being and place it outside. And he said
privately to people, 'A bodhisattva is about to leave.'

"Before ten days had passed he died without illness."

*It was believed that Bodhidharma came to China around 520—after
Pao Chih had already died; internal evidence in *Hsu Kao Seng Chuan*
suggests that Bodhidharma arrived in China during the latter part of
the Liu Sung dynasty (420–479) and was already in northern China
well before the end of the fifth century.

TS'UNG SHEN of Chao Chou (778–897)
CASES 2, 9, 30

Known as Chao Chou, after the place in northern China where
he lived and taught for the last forty years of his long life,
Ts'ung Shen was one of the most famous and revered Ch'an
masters of all time. He claimed to have seen over eighty of Ma
Tsu's successors during his long travels on foot; it was Nan
Ch'uan to whom he succeeded.

One day Chao Chou asked Nan Ch'uan, "What is the Way?"

Nan Ch'uan said, "The ordinary mind is the Way."

Chou said, "Is it still possible to aim for it?"

Ch'uan said, "If you attempt to turn towards it, then you are
turning away from it."

Chou said, "When I make no attempt, how do I know this is the Way?"

Ch'uan said, "The Way is not in the realm of knowing or not knowing; knowing is false consciousness, and not knowing is insensibility. If it is true arrival on the Way where there is no doubt, it is like the great void, like a vacant hall, empty and open; how could one insist on affirming or denying it?"

At these words Chao Chou awakened to the Way. After Nan Ch'uan's death Chao Chou resumed his travels for over twenty years more; only at the age of eighty did he settle down at the Kuan Yin Temple in Chao Chou, where he taught until his death at the age of one hundred and twenty.

Chao Chou was also known for his asceticism: "It was the Master's will to emulate the ancients, and his abbacy was austere. In the monks' hall there were no shelves in front or rear. Vegetarian food was prepared. When one leg of his rope chair broke, he tied on a leftover piece of firewood with rope to support it. There were repeated requests to make a new leg for it, but the Master would not allow it." (This and subsequent citations are taken from the record of Chao Chou's sayings in *Ku Tsun Su Yu Lu* 13–14.)

As abbot, Chao Chou upheld the custom of universal labor in the community of monks, a practice of the Ch'an school initiated by the Fourth Patriarch Tao Hsin and established as a rule by Pai Chang Huai Hai. (In older Chinese Buddhist monastic systems, only novices did manual labor.) One day when he encountered a monk behind the monks' hall, he asked, "Where have all the virtuous ones gone?" That monk said, "They have all gone to work." The master then took a knife out of his sleeve and handed it to the monk, saying, "My tasks as abbot are many; I ask you, Elder, please cut off my head for me." Then he extended his neck; the monk ran off.

Chao Chou's manner of teaching was called "Lip Ch'an," and it was said that light issued from his lips when he spoke. Many sayings of his are recorded, and his repeated appearance in *The Blue Cliff Record* is evidence of their currency. In the closing decades of the ninth century Chao Chou, Hsueh Feng, and Yun Chu (Tao Ying, Tung Shan's great disciple) were the most eminent Ch'an masters in China, but Chao Chou used to say, "Even if you come from Hsueh Feng or Yun Chu, you are still board-carrying fellows." Chao Chou's teaching style was lofty indeed, and he produced thirteen enlightened successors, but there were few who could match, let alone surpass him, so his transmission line died out after a few generations.

A monk asked, "In the aeon of emptiness, is there still someone cultivating practice?" The Master said, "What do you call the aeon of emptiness?" The monk said, "This is where not a single thing exists." The Master said, "Only this can be called real cultivation."

A monk asked, "The Buddha Dharma is remote; how should I concentrate?" The Master said, "Observe how the Former Han and Latter Han dynasties held the whole empire; yet when the end came, they hadn't a farthing."

MA TSU TAO I (709–788)
CASE 3

(Ma Tsu, "Ancestor Ma," also called Great Master Ma, was one of the most illustrious Ch'an masters of all time, the teacher of one hundred and thirty-nine enlightened successors. His teacher was Huai Jang of Nan Yueh, one of the foremost heirs of the Sixth Patriarch Hui Neng. The following is the account of Ma Tsu's meeting with Huai Jang told in the *Ching Te Ch'uan Teng Lu:*)

During the K'ai Yuan era (713–741)* an ascetic named Tao I was dwelling in the Ch'uan Fa Temple; all day he sat meditating. Huai Jang knew that he was a vessel of Dharma, and went to question him; "Great Worthy, what are you aiming at by sitting meditation?" Ma replied, "I aim to become a Buddha." Jang then took a tile and began to rub it on a rock in front of the hermitage; Ma asked him what he was doing rubbing the tile. Jang said, "I am polishing it to make a mirror." Ma said, "How can you make a mirror by polishing a tile?" Jang said, "Granted that rubbing a tile will not make a mirror, how can sitting meditation make a Buddha?" Ma asked, "Then what would be right?" Jang said, "It is like the case of an ox pulling a cart: if the cart does not go, would it be right to hit the cart, or would it be right to hit the ox?" Ma didn't reply.

Jang went on to say, "Do you think you are practicing sitting meditation, or do you think you are practicing sitting Buddhahood? If you are practicing sitting meditation, meditation is not sitting or lying. If you are practicing sitting Buddhahood, 'Buddha' is not a fixed form. In the midst of transitory things, one should neither grasp nor reject. If you keep the Buddha seated, this is murdering the Buddha; if you cling to the form of sitting, this is not attaining its inner principle."

Ma heard this teaching as if he was drinking ambrosia. He bowed and asked, "How shall I concentrate so as to merge with formless absorption?" Jang said, "Your study of the teaching of the mind ground is like planting seeds; my expounding the essence of reality may be likened to the moisture from the sky. Circumstances are meet for you, so you shall see the Way."

Ma also asked, "If the Way is not color or form, how can I see it?" Jang said, "The reality eye of the mind ground can see the Way. Formless absorption is also like this." Ma asked, "Is there becoming and decay, or not?" Jang said, "If one sees the Way as becoming and decaying, compounding and scattering, that is not really seeing the Way. Listen to my verse:

> *Mind ground contains various seeds;*
> *When there is moisture, all of them sprout.*
> *The flower of absorption has no form;*
> *What decays and what becomes?*

Ma heard this and his understanding was opened up. His heart and mind were transcendent. He served his master for ten years, day by day going deeper into the inner sanctum.

*This meeting probably took place in the mid 730's. Huai Jang had six adept pupils, but he said it was Ma Tsu who realized his "heart."

HSUAN CH'IEN of Te Shan (781–867)
CASE 4

(Among Te Shan's nine successors were Yen T'ou Ch'uan Huo and Hsueh Feng I Tsun; he was the ancestor of both the Yun Men and Fa Yen sects of Ch'an. *Ching Te Ch'uan Teng Lu* 15 gives the following account of him:)

Ch'an master Hsuan Ch'ien of Te Shan in Liang Chou was a man of Chien Nan; his surname was Chou. In his youth he left home, and when he came of age he was fully ordained as a monk. He made a thorough study of the collection of regulations, and penetrated the essential import of the various scriptures expounding nature and its phenomenal expressions. He frequently lectured on the Diamond Wisdom Scripture; his contemporaries called him Diamond Chou.

Later he inquired into the Ch'an sect, whereat he said to his fellow students, "A single hair embraces the sea, yet the sea's nature is not diminished; a minute mustard seed falls upon a sword blade—the sharpness of the sword does not move. Whether there is something to learn or nothing more to learn, only I know that." Then he went to Ch'an master Hsin of Lung T'an. . . .

(After the events narrated in case 4, he dwelt in obscurity for some thirty years in Hunan. In 845, when the emperor Wu Tsung of T'ang tried to do away with Buddhism, Te Shan escaped to a stone grotto on a mountain.)

In the beginning of the Ta Chung era (847–860), Hsueh Yen Wang, the governor of Wu Ling (in Hunan), restored the monastery on Te Shan and called it the Meditation Abode of Ancient Worthies. He was going to look for a man of knowledge to dwell there, when he heard of the master's practice of the Way. Though he repeatedly invited him, the master did not come down from the mountain. Yen Wang then fabricated a ruse, sending a runner to falsely accuse the master of having violated the laws regarding tea and salt. Having taken the master into his domain, he looked up to him with reverence and insisted that he dwell there, and reveal the way of the sect.

In the hall, the master said, "There is nothing in the self, so do not seek falsely; what is attained by false seeking is not real attainment. You just have nothing in your mind, and no mind in things; then you will be empty and spiritual, tranquil and sublime. Any talk of beginning or end would all be self-deception. The slightest entanglement of thought is the foundation of the three mires (hell, animality, hungry ghosthood); a momentarily aroused feeling is a hindrance for ten thousand aeons. The name 'sage' and the label 'ordinary man' are merely empty sounds; exceptional form and mean appearance are both illusions. If you want to seek them, how can you avoid trouble? Even if you despise them, they still become a great source of anxiety. In the end there is no benefit."

Hsueh Feng asked, "In the immemorial custom of the sect, what doctrine is used to teach people?" The master said, "Our sect has no words; in reality there is no doctrine to be given to mankind."

Yen T'ou heard of this and said, "The old man of Mount Te has a spine as strong as iron; it cannot be broken. Even so, when it comes to the way of expounding the teaching, he still lacks something."

Before his death he said to his disciples, "Grasping emptiness and pursuing echoes wearies your mind and spirit. When awakened from a dream, you realize it was false; after all, what matter is there?" When he finished speaking, he died sitting at rest.

(Te Shan is perhaps most famous for his use of the staff to strike students.)

LING YU of Kuei Shan (771–854)
CASES 4, 24, 70

(Kuei Shan was the foremost successor of Pai Chang Huai Hai; the whisk which he showed to Te Shan in case 4 was given to him by Pai Chang as a symbol of the transmission. Perhaps the most famous teacher of his time in southern China, Kuei Shan's community numbered fifteen hundred persons, and he produced forty-three enlightened disciples. Among them, the best known were Hsiang Yen Chih Hsien and Yang Shan Hui Chi. Very little is known of Hsiang Yen's successors, but Yang Shan's teaching line remained active for three or four more generations; hence it came to be called the Kuei-Yang Sect, the earliest of the so-called 'Five Houses' of classical Ch'an. The following sermon of Kuei Shan is taken from *Ching Te Ch'uan Teng Lu* 9:)

The mind of a man of the Way is straightforward, without falsehood; there is no turning away nor turning towards, no deceitful false mind. At all times his seeing and hearing are normal; there are no further details or subtleties beyond this. He does not close his eyes or block his ears; it is enough that feelings do not attach to things.

Since time immemorial all the sages have only spoken of the faults of impurity; if there is no such perverted consciousness, opinion and thought habits, then it is like an autumn pond, limpid and clean. Pure and clear, without contrivance, quiescent and still, without hindrance; such is called a man of the Way. He is also called an unconcerned man.

(Kuei Shan also wrote a short book called the *Ching Ts'e,* or 'admonishing stick,' in which he points out the degeneracy of Buddhists in his time, and speaks of the true aim of leaving home. This book gained wide circulation in China, and was the first sectarian Ch'an work to be published in Japan, in the year 1198; it is still current in Rinzai Zen circles.)

I TS'UN of Hsueh Feng (822–908)
CASES 5, 22, 49, 51

Hsueh Feng first wanted to abandon home at the age of nine, but he was prevented from doing so by his parents. At the age of twelve, he went with his father to Yu Chien temple in Fu T'ien (in Foochow): there he saw the preceptual master Ch'ing Hsuan; he said, "This is my teacher," and remained at that temple to serve Ch'ing Hsuan. At age seventeen, he had his head shaved and changed his name to I Ts'un.

When Hsueh Feng was twenty-four, Buddhism was suppressed by the command of the Emperor. In Confucian dress, Hsueh Feng called on the Ch'an teacher Ling Hsun, spiritual grandson of Ma Tsu. The following year, when the suppression had been lifted, Hsueh Feng returned to Ling Hsun as a disciple. Later, when he himself began to teach on Hsueh Feng (one of the names of the mountain where he lived, after which he is usually called, according to Ch'an custom), he modeled the organization of his community after that of Ling Hsun.

At twenty-eight, Hsueh Feng was officially ordained at Pao Ch'a temple in Yu Chou. Two years later his teacher Ling Hsun died; after two more years had passed, at the age of thirty-two Hsueh Feng resumed his travels. He was with Yen T'ou in the community of Huan Chung (780–862, a successor of Pai Chang) at Mt. Ta Tzu in Hang Chou, where they met Ch'in Shan Wen Sui, an outstanding student of Huan Chung. The three of them left Ta Tzu and travelled together to visit other enlightened teachers.

Once in the course of their journey, Ch'in Shan stopped to wash his feet in a stream, when he saw a vegetable leaf floating by. He rejoiced and said, "There must be a man of the Way in

these mountains; let us follow the stream and seek him out."
Hsueh Feng said, "Your eye of wisdom is cloudy; later on, how
will you judge others? His carelessness about material blessings is such as this; what is he doing, dwelling in the mountains?"

Eventually, as the commentary states, Hsueh Feng went to
T'ou Tzu three times and nine times to Tung Shan. The master
Ta T'ung of Mt. T'ou Tzu (819–915) was a successor in the
fourth generation of the Shih T'ou line. Tung Shan Liang
Chieh, patriarch of the Ts'ao-Tung sect, a later branch of the
Shih T'ou (or Ch'ing Yuan) line, was one of the most famous
masters of the time; Ch'in Shan eventually remained and suc-
ceeded to the teaching of Tung Shan, whereas Hsueh Feng and
Yen T'ou succeeded to Te Shan.

Hsueh Feng was already forty years old when he met Te
Shan, who was then over eighty. Although he stayed there for
several years and is reckoned as a successor to Te Shan, in
reality it was by Yen T'ou's exhortation that he was thoroughly
liberated. Later he became a great teacher, a classic illustration
of the Ch'an proverb that "a superior vessel takes a long time
to complete."

After his enlightenment, at the age of forty-five Hsueh Feng
parted company with Yen T'ou and went back to Min
(Foochow): two years later he returned to Mt. Fu Jung ('Lotus
Mountain', where Ling Hsun had taught) and dwelt at ease
there in a stone grotto. Several followers who had sought him
out, especially one Hsing Shih Shih Po, who had been a fellow
student of his long before under Ling Hsun, urged him to "appear in the world" and teach. Finally, at the age of forty-nine,
he went to Hsiang Ku Shan, "Elephant Bone Mountain," where
two donors vied to provide for him. Because the mountaintop
was always covered with snow, it was called Hsueh Feng,
"Snowy Peak"; and at the age of fifty Hsueh Feng went to live
there and spent the next several years with his followers building a place to live and work.

Within ten years, the size of his community had reached
fifteen hundred people; so rapidly did his following increase in
the early years that there was not enough room or ample provisions for them all. Under Hsueh Feng's guidance, the community was exemplary for its industry and austerity. The renown
of Hsueh Feng spread all over China, and in 882 he was given

an honorific purple vestment by the Emperor I Tsung, along with the title Chen Chiao Ta Shih, "Truly Enlightened Great Teacher." By the time of his death at the age of eighty-seven, he had fifty-six enlightened disciples teaching in various places; among them, several who figure in *The Blue Cliff Record* were Hsuan Sha, E Hu, Ch'ang Ch'ing, Ching Ch'ing, Yun Men, Sui Yen, and Pao Fu. Hsueh Feng's teaching line flourished exceedingly through the Fa Yen and Yun Men sects, and lasted about three hundred years in China.

WEN YEN of Yun Men (?–949)
CASES 6, 8, 14, 15, 22, 27, 34

(Successor to Hsueh Feng, Yun Men taught in Kuangtung, southern China; he produced over sixty enlightened disciples, and was known as the founder of the Yun Men school of Ch'an, which lasted into the thirteenth century, and whose masters were responsible for the preservation of a great deal of Ch'an literature. Noted for his wondrous and often abstruse sayings, Yun Men forbade his disciples to record what he said; one of his attendants stealthily wrote down his sayings on a paper robe, preserving in this way an incredibly rich record of Yun Men's words. The practice of reciting and investigating sayings of earlier Ch'an masters seems to have been growing over a long period of time, but Yun Men was one of the first classical masters to make extensive use of the words of Ch'an ancients in guiding his own disciples. He is said to have originated the form of *tai-yu*, or "substitute sayings," in which he answers a question posed by himself, in behalf of his audience, or else supplies an answer to a question or saying of an earlier master, substituting for a speechless monk in a story; he also originated *pieh-yu*, or "alternative saying," a reply or remark given as an alternate to another in a story, or an alternate reply to one of his self-posed self-answered questions. Other members of Hsueh Feng's congregation were known to have discussed ancient and contemporary Ch'an sayings and doings extensively; the Lin Chi school of Ch'an became well known for its use of *k'an-hua ch'an*, or "meditation contemplating sayings," during the Sung dynasty, but the overt recommendation of this practice is in early evidence in Yun Men's sayings. Remember also that Hsueh Tou, who collected the sayings and wrote the poems which are the kernel of *The Blue Cliff Record* was a master of the Yun Men school. The following excerpt from one of Yun Men's speeches recorded in *Ching Te Ch'uan Teng Lu* 19 illustrates his approach to this technique:)

O brethren! You have all called on teachers in various places to settle life and death. Where you went, did not the venerable adepts abiding there utter some compassionate words of help to you? Are there still any phrases you did not penetrate? Come forth and cite them and let's see. This old fellow will haggle with you all. . . .

Ordinary thieving cowards slurp up the spittle of others, memorizing a bunch of miscellaneous trash: wherever they go they run off at the mouth; with asses' lips and horses' chops they boast, 'I know how to pose ten or five pivotal questions.' Even if you go on like this morning to night until the end of time, will you after all have ever seen anything, even in dreams? What use has this in imparting strength to others? Whenever anyone stakes the patchrobed monks to a meal, people like this also say, 'I have food to eat.' How are they even worth talking to? On another day, before the King of Death, he will not accept your verbal explanations.

O brethren, if you have attained, you may spend your days following the crowd in another house; but if you have not attained, just do not pass the time taking it easy. You must be most thoroughgoing.

The Ancients had a lot of problems to help you. These are such as Hsueh Feng's saying, "The whole earth is you." Chia Shan said, "Pick me out in the hundred grasses; recognize the emperor in a bustling market place." Lo P'u said, "As soon as a mote of dust arises, the entire earth is contained therein; on the tip of a hair, the whole body of the Lion is all there." You take hold, and contemplate them over and over again; over long days and many years, you will naturally find a way of entry. In this task, no one can substitute for you; it rests with each individual, without exception.

(The following examples are taken from the *Yun Men Kuang Lu*, to illustrate something of Yun Men's commentary style:)

Quoting Chia Shan's saying, "Find me in the hundred grasses," the master joined his palms and said, "How are you? How are you?" Then he pointed at a pillar with his staff and said, "Chia Shan has turned into a pillar—look! Look!"

Quoting Hsueh Feng's saying, "The Buddhas of past, present, and future turn the Great Wheel of Dharma upon flames of fire," the master said, "The flames of fire expound the Dharma; the Buddhas of past, present, and future stand there and listen."

(The 'three phrases' of Yun Men is a descriptive term first used by Yun Men's successor Te Shan Yuan Mi; the following verses by Yuan Wu describing the three phrases are taken from the *Jen T'ien Yen Mu:*)

> *Fundamental reality, fundamental emptiness;*
> *One form, one flavor—it is not that a subtle*
>   *entity does not exist.*
> *It is not a matter for hesitating over; clear and lucid,*
> *This contains the whole world.*
>
> *It is fundamentally not a matter of interpretation*
>   *or understanding;*
> *When you sum it all up, it's not worth a single let-*
>   *ter.*
> *When myriad activities abruptly cease,*
> *That is cutting off the myriad streams.*
>
> *When you allow the presence of another,*
> *Follow the sprouts to descry the ground,*
> *Understand the person by means of his words;*
> *This is going along with the ripples, following the*
>   *waves.*

FA YEN WEN I (885–958)
CASE 7

Revered as the founder of the Fa Yen sect of Ch'an, he was a successor of Lo Han Kuei Ch'en.* Kuei Ch'en's teacher had been Hsuan Sha, and the compiler of the *Ching Te Ch'uan Teng Lu* refers to Fa Yen as a reviver of the Hsuan Sha sect.

Fa Yen had his head shaved at the age of seven, and subsequently studied both Buddhist and Confucian teachings. Later he gave up these pursuits and headed for southern China to seek sudden enlightenment. First he went to the congregation at Ch'ang Ch'ing in Fu Chou, under the master Hui Leng.

It is said that he was highly esteemed there in spite of the fact that his clinging mind was not yet at rest.

Resuming his travels with several companions, at one point Fa Yen was stopped in his tracks by weather conditions and put up at the Ti Ts'ang temple, where the master Kuei Ch'en was abiding at the time. Kuei Ch'en asked him, "Where are you going?" He replied, "I am going to continue wandering around on foot." Ch'en asked, "What is the purpose of your travel?" He replied, "I do not know." Kuei Ch'en said, "Not knowing is closest to it."

According to the *Ch'uan Teng Lu*, Fa Yen was enlightened at these words, and remained at Ti Ts'ang along with three companions, seeking absolute certainty. The record in the *Wu Teng Hui Yuan* states that they went on to discuss the *Chao Lun,* a fourth century Chinese Buddhist treatise; when they got to the point where it says, "Heaven and earth and I have the same root," Ch'en asked Fa Yen, "Are the mountains, rivers, and earth identical to your own self, or separate?" Fa Yen said, "Separate." Kuei Ch'en held up two fingers; the master said, "Identical." Ch'en again held up two fingers, then got up and left.

When Fa Yen was about to depart, Kuei Ch'en saw him to the gate, whereupon he asked, "You always say that the three worlds are only mind, and myriad things are only consciousness;" then he pointed to a rock in the garden and said, "But tell me, is this rock inside your mind or outside your mind?" Fa Yen said, "It is inside my mind." Kuei Ch'en said, "What reason does a traveller have to put a rock in his head?" Fa Yen was stumped and had no reply. So he put down his bundle and stayed by Kuei Ch'en to seek certainty.

For over a month he daily expressed his understanding and spoke of the principle. Ch'en said to him, "The Buddha Dharma is not like this." Fa Yen said, "My words are exhausted, my reason come to an end." Kuei Ch'en said, "If one were to discuss the Buddha Dharma, all things would appear in full." At these words, Fa Yen was greatly enlightened. (*Wu Teng* 10)

Later, he dwelt in the Ch'iung Shou Temple in Lin Ch'uan, where he began to teach. When Tzu Fang, an elder monk from the Ch'ang Ch'ing community came to call on him, Fa Yen quoted Hui Leng's verse and said, "What is the unique body revealed in the midst of myriad forms?" Tzu Fang raised his whisk; Fa Yen said, "How can you understand it thus?" Tzu Fang said, "What is the master's honorable opinion?" Fa Yen said, "What do you call myriad forms?" Tzu Fang said, "The Ancients did not eliminate myriad forms." Fa Yen said, "In myriad forms there is a single body revealed; why talk about eliminating or not eliminating?" At these words, Tzu Fang was greatly awakened; he expressed himself in verse and submitted in sincerity.

Henceforth, people in congregations everywhere who were conscious of their understanding came in droves; at first they were unyielding, but the Master subtly aroused and awakened them, so that all of them eventually submitted to him. His ocean of followers was never less than one thousand persons. (*Ch'uan Teng Lu* 24)

(Fa Yen, the name by which Wen I is usually known to posterity, is an abbreviation of his posthumous title Ta Fa Yen Ch'an Shih, 'Meditation Master with the Great Eye of Reality.' He was also entitled Ch'ing Hui, 'Pure Wisdom,' and Ta Chih Tsang Ta Tao Shih, 'Great Guide, Repository of Great Knowledge.' His writings were said to have amounted to several tens of thousands of words; much, however, has been lost to posterity. Still extant, however, are a number of poems, and a treatise entitled *Tsung Men Shih Kuei Lun*, 'Ten Guidelines for the School,' an elegant treatise on Ch'an and a denunciation of the decadence of Ch'an schools in his time. Fa Yen had sixty-three enlightened disciples, including Te Shao, National Teacher of Wu-Yueh, Wen Sui, National Guide of Chiang Nan, and Hui Ch'u, National Teacher of Koryo, a Korean kingdom. The Fa Yen school flourished greatly into the third generation, but died out by the fifth, after about one hundred years. Te Shao also did much to revive the T'ien T'ai teachings in China; his disciple Yen Shou was also considered a patriarch of the Pure Land school, and was a great scholar and prodigious author.)

*In some books he is referred to as Ti Ts'ang, in others, Lo Han; he lived for a while in Ti Ts'ang temple, where Fa Yen met him. Later he moved to Lo Han temple in Chang Chou.

TS'UI YEN LING TS'AN (9–10c)
CASE 8

Almost nothing is known of this master, beyond that he was a successor of Hsueh Feng. The compilers of the *Tsu T'ang Chi* state, "We have never seen any record of his doings. King Ch'ien respected him, and bestowed on him a purple vestment and the title Yung Ming Ta Shih, 'Great Teacher of Eternal Brilliance.' "

King Ch'ien* was Ch'ien Liu, entitled King of Yueh in 902, and later became the King of Wu and Yueh in 907, under the new Liang dynasty.

There was a saying that one's eyebrows will fall out if one talks too much; in the version of this example recorded in the *Tsu T'ang Chi,* Ts'ui Yen says 'for the last thirty years' rather than 'this summer.' Judging from the paucity of his record, he died with his eyebrows on. There are, however, one or two sayings left:

A monk once asked, "When the ancients lifted the gavel or stood up the whisk, what was the inner meaning?"

Ts'ui Yen said, "A false teaching is hard to maintain."

The other characters in example 8 were also disciples of Hsueh Feng, and this is, no doubt, where this incident took place. Later on, Ts'ui Yen had two enlightened successors, of whom equally little is known as of their master.

---

*The titular head of the empire being the Emperor, the term *wang* is translated as king, although these were regional titles and there were many such kings.

PAO FU TS'UNG CHAN (?–928)
CASES 8, 22, 23, 95

A man of Fu Chou, his lay surname was Ch'en. At the age of fifteen he went to Hsueh Feng and received instruction from him. At eighteen he was fully ordained at Ta Chung. After traveling in Wu and Chu (southern China), he later returned to Hsueh Feng and served as his attendant.

One day Hsueh Feng suddenly called him and said, "Do you understand?"

Pao Fu was about to approach, when Hsueh Feng poked him with his staff. At that moment, Pao Fu realized the ultimate; he bowed and withdrew. He also always used to ask Master Leng of Ch'ang Ch'ing about the expedient teachings of past and present; Leng deeply approved of him.

A monk asked, "If one wants to arrive on the Birthless Road, he must know the Basic Source; what is the basic source?"

The Master was silent for a long time. Then he asked his attendant, "What did that monk just ask?" When that monk quoted it again, the Master shouted at him and drove him out, saying, "I am not deaf."

Pao Fu's enlightened disciples numbered twenty-five.

CH'ANG CH'ING HUI LENG
(864–932)
CASES 8, 22, 23, 95

According to the *Ch'uan Teng Lu* (18),

"He was a man of Yen Kuan in Hang Chou; his lay surname was Tsun. As a child, he was of pure and peaceful nature. When he was thirteen years old he left home and received the precepts at T'ung Hsuan temple in Su Chou; then he traveled around visiting the Ch'an 'shops'.

"In 878 he went into Min and called on Hsi Yuan; then he visited Ling Yun, but he still had lingering doubts. Later he went to Hsueh Feng, and his feelings of doubt melted like ice."

According to the *Tsu T'ang Chi* (10),

"When he first went to study under Hsueh Feng, his tasks in the study were bitterly painful; he was not too brilliant. Hsueh Feng saw him going on like this and stopped him, saying, 'I am giving you a prescription for medicine for a dead horse; do you find it sweet?'

"He said, 'I will abide by the Master's judgement.'

"Hsueh Feng said, 'You do not need to come up here three or five times every day: just know how to be like a wooden pillar in a blazing fire in the mountain; put your body and mind at rest, for maybe as many as ten years, perhaps seven, or at least three years, and you will surely have understanding.'

"He followed Hsueh Feng's direction for two and a half years; one night his mind was active and he could not sit still, so he went outside the temple building, walked three times around the tea garden, and sat down under a tree. Suddenly, as he was falling asleep, he awoke and returned to the temple. Going up from the eastern hall, the moment he entered the monks' hall he saw the lamp loom large and immediately had understanding. Thereupon he went to the Master Hsueh Feng's place, but before the master got up, he went away instead; leaning on the pillar of the teaching hall, he unconsciously let out a cry.

"The Great Teacher heard it and asked, 'Who is it?'

"Hui Leng called out his name; the Great Teacher said, 'What are you doing, coming here in the middle of the night?'

"He said, 'I have had an extraordinary perception.'

"The Great Teacher himself got up and opened the gate; he grabbed Hui Leng's hand and asked him about his inner condition. The latter, expressing his inner feeling, said in a verse,

> Wonder of wonders!
> Rolling up a bamboo blind, I see the whole world*
> If anyone asks me what sect I understand,
> I would lift up my whisk and hit them right in the
>   mouth!"

According to Wu Teng Hui Yuan (7),

"He asked Ling Yun** 'What is the big idea of the Buddhist teaching?'

"Ling Yung said, 'Before the business with the donkey is over with, a problem comes up with the horse.'

"The master went back and forth between Hsueh Feng and Hsuan Sha like this for a period of twenty years, and wore out seven sitting mats, but still did not clearly understand this matter. One day as he rolled up a bamboo blind, he was suddenly greatly awakened; thereupon he had a verse . . . (same as above).

"Hsueh Feng quoted this to Hsuan Sha and said, 'This lad has finished.' Hsuan Sha said, "Not yet; this is an expression of conscious knowledge. He should be tested again.'

"In the evening, when the community of monks appeared to ask questions, Hsueh Feng said to the master, 'Ascetic Pei (Hsuan Sha) does not approve of you. If you really have correct realization, bring it up before the community.' The master again had a verse, saying,

'Within myriad appearances, a solitary body is re-
    vealed:
Only when a person experiences it personally can
    he be acquainted with it.
In former times I wrongly looked to the road in
    search—
Now I look upon it like ice in fire.'

Hsueh Feng looked at Hsuan Sha and said, 'This can't still be
an expression of conscious knowledge.'"

The master asked Hsueh Feng, "All sages from antiquity
have transmitted and received a single path; please point it out
to me."

Hsueh Feng remained silent; the master bowed and withdrew. Hsueh Feng smiled.

The master entered the abbot's quarters; Hsueh Feng said,
"What is it?"

The master said, "Today the weather is clear, good for asking everyone to work." After this, his replies to questions were
never out of accord with the mysterious meaning.

Ch'ang Ch'ing became a distinguished teacher, producing
twenty-six successors.

*Corrected according to *Wu Teng Hui Yuan*; the earlier version is
somewhat garbled.

**A successor of Kuei Shan Ling You.

TAO TSUNG of Mu Chou (780–877)
CASE 10

Master Ch'en (his lay surname was Ch'en) succeeded to Huang
Po; he lived in Lung Hsing Temple in Mu Chou (in Chekiang).
The master usually carried out his activities in secret; he al-
ways made straw sandals and sent them secretly to people.
Because of this they called him "Ch'en the straw sandal
monk." (*Tsu T'ang Chi* 19)

He first dwelt in Lung Hsing Temple in Mu Chou: he hid his
traces and concealed his activity. He made straw sandals and
secretly placed them on the street; after many years people
came to know of this, so they called him "straw-sandal
Ch'en." At the time, when there were students who sought his

inspiration, he would reply instantly to their questions, and his words were sharp; since he didn't follow a rut, therefore the shallow often derided him. Only profound students who were naturally bright respected and submitted to him; because of this, people from all quarters sought refuge with him and called him Reverend Ch'en. (*Ching Te Ch'uan Teng Lu* 12)

HSI YUN of Huang Po (?–850)
CASE 11

(Huang Po was a successor of Pai Chang, and produced thirteen enlightened disciples, among whom was Lin Chi I Hsuan, founder of the Lin Chi sect of Ch'an. The following sermon is excerpted from the *Ch'uan Hsin Fa Yao*, 'Essential Method of Transmission of Mind,' recorded by prime minister P'ei Hsiu; this version is taken from *Ching Te Ch'uan Teng Lu* 9:)

The Buddhas and all sentient beings are only one mind; there is nothing else. This mind, since beginningless past, has never been born, never perished; it is not green, not yellow; it has no shape or form. It is not subject to existence or non-existence, and is not to be considered new or old. It is not long or short, nor is it large or small; it transcends all limitation, measurement, names, words, traces or oppositions. This very substance is it; stir your thoughts and you miss it. It is like empty space; it has no bounds, and cannot be measured. Just this one mind itself is Buddha. Buddha and sentient beings are no different; it's just that sentient beings grasp appearances— seeking outwardly, they become more and more lost. If you employ Buddha to seek Buddha, use mind to grasp mind, you may go on all your life until the end of time, but will never succeed. Don't you realize that if you cease thinking and forget thought, Buddha will spontaneously appear?

SHOU CH'U TSUNG HUI of Tung Shan (n.d.)
CASE 12

(Not the more famous progenitor of the Ts'ao-Tung School, but one of Yun Men's disciples: the circumstances of his meeting with Yun Men are told in the Commentary to the Verse of Case 12. The following anecdotes are recorded in the *Ching Te Ch'uan Teng Lu 23:*)

A monk asked, "When you're far far on the one road, what's it like?" The master said, "Not agreeing to go while the sky is clear, ending up waiting for the rain to soak your head." The monk said, "What about all the sages?" The master said, "They enter the mud and water."

A monk asked, "Before mind arises, where are things?" The master said, "With no wind, the lotus leaves move: certainly there's a fish swimming through."

A monk asked, "What are the three jewels (Buddha, Dharma, and Sangha, the community of monks)?" The master said, "Impossible to discuss."

A monk asked, "What is the seamless memorial tower?" The master said, "A stone lion at the crossroads."

A monk asked, "What is the proper business of patchrobed monks?" The master said, "Up in the clouds on Mt. Chu, there's certainly a lot of wind and rain."

A monk asked, "What is buddha?" The master said, "Obviously true."

A monk asked, "A great multitude has gathered thick to beg the Master to take hold of the pivotal essentials and reveal a little of the great design." The master said, "A bubble floating on the water displays the five colors; at the bottom of the sea a frog is croaking, 'The moon is bright!'"

Great Master HAO CHIEN of Hsin K'ai in Pa Ling, Yueh Chou (n.d.)
CASES 13, 100

(Pa Ling was a successor of Yun Men; there is no record of his enlightenment story. His nickname 'Mouthy' was because of his eloquence. He had two enlightened disciples.)

A monk asked, "Are the Patriarchal meaning and the meaning of the Teachings the same or different?" He said, "When chickens are cold, they roost in trees; when ducks are cold, they enter the water."

A monk asked, "I do not doubt the twelve part teachings of the three vehicles; what is the business of the Ch'an sect?" He said, "This is not the business of a patchrobed monk." The monk asked, "What is the business of a patchrobed monk?" He said, "If you indulge in watching the foaming waves, you lose the oar in your hands."

He sent a whisk to someone. That person said, "It is fundamentally pure and clean; what is the use of a whisk?" The master said, "If you know it is pure and clean, don't forget it."

CHING CH'ING (863–937)
CASES 16, 23, 46

(The following is from *Tsu T'ang Chi* 10:)

Master Ching Ch'ing succeeded to Hsueh Feng. He lived in Yueh Chou (Fukien). The master's name was Tao Fu; he was (originally) a man of Wen Chou (in Chekiang). When the master first went into Min (Fukien) he called on Ling Yun (a successor of Kuei Shan) and asked, "How do you point out the truth of the great concern of foot travelling?" Yun said, "What is the price of rice in Chekiang?" The master said, "I almost understood it as the price of rice." Then he continued on to Hsiang Ku (Hsueh Feng).

Hsueh Feng asked him, "Where are you from?" He replied, "I'll never say I was born and raised in Wen Chou." Feng said, "Then the Enlightened Overnight Guest (Yung Chia, a successor of the Sixth Patriarch) is a fellow villager of yours." He said, "Where was the Enlightened Overnight Guest from?" Feng said, "This lad deserves to be given a score of blows, but I'll let it go."

The master also asked, "Since antiquity, the ancestral worthies have spoken of the simile of an entry road; is this right or not?" Feng said, "Right." He said, "I am a beginner, only lately come to study; I request you, teacher, to point out an entry road." Feng said, "Just enter from here." The master said, "I am enshrouded with ignorance; again I ask you to point it out." (n.b. Hsueh Feng's answer is not too clear; one character in the text is indistinct. Both the *Ching Te Ch'uan Teng Lu* and the *Wu Teng Hui Yuan* omit this story altogether. Hsueh Feng's answer seems to be, "I don't have many today; why sprawl out and fall right over?" Or it may read, "Hsueh Feng said, 'Today I am not too steady,' and he sprawled himself out and fell over.")

According to *Wu Teng Hui Yuan* 7, at the age of six he didn't eat meat; when his parents force fed him with dried fish, he would immediately vomit it out. Eventually he sought to leave home, and received ordination at the state K'ai Yuan Temple in his native Wen Chou. Then he went foot travelling.

(The following is from *Ching Te Ch'uan Teng Lu* 18; it accords with the *Tsu T'ang Chi* except for slight vocabulary differences:)

One day the Master asked, "Did the ancient worthies not transmit mind by mind?" Hsueh Feng said, "And they did not set up written words or spoken phrases." He said, "If you don't set up written words or spoken phrases, how will you transmit it, teacher?" Hsueh Feng remained silent. The master bowed in thanks. Hsueh Feng said, "Shouldn't you ask something further?" He said, "I ask you for a question, teacher." Hsueh Feng said, "Is it just so, or do you think there is some other consideration besides?" He said, "For you teacher, just so is all right." Hsueh Feng said, "What about for you?" He said, "Turning completely away from people." (The *CTL* stops here; the *TTC* continues,) Hsueh Feng said, "What is the business of not turning away?" The master immediately bade fare-thee-well.

Hsueh Feng once said to the assembly, "Splendidly refined." The master came forth and said, "What splendid refinement is this?" Hsueh Feng got up and said, "What did you say?" The master then retreated and stood there.

Hsueh Feng said, "This matter is so noble, so refined." The master responded by saying, "In the years since (I) Tao Fu has been here, I have never heard the teacher instruct like this." Hsueh Feng said, "Although I hadn't before, now I already have; there's nothing wrong, is there?" He said, "I do not dare (to say so). This is only what the teacher cannot avoid." Hsueh Feng said, "Let me be like this." The master gained true entry by this, but for a while he still followed the congregation. In Min he was called 'Cloth-robed Little Fu.'

As they were working, Hsueh Feng quoted Kuei Shan's saying about seeing mind upon seeing form and asked the master,
"Is there any fault or not?" The master said, "What was the
ancient concerned about?" Hsueh Feng said, "Although you
are right, I still want to deliberate with you." The master said,
"Then it would be better if I went on hoeing."

One day Hsueh Feng asked the master, "Where have you
come from?" He said, "From outside." Hsueh Feng said,
"Where did you meet Bodhidharma?" He said, "Where else?"
Hsueh Feng said, "I still don't believe you yet." He said,
"Teacher, don't vilify me so." Hsueh Feng approved of him.
Later he travelled all over to various places, adding more to his
temporal wisdom.

(First he dwelt at Ching Ch'ing, then at T'ien Lung and Lung
Ts'e temples; King Ch'ien of Min greatly respected him, and
requested him to teach in these places. The *Ch'uan Teng Lu*
says that mystic studies flourished in Wu-Yueh during his
teaching there.)

Someone asked, "An Ancient (Tung Shan) had a saying, 'A
man who is mindless unites with the Way'; how does a man
without mind unite with the Way?" The master said, "Why do
you not ask about 'The Way is mindless of union with man'?"
"How is it that The Way is mindless of union with man'?" The
master said, "Though the white clouds may come to the blue
mountain peak, how can the bright moon descend from the
blue sky?"

(According to the *Tsu T'ang Chi*,) a monk asked, "What is
'leaping high'?" The master said, "Your eyes look upon the
(most rare) Udambara (flower) as like a yellow leaf." "What is
the Udambara like?" The master said, "It appears once in an
aeon." "What is the yellow leaf?" The master said, "This is not
yet real." The monk said, "Then there must still be something
yet more transcendental." The master said, "Obviously."
"What is the transcendental thing?" The master said, "When
you drink the water of the Mirror Lake in one gulp, then I'll tell
you."

"What is the single straight path to the spiritual source?"
The master said, "The water of Mirror Lake is exceedingly
deep."

(Ching Ch'ing had five successors.)

TENG YUAN of Hsiang Lin Temple on Ch'ing Ch'eng Mountain in I Chou (n.d.)
CASE 17

(Hsiang Lin succeeded to Yun Men, and himself produced three successors. He taught in western China. The following is from *Wu Teng Hui Yuan* 15:)

A monk asked, "Why does delicious ghee turn into poison?" The master said, "Tao Chiang paper is expensive." He asked, "How is it when one sees mind upon seeing form?" The master said, "Just then where were you going and coming?" He said, "How is it when mind and objects are both forgotten?" The master said, "Sitting sleeping with your eyes open."

Someone asked, "What is the meaning of 'hiding one's body in the north star (big dipper)'?" The master said, "The moon resembles a drawn bow; little rain and much wind."

Someone asked, "What is the mind of all Buddhas?" The master said, "If it is pure, it is pure from beginning to end." He said, "How can I attain understanding of it?" The master said, "Don't be fooled by people."

Someone asked, "What is the meaning of the Patriarch's coming from the West?" The master said, "Who is the one walking?"

Someone asked, "What is the master's marvelous medicine?" The master said, "It is not apart from the myriad flavors." He said, "How is the one who takes it?" The master said, "Sip some and see."

Someone asked, "What is the one wellspring of Hsiang Lin?" The master said, "Mindfulness without interruption." He said, "How is the one who drinks from it?" The master said, "He measures it out according to his means."

National Teacher HUI CHUNG of Nan Yang (?–776)
CASES 18, 99

(The following biography is from *Tsu T'ang Chi*, 3:)

Hui Chung, the National Teacher, succeeded to the Sixth

Patriarch. His lay surname was Jan; he was a man of Chu Chow district in Yueh Chou (Fukien). When he was a child at home, he never spoke, nor did he ever cross the bridge in front of his house, up until the time he was sixteen years old, when a certain Ch'an master came; as soon as the boy saw him from afar, he ran out and over the bridge to greet him and pay obeisance. . . . His father, mother, relatives and neighbors from far and near all came and discussed this in amazement; they said, "How imponderable it is that since his infancy till his sixteenth year we have never once seen this boy speak, nor have we ever seen him cross the bridge in front of the house. But the moment he saw the monk, he acted like this. Perhaps this boy is different from ordinary people."

The boy then asked the Ch'an master, "I beg the master's compassion, to receive and ordain one of the living. I earnestly wish to take refuge in meditation and leave home."

The Ch'an master said, "The fact is that in the school of our sect, only the crown prince of a silver wheel-turning king, the grandson of a gold wheel-turning king, is able to continue the way of this school without letting it decline; you are a kid reared on a buffalo's back by a man and woman in a village of three families; how could you enter the gate of this sect? It is not something for which you are suited."

The boy said, "I submit to the Ch'an master that this teaching is of equanimity; there is no high or low. How can you speak so as to hinder my good intention? I ask the master again to extend your compassion and admit me."

The Ch'an master observed the boy's state, and said, "You shouldn't leave home like this to follow me."

The boy said, "Then to whom should I resort to leave home? Ch'an teacher, direct me to a master of the sect."

The Ch'an master said, "Have you ever heard of Ts'ao Ch'i?"

The boy said, "I do not even know what region Ts'ao Ch'i is in."

The Ch'an master said, "On Mt. Ts'ao Ch'i in Kuang Nan (Canton) there is a Good Friend; he is called the Sixth Patriarch, and his community is as large as six hundred. You go there to leave home. I am travelling to Mt. T'ien T'ai; you just go by yourself."

The boy then went into the bush and hid; avoiding his parents, he immediately went. Three days' journey he traveled in two days; when it rained, he made a day's journey in one day. When he reached Ts'ao Ch'i, he luckily came at a time when the Patriarch was just about to expound the teaching. Immediately he bowed to the Patriarch. The Patriarch asked him, "Where do you come from?"

He replied, "I have just come near."

The Patriarch said, "Where were you born?"

The boy said, "Since having gotten the five skandhas, I have forgotten."

The Patriarch said, "Come near." The boy approached. The Patriarch said, "Tell me truly where you are from."

The boy said, "I am from Che Chung."

The Patriarch said, "You have come a long way to get here; what did you come for?"

The boy said, "For one thing, an enlightened teacher is difficult to encounter, and the true teaching is hard to hear. Secondly, I want to submit to you and abandon home. I beg the master's compassion to admit me."

The Patriarch said, "I tell you, don't abandon home."

The boy said, "Why do you say this?"

The Patriarch said, "You are a Sovereign; without moving shield or spear, for sixty years the Son of Heaven will be you. Just become an Emperor, and Buddhism will be principal."

The boy said, "I submit to the master that I would not want to be Son of Heaven for one hundred years, let alone sixty. I beg the master's compassion to accept me and let me abandon home."

The master then touched his head and gave him a prediction; "If you abandon home, you will be a Buddha standing alone in the world." Then he took him in and accepted him. He was on Mt. Pai Ya of Nan Yang cultivating his practice for forty years.

In 761 on the sixteenth day of the first month, he obeyed the summons of Emperor Su Tsung calling him to the capital, where he stayed in the western meditation hall of the Temple of a Thousand Blessings. Later he returned to the Abode of Light Temple. Both emperors Su Tsung and Tai Tsung personally accepted the bodhisattva precepts from him, and respectfully entitled him National Teacher.

(The two emperors are usually listed as successors to Hui

med

Chung; the master had three other successors, but Tan Yuan
Ying Chen, who also appears in case 18, is the only one on
whom any information is available. Perhaps the most famous
dialogue recorded between these two is when Hui Chung
called to Ying Chen three times, and three times Ying Chen responded; Chung said, "I had thought that I had turned my back
on you, but it is you who have turned your back on me." Hui
Chung was one of the last surviving successors of the Sixth
Patriarch, and was greatly revered by later generations; see also
case 69.)

CHU TUN of Lung Ya Mountain in Hunan (834–920)
CASE 20

Lung Ya succeeded to Tung Shan Liang Chieh, and produced
five successors. The story of his first awakening is told in the
commentary to the twentieth case; according to the *Tsu T'ang
Chi* and later records, he finally asked Tung Shan, "What is the
meaning of the Patriarch's coming from the West?" Tung Shan
said, "When the Tung River reverses its flow, then I'll tell
you." At this Lung Ya was enlightened. He stayed with Tung
Shan for seven or eight more years. Later he had a following of
five hundred disciples, and was entitled Great Master Witness
to Voidness. Some of his sayings are to be found here and there
in Yuan Wu's commentaries.

WU HSUEH of Ts'ui Wei Temple on Chung Nan Mountain, Ch'ang An (n.d.)
CASE 20

Ts'ui Wei was the successor of Tan Hsia T'ien Jan (738–824);
among Ts'ui Wei's five enlightened successors was the great
Ch'an Master Ta T'ung of Mount T'ou Tzu. The Emperor Hsi
Tsung (r. 874–889) summoned him to the imperial precincts
(Ch'ang An) to teach, and bestowed upon him the honorific
purple robe, and the title Great Master Illumining Everywhere.
    According to the *Ching Te Ch'uan Teng Lu* (14), he first

asked Tan Hsia, "What is the teacher of all Buddhas?" Tan Hsia upbraided him, saying, "Fortunately you are fine on your own; why do you want to hold onto a wiping cloth?" The master retreated three steps; Tan Hsia said, "Wrong!" The master then moved forward; Tan Hsia said, "Wrong! Wrong!" The master lifted one leg, turned his body around, and left; Tan Hsia said, "You've got it, all right, but you're turning away from those Buddhas." The master realized the inner truth from this.

I HSUAN of Lin Chi (?–867)
CASES 20, 32

(The story of Lin Chi's enlightenment given in the *Tsu T'ang Chi* 19 is quite different from that in the *Lin Chi Lu*, the 'Record of Lin Chi,' compiled by his distinguished disciple San Sheng Hui Jan. The latter version is given, with some variation, in the commentary to case 11; the *Tsu T'ang Chi* version is as follows:)

Master Huang Po said to his community, "In the old days I had a companion in the Way, a fellow student of Ta Chi (Ma Tsu), named Ta Yu (according to the *Ch'uan Teng Lu*, Ta Yu was actually a successor of Kuei Tsung Fa Ch'ang, who was a successor to Ma Tsu). This man travelled on foot all over, and his Dharma eye was clear all the way through. Now he is at Ta An; he does not like to dwell among crowds, but lives alone in a mountain hut. When we parted, he made a covenant with me, saying, 'Later on, if you should meet a spiritually sharp person, send one to call on me.'"

At that time the master (Lin Chi) was in the community; after he heard this, he immediately went to call (on Ta Yu). Once he got there, he told (Ta Yu) all of what (Huang Po) had said. In the evening, in the presence of Ta Yu he spoke of the treatise on Yoga and discussed 'only consciousness.' He also asked questions on difficult points, but Ta Yu remained aloof all night and did not answer. When dawn came, (Ta Yu) said to the master (Lin Chi), "This old monk lives alone in a mountain hut; considering that you came a long way, I let you stay for a night. Why have you been shamelessly spewing filth before me all night?" When he had spoken, (Ta Yu) beat (Lin Chi) several times with his staff, pushed him out the door and shut it.

The master returned to Huang Po and told him what had happened. When Huang Po heard this, he lowered his head and said, "An adept is like a blazing fire. It is lucky that you met a man; why then did you go in vain?"

The master again went to see Ta Yu. Ta Yu said, "Before you had no shame; what is your reason for coming again today?" When he finished speaking, he drove him out the door with his staff.

The master again returned to Huang Po and said to him, "This time I have not come back empty." Huang Po said, "Why?" The master said, "At one blow of the staff I entered the realm of Buddhas: even if I had my bones shattered and my body smashed for a hundred aeons and circled Mount Sumeru countless times carrying it on my forehead, I could never requite this profound debt of gratitude."

Huang Po, hearing this, rejoiced exceedingly in it; he said, "You know how to rest, and even assert yourself on your own."

After ten days, the master again took leave of Huang Po and went to Ta Yu's place. As soon as Ta Yu saw him, he immediately went to strike him: the master grabbed the staff and immediately pushed Ta Yu down; then he struck him on the back several times with his fist. Ta Yu then nodded repeatedly and said, "Dwelling alone in a mountain hut, I thought I had spent my whole life in vain; I never expected that today I would after all find a son." . . . Henceforth the master served Ta Yu for over ten years.

(Lin Chi had twenty-one successors, but not very much is known about them. Four of them, including the main figure of case 85, were hermits. One of his successors, Chih Kuan of Kuan Ch'i (cf. verse, case 52), also studied for three years under the nun Mo Shan, who was a disciple of the aforementioned Ta Yu. He served as the gardener in her community; later he said, 'I got half the ladle from poppa Lin Chi and half the ladle from mama Mo Shan; together they made the whole ladle, and having partaken, to this day I've been full, never hungry.' Hsing Hua Tsun Ching, whose line continued longest, also worked with San Sheng, Lin Chi's successor, and Wei Fu Ta Hsueh, another successor of Huang Po, after Lin Chi's death, before he was fully enlightened to Lin Chi's meaning, but he considered Lin Chi his teacher. San Sheng compiled the *Lin Chi Lu*, but the original version is lost, and this text, one of the most important documents of T'ang Ch'an, exists in a compilation made by a later master of the Yun Men sect. The disturbed conditions in Northern China, where the early Lin Chi sect was mainly based, probably contribute to the gaps in our knowledge of this school in the ninth and early tenth centuries. The Lin Chi sect almost died out after the fourth generation, but was greatly revived by the disciples of Shou Shan Hsing Nien (925–993), the successor of Feng Hsueh Yen Chao (896–973; cases 38, 61). During the eleventh century, in the eighth generation of the sect, two outstanding masters appeared, Yang Ch'i Fang Hui and Huang Lung Hui Nan, from whom flowed what came to be known as the Yang Ch'i and Huang Lung branches. It was in the former lineage that Yuan Wu K'o Ch'in, the commentator of *The Blue Cliff Record*, appeared; this branch endured longer than the Huang Lung branch, and flourished exceedingly during the Southern Sung dynasty, with Yuan Wu producing more than one hundred successors, among whom Ta Hui also produced more than fifty. Many streams of Lin Chi Ch'an were introduced to Japan during the twelfth, thirteenth, and fourteenth centuries; by that time contemplation of the *kung an* was firmly established in the Lin Chi sect as a principal method, and this is true in the derivative Japanese Rinzai schools today.)

Teaching Designs of LIN CHI (from the *Lin Chi Lu*)

FOURFOLD HOST AND GUEST

Followers of the Way, according to the understanding of the Ch'an school, death and life are successive. Students, you must be very thorough-going. When host and guest see each other, then there is discussion back and forth. One may show his form to adapt to the person, or one may make use of the entire body; one may use situational strategy with joy or anger, or one may show half of himself; one may ride on a lion, or one may ride on an elephant.

If there is a true student, he will immediately shout, first setting forth a bowl of glue. If the teacher doesn't discern this as an object, then he goes to that object and acts in various ways. The student then shouts, but the former will not agree to let go. This is a mortal disease, and cannot be cured; it is called a guest looking at a host.

Or it may be that the teacher doesn't bring anything out, but just follows the student's questions to dispossess him. The student, being dispossessed, won't let go till the death. This is host looking at guest.

Or there may be a student who comes before the teacher in a state of purity. The teacher, discerning that this is an object, takes it and throws it into a pit. The student says, 'Good teacher!' Then the teacher says, 'Bah! You do not know good from bad.' The student then bows. This is called host looking at host.

Or there may be a student who comes before the teacher wearing stocks and bound with chains. The teacher adds another layer of stocks and chains, and the student rejoices; neither of them are discerning. This is called guest looking at guest.

Worthies, what I have raised here is all to discern demons and pick out heretics, to know their falsehood or verity.

FOURFOLD ILLUMINATION AND FUNCTION

Sometimes I first illumine and then function; sometimes I first function and then illumine. Sometimes illumination and function are at the same time, and sometimes illumination and function are not at the same time.

I first illumine and then function when there is still person (subject). I first function and then illumine when there are still phenomena (object). Illumination and function at the same time is 'driving away the plowman's ox, taking away the hungry man's food, smashing bone and taking the marrow, pressing needle and awl into the sore spot.'

When illumination and function are not at the same time, there are questions, there are answers, guest and host are established; it is mingling with the mud and water, responding to potential in dealing with people.

If one is a man beyond measure, he will immediately get up and go before it is mentioned, and still will get somewhere.

FOUR PROPOSITIONS

Sometimes I take away the subject (person), but not the object (environment); sometimes I take away the object but not the subject. Sometimes subject and object are both taken away, and sometimes neither subject nor object is taken away.

A monk asked, "What is 'taking away subject but not object'?"

The master said, "The warm sun bursts forth, spreading the land with brocade; an infant's hair hangs down white as silk."

"What is 'taking away object but not subject'?"

The Master said, "The king's command is already in effect all over the land; the general beyond the borders is free from smoke and dust."

"What is 'subject and object both taken away' like?"

The master said, "The regions of Fen and P'ing have cut off communication—they occupy one region alone." (*N.b.* Fen and P'ing were two regions which had seceded from the control of the T'ang dynasty.)

"What is 'neither subject nor object taken away' like?"

The master said, "The king ascends his jewel palace, old peasants sing hallelujah."

THE FOUR SHOUTS

The Master asked a monk, "Sometimes a shout is like the Diamond King's jewel sword, sometimes a shout is like a golden haired lion crouching on the ground; sometimes a shout is like a probing pole or reed shade; sometimes a shout does not function as a shout: how do you understand?" The monk hesitated, whereupon the Master shouted.

KUANG TSO of Chih Men in Sui Chou (Ssuchuan) (n.d.)
CASES 21, 90

(Known as Chih Men, he succeeded to Hsiang Lin Teng Yuan, and was the teacher of Hsueh Tou, the poet of *The Blue Cliff*

Record. Besides Hsueh Tou, he had 29 other enlightened successors. The two examples given here are from *Wu Teng Hui Yuan* 15:)

"I remember that in my mother's womb I had a saying: today I quote it for everyone; you can't evaluate it rationally. Is there anyone who can evaluate it? If you can't evaluate it, thirty years hence do not quote it wrongly."

Hsueh Tou asked Chih Men, "When one doesn't arouse a single thought, how can there be any fault?" Men called Hsueh Tou to approach; as soon as Hsueh Tou came near, Chih Men hit him right on the mouth with his whisk. As Hsueh Tou was about to open his mouth, Chih Men hit him again; Hsueh Tou was opened up and enlightened.

Li Tsun Hsu, a military governor under the Sung dynasty and an enlightened lay student of Ch'an, petitioned the Emperor to honor Chih Men with a purple robe, symbolic of highest rank. The Emperor Jen Tsung (r. 1023–1063) granted the purple vestment, but Chih Men refused to accept it. The Emperor, however, did not admit the master's refusal, and finally Chih Men was obliged to accept; he said to his community, "Although this old monk's original intention is to cover this illusory body with shabby garments and fend off the pangs of hunger with coarse food, I can do nothing about the fact that the military governor has asked the Emperor to regale me with a purple robe; if I put it on, it will go against my original intent, yet if I don't put it on, it will go against the will of the Emperor. But leaving aside the issue of putting it on or not for the moment, you tell me: what robe did the patriarchs wear? If you really know, though you wear clothes all day, you have never put on so much as a single thread, and though you eat all day, you have never chewed so much as a single grain of rice. If you don't really know, watch this old monk put on this robe today." (This incident is cited by Kato Totsudo in his *Hekiganrok Daikoza*, vol. 4, page 267.)

GRAND MASTER TSUNG I of Hsuan Sha in Fu Chou (n.d.)
CASES 22, 88

(Hsuan Sha was the spiritual grandfather of Fa Yen Wen I, and the Fa Yen Sect is referred to in the *Ch'uan Teng Lu* as the

Hsuan Sha Sect. He was a successor of Hsueh Feng, and produced thirteen enlightened disciples.)

His Dharma name was Shih Pei; he was a man of Min district in Foochow. His lay surname was Hsieh. When he was young he liked to fish, and used to go out in a little boat on the Nan T'ai river, associating with the fishing folk.

In the beginning of the Hsien T'ung era of the T'ang dynasty (869–873), when he was thirty years old, he suddenly wanted to abandon the world. So he gave up his fish hook and boat, and submitted to Ch'an master Ling Hsun of Lotus Mountain (a successor of Kuei Tsung Fa Ch'ang, also Hsueh Feng's original teacher), who shaved his head. He went to the K'ai Yuan Temple at Yu Chang and received full ordination from preceptual master Tao Hsuan.

He wore a patched robe of coarse cloth and sandals made of straw. He always sat peacefully all day long; the entire community considered him unusual.

He was a later come fellow student with Hsueh Feng I Tsun in their original school (under the teacher Ling Hsun); and he associated with (Hsueh Feng) like master and disciple. Because of his painful practice, Hsueh Feng called him the ascetic.

One day Hsueh Feng asked, "Which one is Ascetic Pei?" He replied, "I would never dare to deceive anyone."

Another day Hsueh Feng called him and said, "Ascetic Pei, why do you not travel to study at other places?" He said, "Bodhidharma did not come to China; the second patriarch did not go to India." Hsueh Feng approved of this. (According to *Tsu T'ang Chi* 10, Shih Pei started off on his journeys, but was suddenly enlightened when he happened to stumble on a rock. Afterwards he shouted and said, "Bodhidharma did not come over; the second patriarch did not obtain the transmission.")

(When Hsueh Feng went to Elephant Bone Mountain in 872, Hsuan Sha accompanied him and helped to build a monastery there. He 'clearly discovered the mindground' when he read the Surangama Sutra, and 'students of the mystery who had some uncertainty would always seek further help from him.')

HERMIT HSIANG of Lotus Flower Peak
CASE 25

After enlightenment, before accepting a request to dwell in a monastery as the guide of a community, Ch'an adepts usually spent years travelling and/or living in seclusion or semi-seclusion, "maturing the holy embryo." Some, like Hsiang, the hermit of Lotus Flower Peak (on Mount T'ien T'ai, one of the five holy mountains of China), remained in humble circumstances as hermits all their lives, though small groups of seekers would come to live near them and call on them for instruction. The following brief sermon of hermit Hsiang, taken from the *Chih Yueh Lu*, "Finger Pointing at the Moon," is the greater part of the very little information we have about this Ch'an master:

"This matter is most urgent: you must clearly apprehend it; once you get it clear, at all times you will avoid being bound up and will be at ease wherever you are. Yet don't use your mind to overcome by force; you must fit into the ancient groove naturally. As soon as you get to study and analysis, you are eager to make some principle into a standard for the Buddhist teaching; (if you go on this way,) when will you ever attain to rest of the mind ground? Elders, I ask you to be thoroughgoing in this way."

The saying in case 25 was spoken by the hermit just before he died.

HUAI HAI of Pai Chang (720–814)
CASES 26, 53, 70, 71, 72, 73

(Pai Chang was one of the foremost successors of Ma Tsu; the circumstances of his enlightenment are told in case 53. Pai Chang compiled the so-called 'pure standards' for Ch'an monasteries, and is thus known as the founder of the independent Ch'an monastic institution in China. From Pai Chang's successors emerged the Kuei-Yang and Lin Chi sects of Ch'an. The following sayings, excerpted from the extensive record of his sermons, are in answer to a question about the essential method for sudden enlightenment in the great vehicle:)

You should all first put an end to all ties, and lay to rest all concerns; whether good or bad, mundane or transmundane, anything at all—do not remember, do not recollect, do not engage your thoughts with them. Abandon body and mind, letting them be free. With mind like wood or stone, mouth makes no object of distinction, mind pursues no activity; then the mind ground becomes like space, wherein the sun of illumination spontaneously appears. It is as though clouds had opened and the sun emerged.

Just put an end to all fettering connections; feelings of greed, anger, love, grasping, defilement and purity, all come to an end: unmoved in the face of five lusts and eight winds, not entangled by seeing, hearing, awareness, or knowledge, not confused by various objective realms, naturally endowed with the wondrous use of paranormal powers, this is a liberated man.

In the presence of all objects, mind being neither still nor disturbed, neither concentrated nor scattered, passing through all sound and form without lingering or obstruction, is called being a man of the Way. Not setting in motion good, evil, right, or wrong; not clinging to a single thing, not rejecting a single thing, is called being a man of the great vehicle. Not bound by any good, evil, emptiness, existence, defilement, purity, doing, non-doing, mundane, supramundane, blessings, virtue, knowledge or wisdom, is called Buddha wisdom.

Once affirmation and negation, like and dislike, approval and disapproval, all various opinions and feelings come to an end and can't bind, then one is free wherever he may be; this is called a bodhisattva with a newly aroused mind immediately ascending to the stage of Buddhahood.

P'U YUAN of Nan Ch'uan (747–834)
CASES 28, 31

The Master's lay surname was Wang, and he often referred to himself as "Old Teacher Wang." In 757, at the age of ten, he received instruction from the meditation master Ta Hui of Mt. Ta Wei; at thirty, he went to Mt. Sung in Honan, one of the five holy mountains of China, where he was formally ordained as a Buddhist monk. He learned the doctrines of the Fa Hsiang school, which analyzes existence into one hundred elements and maintains that the world is created and maintained as it is by the force of mental habit, giving a detailed account of the workings of the mind. He also made a thorough study of the Vinaya, monastic rules of conduct inherited from Indian Buddhism. Then he travelled around, hearing the *Lankavatara* "Entrance (of the Great Vehicle) into Ceylon" and *Avatam-*

saka (*Hua Yen*) "Flower Garland" scriptures expounded. The former scripture maintains that all that can be known of the world is purely subjective, and distinguishes three levels of reality; pure mental construction; relative coexistence—of sense, sense consciousness, and sense data—or interdependent co-production; and perfectly real, which is emptiness: mental construction is projected on relative coexistence, which, being purely relative, has no ultimate basis in fact and is in reality empty. The Flower Garland scripture also speaks of the relative co-production of all things in the cosmos, which means that everything is inherent in everything else; this is expressed symbolically by the net of Indra, made of jewels which each reflect all the other jewels, as well as the reflections of all the jewels in each jewel, and so on, ad infinitum to the power of infinity to an infinite infinity of powers: the ultimate pivot of interdependence is that of mind and matter. Hence this scripture says that the cosmos is produced by the mind, yet the mind does not exist of itself. Nan Ch'uan also studied the *San Lun* or "Three Treatise" school, which teaches the Middle Way based on the works of Nagarjuna and Kanadeva; accordingly, he practiced the contemplations of emptiness, conditional existence, and the mean.

Finally, after many years of study and practice, he called on the great Ch'an Master Ma Tsu Tao I in Hung Chou (in Kiangsi), and attained complete freedom. At the time there were eight hundred people in Ma Tsu's congregation, and P'u Yuan was considered the foremost; no one would dare to debate with him. In 795 he went to Mt. Nan Ch'uan in Ch'ih Chou (in Anwei), built himself a hut, and scratched out his own subsistence from the mountainside. It is said that he didn't come down from the mountain for over thirty years. In the beginning of the Ta Ho era (827–836), he was invited by Lu Hsuan to come down and teach. After that, his followers were never less than several hundred. He had seventeen enlightened disciples, including the famous Chao Chou, Ch'ang Sha, and Tzu Hu. Among Ma Tsu's one hundred and thirty-nine enlightened disciples, Nan Ch'uan is considered along with Pai Chang Huai Hai and Hsi T'ang Chih Ts'ang as the greatest of all time. He once said, "People these days walk around with 'Buddha' on their shoulders; when you hear me say that mind is not Buddha and wisdom is not the Path, you gather together and try to figure me out. You cannot figure me out. If you could wrap empty space up into a staff and hit me with it, then you might figure me out."

FA CHEN of Ta Sui (n.d.)
CASE 29

(Ta Sui succeeded to Ta An, also known as Ta Kuei, or Kuei Shan Ho Shang, who was a disciple of Pai Chang Huai Hai, and later an assistant to Kuei Shan Ling Yu.)

Someone asked, "What happens when birth and death arrive?" The master said, "When there is tea, drink tea; when there is rice, eat rice."

Someone asked, "What is the essential of the Dharma of all Buddhas?" The master raised his whisk and said, "Do you understand?" He said, "I don't understand." The master said, "An elk-tail whisk."

(The lord of Shu summoned Ta Sui repeatedly, but the master refused each time, claiming to be old and sick. The lord bestowed on him the honorific title Spiritual Illumination.)

PAO CHE of Mt. Ma Ku (n.d.)
CASE 31

(Ma Ku was one of Ma Tsu's successors: the following is taken from *Ching Te Ch'uan Teng Lu* 7:)

One day as Ma Ku was walking along with Ma Tsu he asked, "What is great extinction?" Ma Tsu said, "Swift." Ma Ku said, "What's the hurry?" Ma Tsu said, "Look at the river."

Once when Ma Ku was wandering in the mountains with Tan Hsia,* he saw a fish in a stream and pointed to it with his hand. Tan Hsia said, "Naturally, naturally."** The next day Ma Ku again questioned Tan Hsia, "What did you mean yesterday?" Tan Hsia relaxed his body and made the motion of lying down. Ma Ku said, "Heavens!" Another time he travelled with Tan Hsia to Mt. Ma Ku. Ma Ku said, "I'm staying here." Tan Hsia said, "Well, I'll let you stay, but do you still have That One or not?" Ma Ku bade him farewell.

A monk asked, "I am not in doubt about the twelve part

teachings (of the Buddhist canon), but what is the meaning of the coming from the West?" Ma Ku stood up, circled his body once with his staff, raised one foot and said, "Understand?" The monk had no reply, so Ma Ku hit him.

Tan Yuan asked, "Is Twelve-Faced Avalokitesvara ordinary or holy?" Ma Ku said, "Holy," whereupon Tan Yuan struck him a blow. Ma Ku said, "I knew you hadn't gotten to this realm."

*Tan Hsia was a successor of Shih T'ou and also spent time in Ma Tsu's community.

**Tan Hsia's initiatory name, given him by Ma Tsu, was Tzu Jan, "Natural."

HUAI HUI of Chang Ching Temple in the Capital District (?–818)
CASE 31

(The following is taken from the *Ching Te Ch'uan Teng Lu* 7:)

He was from T'ung An in Ch'uan Chou (in Hopei); his surname was Hsieh. He received Ma Tsu's mind seal. First he stayed at Oak Cliff in Ting Chou (in Hopei); then he stayed on Chung T'iao Mountain. In the beginning of the Yuan Ho era (806–820) Emperor Hsien Tsung summoned him to reside at Mystic Temple: there students flocked to him.

The master went up into the Hall and taught his disciples saying, "The ultimate principle is oblivious of words. People these days have not comprehended this, so they force themselves to study extraneous matters, considering this an accomplishment. They do not know that their own nature was originally not the dusty realm (of the senses), but rather the subtle mysterious gate of great liberation. All reflection and awareness neither stains nor obstructs this. This light has never been stopped or nullified: from the primordial past up to now, it has been solid and changeless. It's like the solar disc illuminating far and near: though it touches the many colors, it doesn't mix with them all. The wondrous illumination of the spiritual lamp does not depend on tempering and refining. Since you haven't understood, you cling to the forms of things—it's just like rubbing your eyes and producing false optical illusions. Thus you vainly trouble yourselves, wasting ages of time. If you can turn the light around so that there is no second person, the activities you undertake will not lack the characteristics of reality."

JU PAO of Tzu Fu in Chi Chou (in Kiangsi) (n.d.)
CASE 33

Tzu Fu succeeded to Ch'an master Kuang Mu of the Western Pagoda on Yang Shan; a fourth generation master of the Kuei-Yang lineage, he produced four enlightened disciples. His biography is in *Ching Te Ch'uan Teng Lu* 12.

A monk asked, "What is a phrase responding to potential?" The master was silent. "What is the hidden essence?" The master said, "Close the door for me." "When Lu Tsu sat facing a wall, what was his meaning?" The master said, "Irrelevant." "What is the truly correct eye of all time?" The master struck his breast and said, "Alas! Alas!" "What is the master's family style?" The master said, "Three cups of tea after rice."

HUI CHI of Yang Shan (813–890)
CASES 34, 68

(Yang Shan was a brilliant master, nicknamed 'little Shakyamuni.' According to the *Tsu T'ang Chi*, eleven regional inspectors, officials of the civil government, paid obeisance to him as their teacher. Before he was twenty years old, he had already called on successors of Nan Ch'uan, National Teacher Hui Chung, Ma Tsu, and Pai Chang; he was fully enlightened with Kuei Shan, and stayed there for fifteen years. There are various stories of his awakening. According to the *Jen T'ien Yen Mu*, after he had received the teaching of ninety-seven circular figures from Tan Yuan, who got it from Hui Chung, when he came to Kuei Shan, the latter showed him the figure of the empty circle—the 'full moon,' whereat he was enlightened. According to Dogen, the thirteenth century Japanese master, Kuei Shan first set Yang Shan to work herding buffalo for three years. The following is from the *Ch'uan Teng Lu* 10:)

Yang Shan asked Kuei Shan, "What is the abode of the real Buddha?"

Kuei Shan said, "With the subtlety of thinking the thoughtless, return thought. to the boundlessness of the spiritual effulgence; when thought is exhausted, return to the source, where nature and appearances always abide, phenomena and principle are not two; the true Buddha is thus."

At these words Yang Shan was suddenly enlightened.

(Besides the use of circular figures, the dialogues of Kuei Shan and Yang Shan are known as hallmarks of the Kuei-Yang sect; Yang Shan once said that the essence of the sect was 'two mouths without a single tongue,' symbolizing the meeting of minds. The ninety-seven circular symbols handed down from Hui Chung are now lost; it is said that Yang Shan burned the book which contained them after he had read it once. Tan Yuan, who had given it to him, lamented this, so Yang Shan made another copy from memory and returned it to him. In the twelfth century, a master of the Yun Men sect named P'u Liang made a compilation containing forty or fifty examples, but this work too is lost; it is known, however, that he arranged them into six rubrics: 'circle,' 'merging of personality,' 'ocean of meaning,' 'ocean of characters,' 'speech,' and 'silent discourse.')

Bibliography

I. TEXTS AND COMMENTARIES FOR *Pi Yen Lu*

Hekiganroku Daikoza by Kato Totsudo. Tokyo, Heibonsha, 1940.

Hekiganshu Kogi by Imazu Kogaku, incorporating remarks by Zen Master Shoyaku (1572–1650). Tokyo, Mugazanbo, 1912.

Hekiganshu Shudensho by Daichi Jitto (1656–1735). Kyoto, Bunkyudo.

Hekiganshu Teidokusho by Tenkei Denson (1648–1735), edited as *Hekiganroku Kogi* by Matsuzaki Kakuhon. Tokyo, Koyukan, 1903.

Hekiganshu Teihon edited by Ito Yuten. Tokyo, Risosha, 1963.

Pi Yen Lu Chiang I by Wang Chin Jui. Tainan, 1972.

II. BIOGRAPHIES AND SAYINGS OF CH'AN MASTERS

Ching Te Ch'uan Teng Lu compiled by Tao Yuan, 1004. Taisho Shinshu Daizokyo, vol. 51, no. 2076.

Jen T'ien Yen Mu compiled by Chih Shao, 1188. Taisho Shinshu Daizokyo, vol. 48, no. 2006.

Ku Tsun Su Yu Lu compiled by Yuan Chiao, 1144. Dai Nihon Man Zokuzokyo 2.23.2.

Hsu Ch'uan Teng Lu compiled by Yuan Chi, 14th cent. Taisho Shinshu Daizokyo, vol. 51, no. 2077.

Tsu T'ang Chi compiled by Ching and Ch'un, 952. Kyoto, Chubun Shuppansha, 1972.

Wu Teng Hui Yuan compiled by P'u Ch'i, 1232. Taipei, Kuang Wen Shu Ch'u, 1971.

III. DICTIONARIES AND PHRASE BOOKS

Katto Gosen by Dochu Muchaku (1653–1745). Tokyo, Komazawa Daigaku Jiten Hensansho, 1959.

Zengaku Jiten by Jimbo Nyoten and Ando Bun'ei. Tokyo, Mugazanbo, 1927.

Zengo Ji'i by Nakagawa Shuan. Tokyo, Koshokai Shuppanbu, 1935.

Zenrin Kushu by Toyo Eicho (1429–1504), translated and annotated by Shibayama Zenkei. Kyoto, Kichudo, 1955.

IV. RELATED WORKS

The Zen Koan by Isshu Miura and Ruth Fuller Sasaki. New York, Harcourt, Brace and World, 1965.